Palgrave Studies in Citizenship Transitions series

Series Editors:

Michele Micheletti is Lars Hierta Chair of Political Science at Stockholm University, Sweden.

Ludvig Beckman is Professor of Political Science, Stockholm University, Sweden.

David Owen is Professor of Social and Political Philosophy, University of Southampton, UK.

The Editorial Board:

Keith Banting (Queen's University, Canada), **Rainer Baubock** (European University Institute, Italy), **Russell Dalton** (University of California at Irving, USA), **Avigail Eisenberg** (University of Victoria, Canada), **Nancy Fraser** (The New School for Social Research, USA), **David Jacobson** (University of South Florida, USA) and **Ariadne Vromen** (The University of Sydney, Australia).

This book series focuses on citizenship transitions encompassing contemporary transformations of citizenship as institution, status and practice as well as normative and explanatory analysis of these transformations and their cultural, social, economic and political implications. The series bridges theoretical and empirical debates on democracy, transnationalism, and citizenship that have been too insulated from each other. It takes citizenship transitions as its starting-point and studies the status, role and function of citizenship within contemporary democratic systems and multi-layered governance structures beyond the state. It aims to add a broader array of critical, conceptual, normative and empirical perspectives on the borders, territories, and political agents of citizenship. It scrutinizes the possibilities and challenges of citizenship in light of present broad processes of political fragmentation and pluralisation and the ways emerging ideals and expectations of citizenship are inspired by new social, political and environmental movements. Its cross-disciplinary approach intends to capture the transitions of citizenship from an apparently simple relation between the state and its citizens into a cluster of complex responsibility claims and practices that raise questions concerning citizenship borders and obligations, the public-private scope of citizenship, and even how political actors attempt to and in fact avoid citizenship.

Palgrave Studies In Citizenship Transitions series
Series Standing Order ISBN 978-1-137-33137-3

You can receive future titles in this series as they are published by placing a standing order. Please contact your bookseller or, in case of difficulty, write to us at the address below with your name and address, the title of the series and the ISBNs quoted above.

Customer Services Department, Macmillan Distribution Ltd, Houndmills, Basingstoke, Hampshire RG21 6XS, England

The Political Role of Corporate Citizens

An Interdisciplinary Approach

Edited by

Karin Svedberg Helgesson
Department of Management and Organization,
Stockholm School of Economics, Sweden

and

Ulrika Mörth
Department of Political Science, Stockholm University, Sweden

First published 2013 by
PALGRAVE MACMILLAN

Palgrave Macmillan in the UK is an imprint of Macmillan Publishers Limited, registered in England, company number 785998, of Houndmills, Basingstoke, Hampshire RG21 6XS.

Palgrave Macmillan in the US is a division of St Martin's Press LLC, 175 Fifth Avenue, New York, NY 10010.

Palgrave Macmillan is the global academic imprint of the above companies and has companies and representatives throughout the world.

Palgrave® and Macmillan® are registered trademarks in the United States, the United Kingdom, Europe and other countries.

ISBN 978–1–137–02681–1

This book is printed on paper suitable for recycling and made from fully managed and sustained forest sources. Logging, pulping and manufacturing processes are expected to conform to the environmental regulations of the country of origin.

A catalogue record for this book is available from the British Library.

A catalog record for this book is available from the Library of Congress.

Typeset by MPS Limited, Chennai, India.

Contents

List of Tables

List of Figures

Series Editors' Preface

The goal of the *Palgrave Studies in Citizenship Transitions* series is to contribute to the understanding of the encompassing contemporary transformations that citizenship is undergoing as an institution, a status and a form of practice by individuals and collectivities. This broad perspective on citizenship encourages scholarship that uses a variety of theoretical perspectives, involves many different disciplines and that contributes to the understanding of citizenship transitions by bridging theoretical and empirical debates that have tended to be too insulated from each other in scholarship in general.

As illustrated by its first book, *Territories of Citizenship* (edited by Ludvig Beckman and Eva Erman), the series penetrates the normative and explanatory analysis of an important transformation, namely the development away from the nation-state focus of citizenship. This book aims to explore how norms of citizenship, residence, and territorial jurisdiction contribute to the inclusion and exclusion of people from the enjoyment of rights. The tensions that inclusion and exclusion create and the extent to which they could be resolved are investigated both in the context of nation-states and in the context of multilayered government structures.

The Political Role of Corporate Citizens: An Interdisciplinary Approach is the second volume in the series. It addresses citizenship transitions under a different aspect by contributing to the classical discussion on corporations as political agents of citizenship. It is a significant contribution to the series because it captures the transitions of citizenship from an apparently simple relationship between the state and its citizens into a cluster of complex responsibility claims and practices that raise questions concerning the responsibility for citizenship and, most importantly, the public-private scope of citizenship. It asks: what are the implications of the increased politicization of corporations and their increased presence within the public domain, and how does this development transgress the traditional notions of what corporations are and ought to be? To answer and analyse these questions the book employs the notion of 'corporate citizenship' and is organized along two themes. The first concerns how the state has retreated or transformed and opened up for business to take on societal responsibility. The second theme focuses on the need to develop a new understanding of the political role of business. This theme considers the transformation of corporate responsibility from simply complying with legal standards and conforming with moral rules to one that acknowledges their increased presence in the public domain and their role in taking more independent and forward-looking responsibility for global well-being. As such, the book transfigures the classical debate on the role that the public and private spheres should play in societal affairs.

The series editors would like to thank the support given by the scholars initially involved in helping us develop the theme of citizenship transitions, Andreas Follesdal, Dietlind Stolle and Jonas Tallberg.

Michele Micheletti
Ludvig Beckman
David Owen

Preface and Acknowledgements

The editing of this volume has raised questions relating to participation and identity, as well as on rights and duties. We are very grateful to our esteemed group of co-authors who agreed to participate in the quest to identify and problematize the political role of corporations through the device of corporate citizenship, even more so as the production of an edited volume is not the most democratic of processes. As editors, we have been entrusted with the right to decide on various large and small matters, a duty that we have taken seriously. The book is a result of a collective endeavour, but the mistakes remaining are ours.

We would also like to thank Michelle Micheletti, who persuaded us to edit this volume, Kerstin Sahlin for constructive comments on several chapters during ISA in Montreal, and the participants in the 'Organizing and Leadership' seminar series at the Department of Management and Organization, Stockholm School of Economics for much needed feedback on a late version of Chapter 1.

Our editorial assistant at Palgrave, Harriet Barker, has guided us through the process. Two anonymous reviewers provided important critique on our early efforts, and the comments of a third anonymous reviewer helped polish off the final manuscript.

Finally, we are indebted to Jan Hallenberg for editorial assistance, and good cheer. Claes-Fredrik Helgesson helped with the cheering.

Karin Svedberg Helgesson and Ulrika Mörth

Notes on Contributors

Paula Blomqvist is Associate Professor at the Department of Government, Uppsala University, Sweden. Her research is oriented mainly towards welfare politics, foremost concerning privatization and marketization within the social service sector in Sweden. Her work has appeared in a range of academic journals, including *Social Policy and Administration, Government and Opposition, Social Science and Medicine, Local Government Studies and European Journal of Social Policy.*

Céline Cholez is an Assistant Professor at the Grenoble Institute of Technology and at the PACTE, at the University of Grenoble, France. She specializes in the area of sociology of work and theory of organizations. She is interested in the management of disruptions and unforeseen degradations of expected acting conditions. Her most recent publications have appeared in *Recherches Qualitatives* and *Management.*

Andrew Crane is the George R. Gardiner Professor of Business Ethics and Director of the Centre of Excellence in Responsible Business at the Schulich School of Business, York University, Toronto. He is the co-author or editor of eight books, including an award-winning textbook on business ethics and the *Oxford Handbook of Corporate Social Responsibility.* He also publishes widely on business ethics and CSR in scholarly management journals, and sits on the editorial board of six international journals.

Steven Gerencser is Associate Professor of Political Science at Indiana University South Bend. He writes and teaches in the field of political theory. He has published essays on Michael Oakeshott and as well as a monograph entitled *The Skeptic's Oakeshott* (2000). Besides his work on Oakeshott, Gerencser also writes about the legal status and role of corporations in public life, including 'The corporate person and democratic politics' in *Political Research Quarterly.*

Boris Holzer is Professor of Political Sociology at Bielefeld University, Germany. He acquired his PhD at the London School of Economics and Political Science and subsequently worked at Ludwig-Maximilians-University Munich and at the University of Lucerne. His current research interests include political and economic sociology, social networks and globalization. Among his publications are 'Miracles with a system: the economic rise of East Asia and the role of sociocultural patterns', *International Sociology*; 'Political consumerism between individual choice and collective action: social movements, role mobilization and signaling', *International Journal of Consumer Studies* and the monograph *Moralizing the Corporation*.

Uwafiokun Idemudia is Associate Professor of International Development and African Studies at York University in Toronto, Canada. His research interest lies in the relationship between business and development, and his works have appeared in journals such as *Business and Society, Journal of Cleaner Production, Progress in Development Studies and Journal of International Development*.

Dirk Matten holds the Hewlett-Packard Chair in Corporate Social Responsibility and is a Professor of Strategy at the Schulich School of Business, York University, Toronto. He is also a Visiting Professor at the University of London, the University of Nottingham and at Sabancŷ University in Istanbul. He has taught and undertaken research at academic institutions in Argentina, Australia, Belgium, Britain, Canada, the Czech Republic, France, Germany, India, Italy, Turkey and the USA. His work has appeared in journals including *Academy of Management Review, Journal of Management Studies, Organization Studies, British Journal of Management, the Geneva Papers,* and *Human Research*.

Jeremy Moon is Professor of Corporate Social Responsibility and Founding Director of the International Center for Corporate Social Responsibility at Nottingham University Business School. He has published seven books, five government and other reports, two edited special issues, and over eighty journal articles and book chapters. He received the 'European Faculty Pioneers Award' of the Aspen Institute Beyond Grey Pinstripes awards in 2005 and he has been elected a Fellow of the Royal Society for the Arts.

Fabrizio Panozzo is Professor of Management at Ca' Foscari University Venice and Freie Universität Bozen. His core research interests have been the social and political roles of accounting and calculative practices. From this angle he has published in *Accounting Organizations and Society, Scandinavian Journal of Management, Journal of Management and Governance* on, among other things, public sector modernization, city management, health care reform and the managerialization of nonprofit organizations. He is currently attracted by the ways in which moral, political and philosophical values are manipulated within the ever-changing spirit of capitalism.

Pascale Trompette is a sociologist and CNRS Research Fellow at the PACTE, at the University of Grenoble, France. She works in the area of economic sociology and sociology of markets. Her most recent publications in English have appeared in the *Journal of Cultural Economy, Science Studies, Management and Organization, History, Mind, Culture and activity.*

List of Abbreviations

AML	Anti-Money Laundering
BoP	Bottom of the Pyramid
BCBS	Basel Committee on Banking Supervision
BSC	Balanced Scorecard
BPEO	Best Practicable Environmental Option
CC	Corporate Citizenship
CCBE	Conseil des Barreaux de l'Union Européenne/The Council of Bars and Law Societies of Europe
CSR	Corporate Social Responsibility
CTF	Counter Terrorism Financing
EU	European Union
FATF	Financial Action Task Force
GRI	Global Reporting Initiative
IAIS	International Association of Insurance Supervisors
ILO	International Labour Organization
IOSCO	International Organization of Securities Commissions
LGBT	Lesbian, Gay, Bisexual or Transgendered
NGO	Non-Governmental Organization
NPM	New Public Management
RBA	Risk-Based Approach
SAI	Social Accountability International
SFSA	Swedish Financial Supervisory Authority
TBL	Triple Bottom Line
TNC	Transnational Corporation
UDHR	Universal Declaration of Human Rights
UN	United Nations

1
Introduction: Corporate Citizenship and the Political Role of the Corporation

Karin Svedberg Helgesson and Ulrika Mörth

Introduction

The role of corporations in modern society is in flux, and the state is not what it used to be. During recent years the scholarly debate on the borders between the public and private domains has focused on how large transnational companies have gained authority in areas of global governance and regulation that traditionally belonged to the state, intergovernmental organizations and the public sector (Jordana and Levi-Faur, 2004; Djelic and Sahlin, 2006; Kobrin, 2009). This trend comes in many shapes and forms. Increased co-operation and boundary-blurring are conceptualized as network governance (Bäckstrand, 2008), multi-sectoral or global policy networks (Benner et al., 2005), forms of neo-liberal governmentality (Lipschutz, 2005), a manifestation of an emerging global public domain (Ruggie, 2004; Helgesson and Mörth, 2012), private international authority (Cutler, 2003; Hall and Biersteker, 2002), private government (Crane et al., 2008), and public-private part-nerships (Dingwerth, 2007; Schäferhoff et al., 2009; Bexell and Mörth, 2010). A common theme in the literature is that the state and the public sector have become more dependent on business norms and resources, to what is in national and European contexts referred to as New Public Management (Lane, 2000; Mörth, 2008), and in the global context dis-cussed in terms of market multilateralism (Bull and McNeill, 2007).

Of course, the scholarly debate on the role of business in society has long roots. The concept of private government was contemplated by Merriam (1944), and others. Around two decades later, Peter Bachrach (1967) argued that there were important similarities between General Motors and the United States government. Bachrach (1967: 102, in Vogel, 1975: 15) proposed that these entities 'both authoritatively allocate values for the society. It is on the basis of this resemblance that General Motors and other giant private governments should be considered a part of the political sector in which democratic norms apply'. In a similar vein, James March observed that the business firm is a political coalition (March, 1962). A large corporation was thus not only to be thought of as a social enterprise but as a political system as well (Dahl, 1972). Although the political system of the state in principle had the legitimate authority to its citizens, an authority that the large corporations lacked, the distinction between the systems was blurred in practice (Dahl, 1972). Dahl argued that large corporations may cause death and injuries by decisions on pollution, working conditions, impose severe deprivations of income by making decisions on plant location, and 'exercise influence, power, control, and even coercion over employees, customers, suppliers ... by advertising, propaganda, promotions, and demotions, not to mention possible illegal practices' (Dahl, 1972: 18). For Dahl, the implication of this similarity between the political system of the state and the enterprise was the obligation to examine the corporations. They were a public matter.

The quote from Dahl (Dahl, 1972: 18) illustrates the wave of the publicization of the corporation that was so strongly advocated in the 1960s and 1970s (Vogel, 1975). The aim was not only to raise questions on the internal legitimacy of management, but to challenge, and expand 'the accountability of the corporation as a whole to the society' (Vogel, 1975: 16). The collapse of the distinction between government and business, expressed in the buzzwords at the time – the military-industrial complex and the corporate state – made it necessary to analyse the corporation as a form of governmental authority and public institution.

Currently, we still grapple with questions on the borders between the public and private, and the role of corporations in society. In the early 2000s they appear perhaps more pressing than ever. The classic Friedman approach towards business – that businesses should 'stick to the knitting and attend exclusively to their interests of their shareholders' (Néron and Norman, 2008: 1) – is challenged, though advocates are also around (Pies et al., 2010). New demands on legitimacy standards are being raised for governance beyond the state and by the for-profit sector (Dingwerth and Hanrieder, 2010; Dingwerth, 2007). These demands are often about democratic legitimacy and accountability, as the power to act on public matters is not always grounded in a legitimate authority to do so (Kobrin, 2009). Far from it, irrespective of whether transnational corporations are deemed democratically legitimate or not, they do 'operate directly as powerful autonomous actors in international politics'

(Kobrin, 2009: 354), and capital markets are intertwined with national politics:

> The formation of a global capital market represents a concentration of power capable of influencing national government economic policy, and, by extension, other policies as well. These markets now exercise the accountability functions associated with citizenship: they can vote governments' economic policies down or in; they can force governments to take certain measures and not others. (Sassen, 1996: 42, see also Lindblom, 2001)

The political dimension is not necessarily about party politics but on how political values and norms are involved when corporations provide welfare services, or protect citizens from terrorist attacks (den Boer and van Buuren, 2012). We are witnessing an increased politicization of corporations when they increasingly populate the public domain. Studies by Drache, Ruggie and Dryzek deal with how states and non-state actors are embedded in a broader institutionalized arena concerned with the production of global goods and services (Drache 2001; Ruggie 2004; Dryzek 2000). Their works deal with how different values and norms from the public and private are intertwined, and re-mixed, and the normative implications of this embeddedness. One implication is a state of confusion of what norms and values are applicable in politics as argued by Sennett (1974). We believe that the stronger presence of corporations in the public domain may depoliticize this domain also in the sense that the democratic system, the elected politicians and citizens, will have less influence over welfare and other core policy areas.

The implications of an increasing publicization of corporations – that they take on important roles in societies – and how it affects the public domain, the welfare state and democracy is multifaceted. In this volume we analyse the current state of the role of corporations in societies with a view to the political role of corporations. Drawing on a range of disciplines, including political science, organization and management, sociology, and accounting, we make use of the notion of a citizenship for corporations as a device for delineating and analysing the political role of the corporation in the public domain. The political role of corporations is understood here as a role that goes beyond the traditional understanding of corporations and politics. Traditionally, corporations are perceived to act and react towards the political system by lobbying and other activities in order to influence public policy. This volume is about boundary blurring between the world of corporations and politics.

Corporations are not outside the political process. They are influencing the playing field of politics by enacting different societal roles. We ask what ideas on corporate citizenship may be voiced about this ongoing publicization of the corporation. What are the roles of the corporate citizen in the public domain and how do these new roles transgress traditional notions of what corporations are and ought to be?

Frame of reference

The volume addresses the complex and classic questions on the roles of states and markets by analysing how this longstanding debate is manifested in corporate citizenship. Corporations may not be citizens, but 'corporations could reasonably claim to act "as if" they were metaphorically citizens in that their engagement in society resembles that of citizens' (Moon et al., 2005: 448).

What then is it that such an 'as if' position of citizen may entail for corporations? How is corporate citizenship to be defined? One influential template in the literature on corporate responsibility and citizenship is that of Carroll (1991, 1997, 2003). He proposes that corporate citizenship has four facets, or levels, to do with being profitable, obeying the law, behaving ethically and engaging in philanthropy. Here, we have opted for using a template that draws more explicitly on traditional notions of individual citizenship. One important reason for this, we argue, is that for the concept of corporate citizenship to serve as a device for understanding the political role of corporations in the public domain, one needs to acknowledge that 'citizen' and 'citizenship' are powerful and multifaceted concepts. They are powerful because they speak of rights, duties/responsibilities, participation/deliberation and identities. They are multifaceted because these values can be categorized into different types of rights, duties, participation and identity (Delanty, 2000). Citizenship can further be regarded as an individual membership or as a social citizenship in the welfare state alleviating socio-economic inequality (Delanty, 2000).

Importantly, there exist various theoretical traditions in modern social and political thought on how to interpret citizenship, that have different implications for the conceptualization of corporate citizenship. Put simply, the liberal tradition emphasizes rights, the conservative tradition stresses duties, and the republican and communitarian tradition focuses on participation and identity as being linked to the nation-state project (Delanty, 2000). This implies that what corporate citizenship is and can be varies depending on what tradition is placed at the fore, and which constituent parts and sub-categories are emphasized. In this volume, we will make use of Delanty's categorizations and discuss the realm of corporate citizenship in terms of rights, duties, participation and identity (cf. Crane et al., 2008).

The idea of a citizenship for corporations can be seen as provocative in that it implies that corporate actors could be similar to individuals in important matters of citizenship. To be sure, neither the concept nor the phenomenon of corporate citizenship exists in the classical literature on citizenship, and the notion of a citizenship for corporations tends to be regarded as an oxymoron (Delanty, 2000). Here we do not attempt to claim that corporations can be equals among other citizens. However, we do believe that the friction and resistance the concept of corporate citizenship encounters are useful for analytical purposes, and make the notion of citizenship more challenging than related concepts like corporate social responsibility and corporate accountability (see the comparative analysis of these concepts in Waddock, 2004). It is precisely because the fit is not perfect that the idea of a citizenship for corporations can serve as a device for delineating the political role of corporations that spans the public-private divide, we suggest.

Two recurrent themes

Our analyses of the following are grounded in two recurrent themes from discussions of the role of corporations in the general literature on politics and business. The first theme is how the state has retreated or transformed and opened up for business to take on societal responsibility. The second theme is that this development, in turn, requires a new understanding of the political role of business that goes beyond 'mere compliance with legal standards and conformity with moral rules' (Scherer and Palazzo, 2008). In summary, there is a call for a political theory of the firm (Néron, 2010).

The first theme – the retreat or transformation of the state – is an important premise in the literature for the very notion of bringing in citizenship into the world of business that goes beyond the traditional legal-rationalistic perspective on corporations (Scherer and Palazzo, 2011). The marketization of the public and/or the privatization of the state create spaces that may be filled by (more engaged) corporate citizens. Globalization and the post-Westphalian order or the post-national constellation has created new challenges for business. The erosion of the division of labour between business and government accentuates and emphasizes the need for the business to take on societal responsibility (Crane et al., 2008; Scherer and Palazzo, 2011).

Thus, the theme in the literature on the retreat or the transformation of the state has to do with the complex issue of whether the emergence of corporate citizenship is a function of a changed or a weak state. The question is seldom the object of empirical scrutiny in the literature on corporate citizenship. We believe that this volume contributes to the theorization of the relationship between states and corporations. The 'commodification' or the 'choice revolution' (Blomqvist, 2004 and Blomqvist, this volume) in the welfare states in the western world have created new rights and obligations for corporations, whether they want to take on such a role or not. What is less problematized is that in some cases there was no prior state, only failed state-building efforts, in need of responsible actors, private or public (Matten and Crane, 2005; Idemudia, 2010). We have limited knowledge on if, and how, governments or local authorities respond to a societal role by corporations in cases of weak states. Furthermore, we have limited empirical studies on the various manifestations an increased publicization may take in the western world. The advent of new existential threats raises demands for a more proactive engagement on behalf of corporate actors as agents in process of securitization with associated conflicts of interests and values (Helgesson and Mörth, 2012).

The second theme from the literature is that corporate citizenship helps bring politics into the world of business and business into the world of politics (Moon et al., 2005; Edward and Willmott, 2008a, 2008b). The concept of citizenship may thus open up for a more explicit analysis of the firm as a political actor in contrast to the traditional view of corporations in societies (Néron, 2010). As Néron and Norman (2008), who are critical to many aspects of corporate citizenship, acknowledge: 'if we take seriously the conceptual resources of citizenship, it will focus our attention back on a number of important virtues that are surprisingly neglected in discussions framed under the rubrics of business ethics, CSR and sustainability' (Néron and Norman, 2008: 18). Or as Edward and Willmot (2008b: 772) put it: 'An alternative to dropping the corporate citizenship term is to advance a more powerful case for its retention in order to promote greater politicization of the corporation as a means towards social and corporate transformations.' One recent suggestion along these lines is to aim to democratize corporations from within (Scherer et al., 2012).

A note on the public–private divide

Returning to the topic of the (non) existence of the public-private divide, our stance is something of a middle ground approach. As we have discussed above, the literature on states and markets has repeatedly argued (Dahl, 1972) that there has never been a viable distinction between the sphere of politics and the sphere of economic organization in the first place. A similar critique can be found in the literature on corporate citizenship (Van Oosterhout, 2008), a critique that relates to the wider questioning of the explanatory powers of reductionist categorizations (cf. Zelizer, 1997, 2005). As far as the aims of present volume are concerned, this critique somewhat contradicts the novelty of the new role for the corporate actors. An identification of the 'new' role rests on the premise that there is an 'old' one at hand to serve as a point of reference. On the other hand it draws attention to the condition that corporate actors are already engaged in politics, whether we like it or not. Hence, either way, the presence of corporate actors that participate in the public domain needs to be analysed further.

Our position on this issue is that we do agree that the liberal democratic understanding of the public-private divide is a salient condition in contemporary society (Geuss, 2003; Mörth, 2009). Simultaneously we acknowledge that this distinction is by no means self-evident or given. In order to strike a balance between these diverging views, we will treat the public-private divide as a form of rationalized institutional myth (Meyer and Rowan, 1979). The existence of identifiable borders between the public and the private sectors may be one of the great myths of liberal democracy, but it is one that is still alive (cf. Cutler, 2003). Here, we will therefore treat the liberal understanding of democracy as a rationalized part of modern democracies. It does not mean, however, that the divide is not there to be questioned. On the contrary, an overarching theme of the volume is to analyse the assigned new political role of the corporation in the public domain, and this includes casting a critical eye on traditional boundaries and identities.

In the next section, we will expand on how ideas on corporate citizenship can be used as analytical devices to better depict and understand some of the core aspects of the new role of corporate actors in the public domain, including their political role. We will start out with a discussion of the publicization of corporations. We then turn to the set of core properties of citizenship laid out above and discuss some of the implications these may have for the delineation of corporate citizenship.

Publicization, politicization and corporate citizenship

The publicization of the corporation can be understood in several dimensions, some of which overlap with notions of politicization. Publicization and politicization are both signifiers of processes whereby corporate actors are being situated in new positions as compared to their traditional ones as, primarily, economic actors. Though overlapping concepts, publicization can be conceived as the more general concept of the two, and one that is less overtly politically laden. In its basic form, publicization is as a process through which corporations become (more) public. However, what this means in practice varies depending on different conceptions of what the category of 'public' contains. In Bozeman's (1987) view, being 'public' is not a state of either-or. Rather, a specific organization can be deemed public 'to the extent that it exerts or is constrained by political authority' (Bozeman, 1987: 84). Similarly, in his seminal text, Vogel (1976) argues that publicization could be understood in terms of a set of interrelated dimensions that places the corporation in the position of a de facto public institution:

> First, citizens must make demands directly on it [the corporation]. Secondly, they should behave towards it in ways that are similar to their behavior to-ward the state. Thirdly, they should seek to apply to it modes of accountability and responsibility similar to those they apply to the public government. These three aspects of corporate publicization are not empirically distinct; they are dimensions of any behavior that deals with the corporation as a public institution. (Vogel, 1976: 17)

Vogel (1976) frames the publicization of corporations as resulting from the relationship to, and activities of, its clients. The process of publicization arises from demands made on the corporation from the side of the citizens. This is a notion that resonates with contemporary work on stakeholder theory (Jamali, 2008) that underscores the importance of clients and their activities in relation to the focal organization. Modern corporations are expected to contribute to society by taking on more responsibilities and helping out with problem solving in the political arena (Bexell and Mörth, 2010). The emphasis on responsibilities and duties on behalf of corporations in relation to various stakeholders in society is a common denominator across notions of corporate citizenship and related concepts (e.g. Carroll, 1997; Waddock, 2004), Thus, the duties and responsibilities of the corporations for 'the other' (Scherer, 2002) are underscored.

Vogel's (1976) proposition further suggests that it is through the activities of individual citizens that corporations can become corporate citizens. Without other actors taking on the role of citizens, there are no corporate citizens. Notions of political consumerism (Micheletti, 2003) give emphasis to this point. Political consumers are actors that have opted for defining themselves as democratic agents even within the realm of the market. Thus, by acting as citizens they help reconfigure the corporation like a public institution.

Other authors put a larger emphasis on the corporation itself as an actor driving publicization. Moon et al. (2005) portray the corporate actor as an agent engaged in deciding how public it is to be itself. By acting like a citizen the corporation becomes more of one:

> While corporations therefore 'are' not citizens (in the sense of status) we contend that corporations could reasonably claim to act 'as if' they were metaphorically citizens in that their engagement in society resembles that of citizens. (Moon et al., 2005: 448)

What complicates matter is that citizens can be passive or very active members of civil society. It follows, that if corporations act 'as if' (Moon et al., 2005) they were citizens, their behaviour is not necessarily of the active variety. Corporate citizens may thus not be good citizens, and their behaviour may be irresponsible (cf. Lange and Washburn, 2012). As Andriof and Waddock (2002) put it:

> Companies, as independent legal entities, are members of countries and can be thought of as corporate citizens with legal rights and duties—responsibilities. All companies, therefore, are corporate citizens but their citizenship performance varies just as it does for any individual citizen. (Andriof and Waddock, 2002: 26)

With respect to duties, van Oosterhout (2008) has also argued that the use of citizenship in relation to corporations is misleading as corporate actors are not subjects that are to comply, but part of the governance system, 'of the institutional matrix that facilitates and enforces compliance' (van Oosterhout, 2008: 36). Then again, according to Crane et al. (2008), one way for corporate actors to be citizens is perform precisely the kind of governing activities that van Oosterhout calls into question. This leads us back to Peter Bachrach's (1967) thesis that there existed important similarities between General Motors and the United States government.

Responsibilities and duties constitute only one part of citizenship. Following the liberal tradition, rights are at the core of citizenship. This implies that corporate citizens, like other citizens, can be considered as having certain rights and a legitimate sense of entitlement (in relation to their community). Of course, it is difficult to envisage large transnational corporations in the same position as an individual human with respect to human rights, for example. We suggest that such an implied sense of entitlement can however serve as an additional tool to understand corporations as political actors. In particular, with reference to the profit-interest of market actors, and the widespread emphasis on 'the business case' in favour of corporations becoming more pro-active member of society (Roberts et al., 2002; Carroll and Shaban, 2010), the benefits that citizenship connotes for those concerned need to be analysed as well. In the words of Vogel (2009: 79): 'many business firms have now concluded that professing to "good global corporate citizenship", often by subscribing to a civil regulation, makes business sense'. The notion by corporations that they have rights and not only responsibilities might of course create controversy in different political and societal settings. These rights might concern free speech which could be profitable for the corporations because it could allow them greater freedom when marketing their products.

There also exists discussion on identity in relation to corporate citizenship. Above, we touched upon how the placing of the corporate citizen in relation to the public-private dichotomy affects how it is portrayed and identified. In fact, it can be argued that acts of citizenship signify a process of publicization to the effect that the corporate identity becomes (more) public in character. By taking on public tasks and obligations, the corporation becomes less of a private actor. Through its changed behaviour the corporation may take on a new corporate citizenship identity or 'persona' (Burchell and Cook, 2006). The identity of the corporate citizen can thus be seen as stemming from the corporation changing its affiliation from one particular domain, the private domain of the market, to the public domain (see Brunsson, 1994; Jansson and Forssell, 1996 for discussions of shifts in institutional affiliation), From a strategy point of view, there are also discussions on whether the identity of the corporate citizen is to be kept stable, or whether it can, and should, be adapted to local contexts (Huemer, 2010).

Moreover, the idea of citizenship evokes an associated community. Indeed, one important common denominator across theoretical traditions is the notion of how citizenship is about political membership (Beckman and Erman, 2012). As Marshall emphasized: 'Citizenship is a status bestowed on those who are full members of a community' (Marshall, 1992: 18). The members of a community are equal in the sense that they can claim the same civic, social and political rights, and in that they are expected to fulfil the same duties to vote in general elections, for example. Erman (2012) analyses different kinds of political actors or agencies involved in political rule – and decision-making and the different kinds of boundaries and territories within which these practices take place (Erman, 2012). She argues that we need to assess the different roles that political subjects can and ought to play in governance structures. Citizens as political agents can perform many roles in different governance structures and communities. An apposite question is here how this reasoning can be applied to business firms. If a corporation is viewed as a citizen, this means that it is being identified as a political actor within a community, but what kind of political actor, one may ask. Following Erman (2012) the potential territory of corporate citizenship is necessarily limited. She argues that firms may be agents of democracy – they can push for various democratic values – but they are hardly democratic agents since this would require political equality and political restraints (Erman 2012). According to Scherer and Palazzo (2011: 918), however, the politicization of corporations is a result of their operating 'with an enlarged understanding of responsibility', and through their assisting the state in solving 'political problems' along with actors in civil society. Here the political role of corporations appears a more open-ended question.

Furthermore, a growing concern in the citizenship literature is how the community is to be delineated. Communities can be local, national, regional or global. Delanty's discussion views citizenship as being grounded in the nation state project, but this privileging of a state centred community is challenged by contemporary theorizing on political and social transformations:

> Concern about what citizenship is and ought to be is fuelled by the sense that traditional understandings of what it means to be a member of a political community, and what the conditions for membership should be, stand in need of revision as a result of current social and political transformations, in the form of increasingly diversity within states and as a result of new and overlapping governance structures appearing above and in between states. (Beckman and Erman, 2012: ix)

In parallel, authors occupied with corporate citizenship have discussed how a global corporate citizenship can be conceptualized, and differentiated from, one that is embedded in a local or national context. For instance, Logsdon and Wood (2002) distinguish between the propose that the term 'business citizenship' should be used to denote a more global corporate citizenship.

Table 1.1   Corporate citizenship

Citizen traits of corporations	Possible implications for corporate actors
Rights	• By law
Duties	• Problem-solving in society (incl. governing)
	• Responsibilities towards 'the other'
Participation	• Local community
	• National community
	• Transnational community
Identity	• Citizen
	• Public actor

The transformations Beckman and Erman discuss include how reforms in welfare states generate new challenges to social citizenship, and how businesses increasingly provide citizens with public goods and services (Taylor-Gooby, 2008). To be certain, Scherer and Palazzo (2011) stress that globalization promotes the creation of a space for corporations as political actors. Taken together, this challenges the very idea of what it means to be a political member, a citizen, of a community.

Summing up, apart from the traditional public–private divide we can see processes of boundary blurring that call for a new role for private actors in the public domain. This new role can be analysed through the device of corporate citizenship that calls the divide into question. Established notions of citizenship emphasize rights and duties, identity, and participation in the community. These citizenship traits will serve as a framing of the concept of corporate citizenship in this volume, as outlined in Table 1.1.

Contents

The following chapters will look this into questions of the rights and duties of corporate citizens, of their identity, and, not least, the participation of corporate citizens and their political role. In Chapter 2, Steven Gerencser analyses the relationship between the corporate actor and other citizens, and reflects on processes of publicization and the accountability of corporate citizens. Gerencser starts out by highlighting the complexities of the role of corporate citizens as bearers of rights, on the one hand, and as bodies with the capacity to take responsibility for the rights of others, on the other. He then outlines a theoretical framework for analysing the governing role of corporate citizens that draws on ideas on clientelism and the client-patron relationship. This includes viewing the corporation as patron in relationships with other actors, and a placing of asymmetries of power and political problems centre stage in the analysis. The next chapter also draws attention to the relationship between corporate citizens and individual citizens. In Chapter 3, Andrew Crane, Dirk Matten and Jeremy Moon analyse questions on how corporate citizens are implicated in the construction of citizenship of other members of the community, in particular in the construction of citizenship based on identity and difference. In the chapter, Crane et al. elaborate on different facets of the multifaceted role of corporations in identity politics, including their enabling and inhibiting of particular identities. They further argue that economic self-interest is not in and of itself incompatible with the roles they describe.

In Chapter 4, by Boris Holzer, the duties of corporate actors in the transnational public domain are placed at the fore. Holzer discusses how corporations are becoming more like public actors in that they are increasingly being pressured to be transparent about their activities, and open to outside interests and demands. Using Shell as an example, Holzer shows how a number of actors, such as clients, drive the configuring of corporations as moralized actors. In Chapter 5, Fabrizio Panozzo continues the analysis of the reconfiguring of the corporations. One premise for his discussion is that it is inherently difficult for corporations to provide answers to questions concerning who they are, to whom they are accountable and for what, and even more so for corporations aiming to adopt the role of corporate citizens. He then goes on to argue that programmatic ideas of accountable corporate citizens are dependent on the existence of particular techniques that render such accountabilities visible and manageable. In the chapter, this argument is demonstrated through analyses of the SA8000 standard (www.sa-intl.org), the notion of 'Triple Bottom Line' (TBL), and the 'Balanced Scorecard'.

Uwafiokun Idemudia, Chapter 6, seeks to create more space for the marginalized in discourses on corporate citizenship. In the chapter, Idemudia problematizes issues of community and corporate citizenship in relation to large transnational corporations (TNCs). In so doing, he provides an empirical illustration of how the transnational and the local can be very much intertwined aspects of corporate citizenship in practice. One focus for the empirical analysis is to link the expectations of local communities in the Niger delta to the obligations of the oil TNC present in the area, including questions on reciprocal responsibility. Idemudia concludes by discussing how his results support a view of corporate citizenship as a contested domain involving stakeholders at multiple levels in society. Chapter 7, by Céline Cholez and Pascale Trompette, further contributes to the critical analyses of the interrelationship between corporate citizenship and communities in their study of electrification in Madagascar. In this project, the actors in a Bottom of the Pyramid project faced various political concerns and demands to reconcile diverse and opposing aims like responsibility and mass consumption or ecological norms and low-cost criteria in the construction of a market. Cholez and Trompette analyse how the multiple actors and interests concerned could both be included, or marginalized, depending on the market design. They further discuss which community is to be the target one for corporate citizenship when the membership obligations or preferred values in different communities clash. One conclusion from the chapter is that being a good corporate citizen that is legitimate in the eyes of wider institutional settings may equal being a bad corporate citizen in the local community, and vice versa.

In Chapter 8, Paula Blomqvist shifts the perspective to corporate citizenship in (post) New Public Management (NPM) welfare states, as illustrated by the case of Sweden. Sweden was an early adopter of NPM but is also a country where values of social citizenship rights and egalitarianism are still strong, which makes it an interesting case. Indeed, the case of Sweden shows how the publicization of corporations goes hand in hand with a shift from social citizenship to individual citizenship. In the chapter, Blomqvist pays particular attention to the role of corporate citizens as providers of welfare services. One finding is that there are as yet no marked differences in the quality of services across different types of providers, private or public. However, Blomqvist does point to some 'warning signs' for the future, that may cause increased stratification and undermine egalitarian values in society. A starting point for the analysis in Chapter 9, by the editors, is that devolution of (public) authority to corporations points to a renegotiation of the public-private divide emphasizing the duties of corporations to take responsibility for public aims. Using empirical vignettes from a study of the role of private actors in the prevention of money laundering and the financing of terrorism, the chapter analyses the reactions of designated corporate citizens to these demands – and some of the problems they caused. One question discussed is how lawyers and bank employees are to handle the dilemma between being good corporate citizens on the one hand, and serving their clients on the other. Or is being loyal to clients a way of being a good citizen? The empirical illustrations from Swedish private actors are highly interesting at a time when Sweden is reinventing its model of capitalism which has important ramifications for the public-private divide (Greve and Mörth, 2010; Blomqvist, 2004; see also *The Economist* 2013).

In Chapter ten the editors revisit our main research questions. First we provide a summary of what the chapters have had to say concerning what a citizenship for corporations entails, and what the everyday business of citizenship is about. Here we also provide examples of how such practices engage with established ideas on citizenship – corporate and social. We then elaborate on how the previous chapters have contributed to a better understanding of the role of the corporate citizen in the public domain, and discuss to what extent enacted new roles transgress traditional notions of what corporations are and ought to be. Finally we revisit the question of what political role corporate citizens may have.

References

Andriof, J. and S. Waddock (2002) 'Unfolding Stakeholder Engagement', in J. Andriof, S. Waddock, B. Husted and S. Sutherland Rahman (eds) *Unfolding Stakeholder Thinking: Theory, Responsibility and Engagement*, Sheffield: Greenleaf, pp. 19–42.

Bexell, M. and U. Mörth (eds) (2010) *Democracy and Public–Private Partnerships in Global Governance*, London: Palgrave Macmillan.

Blomqvist, P. (2004) 'The Choice Revolution: Privatization of Swedish Welfare Services in the 1990s', *Social Policy and Administration*, 38, 2: 139–155.

den Boer, M. and J. van Buuren (2012) 'Security Clouds', *Journal of Cultural Economy*, 5, 1: 85–103.

Bozeman, B. (1987) *All Organizations Are Public. Bridging Public and Private Organization Theories*, San Francisco, CA: Jossey-Bass.

Brunsson, N. (1994) 'Politicization and "Company-ization" – On Institutional Affiliation and Confusion in the Organizational World', *Management Accounting Research*, 5: 323–335.

Burchell, J. and J. Cook (2006) 'Confronting the "Corporate Citizen". Shaping the Discourse of Corporate Social Responsibility', *International Journal of Sociology and Social Policy*, 26, 3/4: 121–137.

Carroll, A. B. (1991) 'The Pyramid of Corporate Social Responsibility. Towards the Moral Management of Organizational Stakeholders', *Business Horizons*, July–August, 39–48.

Carroll, A. B. (1997) 'Understanding Stakeholder Thinking', *Business Ethics: A European Review*, January, 46–51.

Carroll, A. B. (2003) 'The Four Faces of Corporate Citizenship', *Business and Society Review*, 100/101: 1–7.

Crane, A., D. Matten and J. Moon (2008) *Corporations and Citizenship*, Cambridge: Cambridge University Press.

Cutler, C. A. (2003) *Transnational Merchant Law in the Global Political Economy*, Cambridge: Cambridge University Press.

Dahl, R. (1972) 'A Prelude to Corporate Reform', *Business and Society Review*, 1, Spring, 17–23.

Dingwerth, K. (2007) *The New Transnationalism: Transnational Governance and Democratic Legitimacy*, Basingstoke: Palgrave Macmillan.

Dingwerth, K. and T. Hanrieder (2002) 'Public Markets and Private Democracy?', in Magdalena Bexell and Ulrika Mörth (eds), *Democracy and Public–Private Partnerships in Global Governance*, Basingstoke: Palgrave Macmillan.

Djelic, M.-L. and K. Sahlin-Andersson (2006) *Transnational Governance. Institutional Dynamics of Regulation*, Cambridge: Cambridge University Press.

Drache, D. (2001) (ed.) *The Market or the Public Domain: Global Governance and the Asymmetry of Power*, London: Routledge.

Dryzek, J. (2000) *Deliberative Democracy and Beyond: Liberals, Critics, Contestations*, Oxford: Oxford University Press.

The Economist (2013) 'Northern Lights', February 11–15.

Edward, P. and H. Willmott (2008a) 'Structures, Identities and Politics: Brining Corporate Citizenship into the Corporation', in A. G. Scherer and G. Palazzo (eds) *Handbook of Research on Global Corporate Citizenship*, Cheltenham: Edward Elgar, pp. 405–429.

Edward, P. and H. Willmott (2008b) 'Corporate Citizenship: Rise or Demise of a Myth', *Academy of Management Review*, 33, 3: 771–775.

Geuss, R. (2003) *Public Goods, Private Goods*, Stanford, CA: Stanford University Press.

Greve, C. (2010) 'Public–Private Partnerships: The Scandinavian Experience', in G. A. Hodge, C. Greve and A. E. Boardman (eds) *International Handbook on Public–Private Partnerships*, Cheltenham: Edward Elgar.

Giddens, A. (1990) *The Consequences of Modernity*, Stanford, CA: Stanford University Press.

Helgesson, K. S. and U. Mörth (eds) (2012) *Securitization, Accountability and Risk Management. Transforming the Public Security Domain*, London: Routledge.

Huemer, L. (2010) 'Corporate Social Responsibility and Multinational Corporate Identity: Norwegian Strategies in the Chilean Aquaculture Industry', *Journal of Business Ethics*, 91: 265–277. http://www.sa-intl.org/index.cfm?fuseaction=Page. ViewPage&PageID=937 (accessed September 20, 2012).

Idemudia, U. (2010) 'Corporate Social Responsibility and the Rentier Nigerian State: Rethinking the Role of Government and the Possibility of Corporate Social Development in the Niger Delta', *Canadian Journal of Development Studies*, 30, 1–2: 131–153.

Jamali, D. (2008) 'A Stakeholder Approach to Corporate Social Responsibility: A Fresh Perspective into Theory and Practice', *Journal of Business Ethics*, 82: 213–231.

Jansson, D. and A. Forssell (1996) 'The Logic of Organizational Transformation: On the Conversion of Non-Business Organizations', in B. Czarniawska and G. Sevón (eds) *Translating Organizational Change*, Berlin: Walter de Gruyter.

Kobrin, S. J. (2009) 'Private Political Authority and Public Responsibility: Transnational Politics, Transnational Firms and Human Rights', *Business Ethics Quarterly*, 19, 3: 349–374.

Lange, D. and N. T. Washburn (2012) 'Understanding Attributions of Corporate Social Irresponsibility', *Academy of Management Review*, 37, 2: 300–326.

Logsdon, D. J. and J. M. Wood (2002) 'Business Citizenship: From Domestic to Global Level of Analysis', *Business Ethics Quarterly*, 12, 2: 155–187.

Lindblom, C. (2001) *The Market System. What It Is, How It Works and What to Make of It*, New Haven, CN: Yale University Press.

March, J. G. (1962) 'The Business Firm as a Political Coalition', *Journal of Politics*, 25: 662–678.

Merriam, C. F. (1944) *Public and Private Government*, New Haven, CN: Yale University Press.

Micheletti, M. (2003) *Political Virtue and Shopping: Individuals, Consumerism, and Collective Action*, New York: Palgrave.

Moon, J., A. Crane and D. Matten (2005) 'Can Corporations Be Citizens? Corporate Citizenship as a Metaphor for Business Participation in Society', *Business Ethics Quarterly*, 15, 3: 429–453.

Mörth, U. (2008) *European Public–Private Collaboration. A Choice between Efficiency and Democratic Accountability?* Cheltenham: Edward Elgar.

Mörth, U. (2009) 'The Market Turn in EU Governance – The Emergence of Public–Private Collaboration', *Governance*, 22, 1: 99–120.

Neron, P.-Y. (2010) 'Business and the *Polis*: What Does It Mean to See Corporations as Political Actors?', *Journal of Business Ethics*, 94: 333–352.

Néron, P.-Y. and W. Norman (2008) 'Citizenship, Inc. Do We Really Want Businesses to Be Good Corporate Citizens?', *Business Ethics Quarterly*, 18, 1: 1–26.

Ruggie, J. G. (2004) 'Reconstituting the Global Public Domain: Issues, Actors and Practices', *European Journal of International Relations*, 10, 4: 499–531.

Pies, I., Beckman, M. and S. Hielscher (2010) 'Value Creation, Management Competencies, and Global Corporate Citizenship: An Ordonomic Approach to Ethics in the Age of Globalization', *Journal of Business Ethics*, 94: 265–278.

Sassen, S. (1996) *Losing Control? Sovereignty in an Age of Globalization*, New York: Columbia University Press.

Scherer, A. G. and G. Palazzo (2011) 'The New Political Role of Business in a Globalized World: A Review of New Perspectives on CSR and Its Implications for the Firm, Governance, and Democracy', *Journal of Management Studies*, 48, 4: 899–931.

Scherer, A. G., D. Baumann-Pauly and A. Schneider (2013) 'Democratizing Corporate Governance: Compensating for the Democratic Deficit of Corporate Political Activity and Corporate Citizenship', *Business & Society*, DOI: 10.1177/0 007650312446931.

Sennett, R. (1974) *The Fall of the Public Man*, London: Penguin.

Van Oosterhout, J. (2008) 'Transcending the Confines of Economic and Political Organization? The Misguided Metaphor of Corporate Citizenship', *Business Ethics Quarterly*, 18, 1: 35–42.

Vogel, D. (1975) 'The Corporation as Government: Challenges and Dilemmas', *Polity*, 8, 1: 5–37.

Vogel, D. (2009) 'The Private Regulation of Global Corporate Conduct: Achievements and Limitations', *Business & Society*, 49, 1: 68–87.

Waddock, S. (2004) 'Parallel Universes: Companies, Academics, and the Progress of Corporate Citizenship', *Business and Society Review*, 109, 1: 5–42.

Zelizer, V. A. (1994) *The Social Meaning of Money*, New York: Basic Books.

Zelizer, V. A. (2005) *The Purchase of Intimacy*, Princeton, NJ: Princeton University Press.

2
Corporations and Clientelism: The Problem of Democratic Accountability for Corporate Citizenship

Steven Gerencser

Introduction

The status of the rights of all humans anywhere on the earth has been a concern of the United Nations for the more than sixty years since the adoption of the Universal Declaration of Human Rights in 1948. Such a declaration immediately reveals a long-standing complexity in all discussions of rights. The rights of humans have been understood for centuries by many as the reflection of the dignity that is owed to all humans by others out of respect for their common situation as fundamentally equal moral creatures, notwithstanding the society or state in which they live. Yet rights also have been understood as the particular sets of guarantees of treatment and support that the governments of various individual sovereign states secure for those within their borders, and especially the citizens who are the formal members of their polity. The UDHR attempts to reflect both the universal and general aspect of rights and their particular and historical side as well. It speaks to the universal character of the moral standing of all humans, founding itself upon 'recognition of the inherent dignity and of the equal and inalienable rights of all members of the human family' and yet its mechanism for supporting these rights is the obligation created when 'Member States have pledged themselves to achieve, in co-operation with the United Nations, the promotion of universal respect for and observance of human rights and fundamental freedoms' (United Nations, 1948: Preamble). This complex structure reflects two primary sets of actors: individual humans and sovereign states; the United Nations presents itself as an arena within which the relations of individuals and states can be seen and monitored. Yet while states may claim a status as the unique arbiters and enforcers of rights, and human individuals the unique bearers of those rights, other groups and institutions also situate themselves in some relation to those rights. NGOs act as monitors and advocates of rights and now corporations act both as bearers of rights and importantly as institutions in some way responsible for the supporting and securing rights of citizens.

Corporations' relationship to the rights of citizenship increases the complexity of rights' discussions and introduces confusion because corporations fit easily into neither the position of the protected citizen, not themselves being humans with fundamental dignity to be respected, nor the role of rights' securer and enforcer, lacking the traditional foundations of authority and legitimacy that sovereign governments can claim. Furthermore, corporations are a significant lacuna in the UDHR, which lacks any mention of them at all. However, given the power that corporations possess, especially large transnational corporations, they have often been drafted into the discourse of human rights and citizenship. Notably the United Nations has itself addressed its omission of corporations in the UDHR by the development of the United Nations Global Compact, 'a strategic policy initiative for businesses that are committed to aligning their operations and strategies with ten universally accepted principles in the areas of human rights, labour, environment and anti-corruption' (Global Compact, 2010). The UN Global Compact however establishes relationships that are distinct from common understandings of the relationship of corporations or citizens to governments. Most importantly, the UN Global Compact encourages, exhorts, and makes a business case and even a moral case for why corporations should respect human rights;[1] yet, the Global Compact is clear that its principles and commitments are voluntary, not obligatory.[2] Yet while describing standards and expectations, these documents do not reflect the long-standing discussions, debates and controversies upon which the legitimacy of authoritative institutions of government might be based; while the United Nation is made from sovereign states, of course it does not claim sovereignty, and neither do the corporations being called upon to act in ways as do sovereign states. Thus, the Global Compact does not reflect the contested discourses and debates of democratic deliberation and accountability that seek and challenge the grounds of the sovereign authority of governments and states. Instead the assumptions and claims of the Global Compact seem to be based upon capacity or power; that is, it assumes that because corporations can and do affect the lives of many people beyond the marketplace, corporations then have responsibilities to act in certain ways toward them. Accurate or not, this is a long remove from suggesting they have responsibilities or rights that reflect either those of governments or citizens. Below I consider the complications of moving to an understanding of corporations in the role of fulfilling governing responsibilities as citizens and for citizens. I begin by reviewing some traditional arguments and discussions about citizenship and governance in the liberal democratic framework, and reflect how corporations frustrate those frameworks. I then review some of the claims made regarding how and when corporations have a role for governing. I then turn to a social science framework that reveals complications and limitations for moving toward corporations as governing intuitions that are democratically accountable.

Liberal democracy, markets, and citizens

In standard liberal economic theory, whether paleo or neo, markets and their participants are seen primarily as responding to and creating aggregated individual needs and desires, following principles of supply and demand. The supposed genius of the system 'à la' Adam Smith is that individual market participants, in seeking their private gain, produce a positive unintended public good: a prosperous economy benefiting those individuals in the aggregate and a nation's economy as a whole. The ingenious paradox of the system is that no market actor seeks, or needs to seek, the public good; rather, each is encouraged to seek only its own interests, yet the public good results. Conversely, not only individual market actors need to seek the public good, but such ironically can be deleterious to the provision of the public good. If 'market actor' seems like an odd locution, it is because significant actors in the liberal market economy – if not the most numerous – are not only the individual human actors of whom Smith wrote, but corporations.

From this model of market economics, regardless of how well it works to explain economic behaviour, it is tempting to ask how well it might serve as a model for broader social and political life. That is, if in a market economy actors only need pursue their own self-interests and the common good results, then is this also the case for members of a society in all their actions or for citizens in a polity? Will a public good result when citizens only pursue their self-interests? Indeed much of the history of liberal theory and politics has centred on an on-going set of debates about such questions. Strong proponents of liberalism have advocated for the primacy of the individual and posit the core task of politics as the need to protect the individual's choices regarding how she will lead her life. Conversely many communal, republican, social-ist and even conservative critics of liberalism have to a greater or lesser extent emphasized the need for citizens to identify with and accept responsibilities to serve a public or shared good of some sort.

Consider Jean Jacques Rousseau as an example of a political thinker who has been adopted by almost the whole variety of critics of liberal-ism as well as some liberals. Rousseau differentiates two identities for members of a community living in a just polity; each person needs to hold both of these identities and know when to act with the one pre-dominating or the other. In most of daily life, when interacting in the market place or with one's neighbours, the member of a community may act justly when pursuing even narrow self-interest as long as in doing so he is following the law. Self-conscious consideration of the public good is not necessary as long as one accepts being subject to the laws; and thus Rousseau calls this identity a subject. As a subject, the guiding principles of Adam Smith or the market may play out perfectly well. However, Rousseau holds out a second, necessary if more rarely engaged identity: the citizen. The same person who may freely and justly pursue self-interest in private life must adopt a new perspective when undertak-ing actions in public life. It is with this identity, when being part of an active polity that considers public issues, one that deliberates laws that affect all and the conditions of life that all must share, that a different identity, that of the citizen, must be adopted. When acting as a citizen one is an active member of a community, and it is not self-interest but the public good that one must pursue with others, and the sovereign will that enacts the laws under which those same citizens go on to live their lives as subjects is what Rousseau calls the general will.[3]

Rousseau handles these issues by presenting in one framework the two different ways of understanding the identities, motivations and expectations of members of communities which are reflected in two basic competing models of politics and citizenship. The first is a com-munitarian or participatory model of politics and citizenship that relies on traditional republican ideals, those emphasizing responsibili-ties of on-going and active service to the polity by its citizens and in which freedom is seen in the rights to participate in communal self-governance. This model is often praised and idealized, but in practice often fades relative to a second model, a more liberal model. This liberal model emphasizes the rights of individuals to make choices about their lives within the broadest range of freedom possible while accepting a modicum of limitation upon that freedom to gain the stability offered by the rule of law, common security, and perhaps some other limited list of public goods that cannot otherwise easily be achieved. This bargain between seeking greater amounts of freedom within a framework of limitation, whether seen as law, regulation, or taxation, also orients much of the debate within liberalism; government is given the sole responsibility for enforcing law, protecting rights. Politics in this liberal framework serves primarily to establish and alter the common rules by which all should live; furthermore, politics serves to assure that whatever power is established to protect rights does not itself become abusive of rights. The more democratic the politics in this framework, the more the government is accountable to those over whom it exercises such an awesome responsibility, and accountability is a fundamental feature since government is only authoritative because its rests on the acceptance of those over whom it exercises such power.

This brief rehearsal of some central features of liberal democratic theory and the competing ideas regarding identities and of citizens and the role for government likely covers familiar ground. There are of course many alternate political theories and social/political economic arrangements than liberal ones, and I do not assume liberal frameworks – and debates about it them – are the only insightful ones. However, central features of market economies, the grounding of rights, and understandings of the rule of law have routinely reflected this liberal framework. Furthermore, this understanding of liberalisms' framing of these discussions reveals some of the complexities of understanding what role corporations might or should play in avenues of life that have traditionally been conceived without their presence, particularly society and politics. Thus, in the liberal political framework that has supported market economics, the debates have often centred on the following types of questions: how much or how little or under what circumstances should a member of a political community pursue self-interest versus pursuing the good of the whole? How active and vigorous should government be in protecting the rights of citizens, and which sets of rights are appropriate for government action to secure, and what procedures are necessary for assuring that when the government acts it does so in such a way to be accountable to those it claims to act on behalf of?

The debates about those questions above, which are played out in the skirmishes between liberal and republican or communitarian theorists are complicated enough to generate centuries of political and theoretical disagreements; these debates are made even more difficult in several ways by corporations. First, this way of debating rights and responsibilities of individual actors is complicated by the variegated history of corporations which begins with them being established to achieve distinctly public goods, an identity that lingers in school corporations or port authorities, but in which they become transformed into distinct and powerful market actors for the narrow purpose of the benefit of their investors.[4] Second, there have been on-going philosophical debates about the pre-political status of the human individuals that become citizens and provenance of the rights they bear. Yet the basis of rights of corporations has been less theorized, even while it is similarly complicated, legally confusing, and politically contested, especially when trying to plumb whether the rights corporations claim are manifestations of or independent from the individual humans who make them up. Third, and related, as such powerful actors, corporations are capable of generating enormous resources and in doing so have enormous impact upon the lives of those around them in a way that is all but impossible for individual human citizens to accomplish; thus corporations are seen at times as just one more economic actor on the model of human agents, and at others like larger social institutions such as churches or hospitals, or even governments.

Corporations, then, frustrate common ways of understanding and questioning the basis of citizenship: considering whose rights are to be protected, what are primary threats to individuals' rights, which institutions are to protect those rights, and who or what cares for the public and political goods of the citizens of any polity. The practices of looking to corporations to take up responsibilities in society more generally is not new, of course, and if using the language of citizenship as a way to characterize these responsibilities is more recent, it has in a short time generated a significant outpouring of debate and scholarship. The history of political philosophy about the appropriate roles of government, citizens, the economy, and civil society need not limit that debate, but it is at least worth remembering that the questions regarding who has rights, who is responsible for protecting those rights, and what those rights should be has a history.

Corporations as citizens and governments

As suggested above, the social role of corporations has been contested by economists, business ethicists, business practitioners, and social activists who have wrestled over what, if any, responsibilities the modern business corporation should undertake in society.[5] While much of this debate has centred on the identity of corporate (or business) citizen, a recent and potentially helpful debate has centred on understanding corporations not primarily through the concept of citizenship, but through the concept of governance. Indeed the primary innovation of the works of scholars such as Andreas Georg Scherer, Guido Palazzo, Wendy Chapple, Andrew Crane, Dirk Matten, and Donald Moon has been to challenge the idea of corporate citizenship, not by rejecting in whole, but by understanding how corporations play at least a dual role in society.[6] While sometimes corporations may act as individual entities that may have certain rights and duties just as individual citizens, they can and should be understood as having a 'political role' (Scherer and Palazzo, 2011: 900), and that increasingly 'corporations take over many of the roles and actions previously associated with government' (Matten and Crane, 2005: 170). I will not examine that argument in its entirety, but I will review its main elements as found in the especially of Crane et al. to judge how it might assist or limit thinking about the protection and promotion of citizenship. It further must be noted that while this proposal has freshened the debate about corporations' social and political roles, it has also been a source of some controversy, generating critics as well as supporters.

Crane et al. acknowledge the complex nature of the concept of citizenship, arguing it is 'an essentially contested concept' and not only because there are competing normative claims about it, but because it can be employed normatively, empirically, and analytically (Moon, Crane and Matten, 2005: 433). They further recognize that much of the debate about corporate citizenship has taken place in a normative vein, where corporate citizenship (CC) is viewed primarily as one more version of corporate social responsibility (CSR). Granting, or saddling, corporations with the identity of citizen however generates theoretical, legal, as well as practical problems because it remains unclear whether the title is meant metaphorically or that corporations can be actual citizens. Furthermore, that so many corporations so happily adopt the identity of citizen may show that is has been a successful strategy to corral their poor behaviour as well as to encourage better social engagement from corporations, yet simultaneously this adoption raises suspicion regarding why corporations might be so open to it. Corporate interest in CC is at least in part grounded in the positive valuation that comes from a successful claim to the status of citizen; further unlike CSR, which focuses almost exclusively upon duties, citizenship encompasses a measure of rights as well as responsibilities. Thus, Bernhagen and Mitchell suggest the importance of understanding firms' 'decision to join the [UN] Global Compact as a form of corporate political activity ... a generalized "investment" in political capital, which they expect to yield non-specific payoffs' (Bernhagen and Mitchell, 2010: 1177). As in the title of the groundbreaking article by Crane et al., corporations can the act 'Behind the Mask' of citizenship, accepting the plaudits for their CSR activities, while claiming rights relative to other traditionally conceived citizens. Here, however, Crane et al. argue that while corporations may not be best understood as citizens, there is no escaping that in contemporary political, social and economic life corporations are connected to citizenship. This connection, they argue, is not simply in undertaking the activities of citizens, but in producing citizenship and affecting the lives of citizens. Traditional CSR and even CC activities have challenged how corporations should act in society based on the model of what citizens ought to do; but beyond this, Crane et al. suggest corporations affect and in many cases effect citizenship.

Citizenship is a bundle of more or less well defined rights, and the corporate involvement in this context does not mean that corporations bravely share in these, but that they have gradually amounted to replace the most powerful institution in the traditional concept of citizenship, namely government. corporations, and to a decreasing amount governmental institutions, assume responsibility for the protection and facilitation of social, civil and political rights and corporate 'citizenship', we would suggest, can and should be reconceptualized to mean exactly this. The implications are that corporations are engaging as facilitators of the citizen process, regardless of whether they are explicitly setting out to be 'good corporate citizens' (Matten, Crane and Chapple, 2003: 117).

This changes significantly the discussion of corporations because the questions shift from how much they can or should act like citizens to how much they can and should act like governments, the institutions which have had the primary focus of supporting and protecting citizens in the modern state.

Crane et al. arrive at this conclusion by drawing together for observation a variety of developments in the realm of citizenship and governance of the last few decades. One such trend has been a diminished capacity of the governments of states to respond to the needs and demands of citizens, resulting in a so-called retreat of the state, whether in developed liberal states that are primarily affected by globalization and neo-liberal political policies or in less developed states whose governments never fully established the capacity to secure citizenship. A second development has been corporations increasingly providing the type of citizenship benefits and protections in the sense of civil and social rights that in the recent past governments have been expected to provide. Thus when corporations undertake some activities associated with traditional CSR, one way to understand what they are doing is filling in the gaps left when states retreat from earlier commitments or fail even to attempt them.[7] Leaving aside the question of whether this is a useful way of understanding the roles of corporations in society, it is easy to see that doing so raises many challenging analytical and empirical questions, such as: to what extent do corporations actually do this? Which corporations (or types) act in a governing role? Are the governing activities evenly distributed over all corporations? Are there areas of governance that corporations can – or cannot – accomplish well? Do differing state relations to corporations make their capacity to participate as governors more effective? Do corporations seek this role? Is the interest in this role even across sectors? What social or political vulnerabilities are created in the context of general market failures or the specific failure of a corporation in a market? These empirical and analytical issues slide into a second set of fundamentally critical and normative questions as well. Fundamentally: on what basis do corporations claim legitimacy for acting with governing authority? Viewing corporate citizens as corporate governors also raised questions such as: can institutions whose primary interest is in profit be expected to serve interests and needs which detract from or conflict with profitability? Should citizens expect a role for self-governance when being governed by corporations? How can corporations be held democratically accountable for their governmental like actions?

In their work, Crane et al. have addressed many of these issues, and I will stay focused upon the latter set of these questions as they attend to issues of citizenship. But I note first that while the discussion surrounding CSR and CC is mostly hortatory or laudatory, such approaches do have their critics, including when corporations are viewed through their governing functions. The array of such criticism is broad, ranging from defenders of a traditional view of the corporation (e.g. Sundaram and Inkpen, 2004) to those that object specifically to idea of corporations as citizens with rights (e.g. van Oosterhut, 2005). Citizenship is almost always seen to include some attention to a set of rights and obligations; and certainly much political debate surrounds what the content and balance of those rights and obligations should be. Not surprisingly one of the controversies about seeing corporations through the lens of citizenship is that it secures for them an identity with a set of the rights that have commonly been understood to be the claims of human individuals. If CSR focused upon obligations, then adopting the language of citizenship allows corporations to graft on a set of rights. Retaining the language of citizenship in connection with corporations thus threatens to empower them with rights over and against the human individuals and even the states that create and charter them. Much of the reaction to the 2010 Supreme Court of the United States' ruling *Citizens United v. FEC* (494 U.S. 652, 2010) expresses this type of concern.[8] Yet, prior to this ruling, critics had pointed out the problems of political equality subsumed in the notion of corporate citizenship. If the point of attention to corporations as governments by Crane et al., as noted above, is to recognize that governance function of corporations in connection to citizenship, then, critics have also pointed out some fundamental problems with this approach. Van Oosterhout, for instance, asks '(1) why corporations would be more efficient administrators of citizenship rights than states or other intra- or international public entities, and (2) why they might choose to take up these responsibilities in the first place. This is particularly problematic given that most citizenship rights have a public goods character, making their administration by corporations result in vast collective action problems' (2005: 678). These questions point to the dilemma that modern corporations are primarily market institutions, and van Oosterhout (2005) suggests there is neither the market justification for corporations acting as governments, nor is there any empirical evidence that suggests that when they do so, it is in a fashion more efficient that states.

The observations research identifying the increasing governance role corporations do, however, obscure one important element. Crane et al. argue ideological realignments and globalization have combined with and accelerated an 'institutional failure of the classic welfare state' (Crane, Matten and Moon, 2008: 56). The state has retreated and thus is no longer capable of providing enough by way of securing and administering citizenship rights, leaving the field open for those institutions which can: corporations. The suggestion that the state has declined – both as concept for study and an institution capable of governing – has been a significant point of contention in the study of politics. The claim itself varies between empirical claims about the size and scope of modern welfare states to more interpretative judgments about declining legitimacy of the modern welfare state. However, the meaning of the discussion and any actuality of decline of the state needs to be studied in the context of corporations and their political activities. The retreat or failure of the state cannot be viewed like that of a natural event that simply has occurred and must be reckoned with. Rather, when the state deregulates parts of its economy, privatizes central functions, fails to address a public needs, comes to be viewed as illegitimate by its citizens, or is exposed as vulnerable to global pressures, these are the results of complex political actions and rhetorical framings, contributed to by corporations and their intellectual defenders, among others.[9]

Views that an economy is over-regulated, that the government is not able to offer services efficiently, and that citizens or businesses are over-taxed are all important judgments for citizens to render and they may be fair or even accurate assessments of a situation. But they also reflect ideological positions and power interests of some actors who affect the situation. While Crane et al. acknowledge ideological formations such as the 'New Right' and its contributions to changing assessments of the value and efficiency of the state; this is done primarily to set the scene in which corporations' new role might come to be discussed (Crane, Matten and Moon, 2008: 57). However, corporate actors must themselves be understood to be part of the creators of the conditions in which states find themselves vulnerable to forces of globalization and less able to secure basic levels of equality for their citizens. It ought not to be surprising that corporate actors will often lobby for less regulation and less market control by governments and support political parties, politicians, and ideological opinion leaders who are predisposed to find government failure or argue for a reduced role for government. Similarly, globalization is not simply a natural process that unfolds; rather, globalization reflects choices that favour some interests over others, certain political structures over others. Crane et al., for instance, suggest as an 'indicator of the declining effect of the welfare state is the growing levels of inequality between citizens in many liberal democracies such as the US' (Crane, Matten and Moon, 2008: 55). While it is no doubt true that levels of inequality have grown in the United States, this trend has been brought about, in part, by a sustained political assault on unionization and the adoption of taxation policies that have served to create such conditions. In each of these cases corporations have not been bystanders but participants.[10]

Clientelism and corporations: a framework for analysing corporations' governing role

The model of corporations as exercisers of governance in society as a whole proposed by scholars like Crane et al. is provocative in part because it expands the field of analysis with which we can understand both the relations between corporations and society and then also the affects those relations have upon other significant social, political, and economic relations and values. One potential advantage of seeing corporations through the lens of governments is that we have centuries of theory, analysis, and practice for examining governments, for judging their effectiveness, for discussing their justness, for scrutinizing different forms of government both their strengths and vulnerabilities, and for understanding how citizens can hold them accountable. How well these are all applicable to corporations is a question worth significant study, but Crane et al. broaden the range of study beyond inquiring how much corporations are like citizens to other analytical frameworks. One such framework is clientelism, or the study of patron-client relations, an approach used in anthropology, comparative sociology, and political science to study societies in which a distinct type of social relation frustrates the development of legitimate and accountable practices of power. With corporations understood as exercising power more broadly in society, clientelism, or the patron-client framework, focuses upon the relations of a corporation to those stakeholders with whom it has a governance relationship, illuminating how these often reflect a patron using its significant resources to grant favours to its clients. Furthermore, this framework of patrons governing over clients provides insight to the difficulty in creating avenues by which those subject to power can hold accountable those who exercise power over them.

Patrons and clients

There is a long history of analysis of patron-client relations in a number of historical and social science fields with various emphases, however some central themes emerge. Luigi Graziano provides a theoretical review of some of clientelism's core conceptual and theoretical elements, starting with a basic definition from James Scott, 'The patron-client relationship – an exchange relation between roles – may be defined as a special case of dyadic (two-person) ties involving a largely instrumental friendship in which an individual of higher socio-economic status (patron) uses his own resources and influence to provide protection or benefits, for a person of lower status (client) who, for his part, reciprocates by offering general support and assistance, including personal services, to the patron' (Graziano, 1976: 152, quoting Scott, 1972: 92). Graziano identifies the three main properties that more fully detail a clientelist relationship. It features particular structural relationships that are 'dyadic'; next, it exhibits political relationships that are 'power relationships'; and finally, such relations are 'a factor affecting the political and social development of a society' (Graziano, 1976: 151). His elaboration of the first presents an interesting hurdle to applying this framework to analysing corporations' relations to society; the dyads that Graziano discusses emphasize personal relations between patron and client. Almost all discussions of clientelism emphasize this characteristic; further, this is one of the reasons why it is seen as a more primitive form of power relationship: patron-client relations are not institutionalized but unique, personal, and even intimate. Further, the patron will have a number of such relationships with many different clients and each of these, because personal, need not be equal to or consistent with the others. This property of clientelism significantly limits the relationship to particular and individual dyads, and thus when either side of that dyad ends the relationship, or perhaps even dies, that particular patron-client relationship is over. This property then serves to isolate clients from each other since each client has a unique, personal relation to the patron. Finally, these relations are not specific and satisfied upon a particular action; they are not contractual but organic and amorphous.

The second of the properties of patron-client relations emphasizes the power relations involved between the sides of the dyad, in particular the asymmetrical character of that relationship. This feature is emblematic of the clientelist of relationship, the patron has power and resources which he can exert on behalf of or bestow upon – and also withhold from – the client, creating an obligation on behalf of the client. Again this is not a contractual relationship of bargained exchange; the exchange, while reciprocal, is not equal. The patron offers a favour with the expectation of some future return, but unlike a contract it is not specified exactly what and when it will be repaid; neither does it presume that whatever the client can offer in the exchange actually or fully pays for the benefits received. This is an asymmetrical power relationship because the patron offers something that the client needs or desires while the client cannot offer something of equivalent value or need to the patron, and thus remains in a state of sustained indebtedness, held hostage to the benefits that are accepted and thus to the patron who offers them. This is not to say the relationship is purely unidirectional. The patron receives some benefit as well, but while the initial favour is clear and specific, and perhaps on-going, the return is unspecified. Thus, Graziano emphasizes that while each side may benefit, the granting of a favour or gift by the patron establishes a relationship in a way that enhances his power, creating a client who is a supplicant, dependent, and obligated. '[A patron] gives because in highly stratified societies an effective way to control conflict is to establish a network of personal obligations; one gives, at the same time, in order to crush clients and rivals with onerous obligations sanctioned by personal submission of the defaulting debtor. One gives, in summary, because this is a rational means for accumulating power, a means which is *typical* in "primitive" society and *subsidiary* to the market in advanced capitalist societies' (Graziano, 1976: 162, emphasis in original). Thus, the granting of gifts and benefits is not merely a sign of asymmetrical power relations, but a mechanism for perpetuating the asymmetry.

The idea of the gift as an obligating source of power was also recognized by Marcel Mauss, the early twentieth-century sociologist, in his monograph titled *The Gift*. Studying non-industrial societies, Mauss suggested that in such 'civilizations contracts are fulfilled and exchanges of goods are made by means of gifts' (Mauss, 1954: 1). It would be a mistake, however, to see these gifts as purely charitable, given with no expectation of return. Instead, Mauss observed gifts 'are in theory voluntary, disinterested and spontaneous, but in fact are obligatory and interested. The form usually taken is the gift generously offered; but the accompanying behaviour is formal pretence and social deception, while the transaction itself is based on obligation and self-interest' (Mauss, 1954: 1). While this may seem cynical, Mauss's purpose is analytical, to illuminate how beside an altruistic element of gifts there may be an exchange character of gifts, gifts given out of expectation and how then gift giving generates or satisfies obligation.

Graziano's emphasis, like Mauss's, on the way gift giving perpetuates asymmetries leads to the third property of patron-client relations: they negatively affect political development. Patron and client do not simply describe static identities in relation, but a self-re-enforcing relationship that anchors an asymmetric distribution of power; thus this relation also serves to limit political possibilities. Graziano suggests that political development past patron-client relations occurs only when power becomes legitimate through the process of increasing 'indirect exchanges', those not based on personal relations or 'direct exchanges', but upon mediated forms of exchange (like markets and bureaucratic institutions) and expressing widely acknowledged values. Political development requires a movement to secular 'Authority [which] stabilizes power in a way that personal influence, based as it is on vertical controls of the leader over single subordinates, cannot possibly do' (Graziano, 1976: 168). 'Authority' in this context reflects the achievement of a stabilized and legitimate form of power which further can accept 'organized opposition ... which makes it possible for people to unite and react collectively', breaking the isolation of the various clients' position (Graziano, 1976: 170). On the other hand 'individual incentives typical of direct exchange make collective mobilization for long-term objectives infinitely more difficult' (Graziano, 1976: 169). Again, because the personal exchange relations between patron and client isolate clients, they limit the development of shared expectations while narrowing the capacity for deliberation and common account-ability. Thus the maintenance of the central properties of clientelism prevents a movement to power relations that reflect formal authority with a capacity for public deliberation, a discourse of accountability and democratic action.[11]

Before suggesting ways in which this approach may be insightful in understanding corporations' role as social benefactors, I acknowledge a caution. Hilgers appropriately counsels against excessive 'conceptual stretching' when discussing clientelism warning that it empties it of any distinct meaning (Hilgers, 2011: 576). Reviewing all the different behaviours and interactions that social scientists have stretched to apply clientelism she observes:

> Candidates for public election buy votes; certain electoral districts benefit unfairly from public works programs based on their repre-sentatives' bargaining power in various governmental fora; citizens bribe officials; governing parties bribe members of the opposition; friends and supporters receive jobs that they do not merit; citizens – individually or in groups – and their patrons build lasting relationships in which they exchange all manner of goods and services; dissidents are economically or physically threatened; and some political parties or governments engage in all of these practices. All of this is described as clientelism. Despite the intrinsic value of these research contribu-tions, their indiscriminate use of the term clientelism has voided the concept of descriptive power and makes it difficult to compare a case described in one study to that in another. (Hilgers, 2011: 572)

The application of clientelism is not my attempt to 'void the concept of value', but to determine how much of its insights can help analysts see corporate social power and governance activities in a new light.

Corporations as patrons

Based on this review of some basic features of clientelism, how well might this framework provide analytical insight to corporations' partici-pation in social governance? On the surface, at least, it appears that the provision of benefits and protections that corporations offer in their gov-ernance roles do fit them in the identity of patron. Either when engaged in the activities of philanthropy in an advanced industrial state or when providing basic benefits such as clean water, roads, or health clinics in less developed states with weak governments, corporations use their greater resources to grant to those in need; they clearly are benefactors in these social and governance roles. Yet other features of the framework may reveal some limitations in applying it to corporations. Most importantly, the first of the properties that Graziano discusses emphasizes the personal element in the patron-client relationship. Traditionally, an individual land holder may grant benefits to a worker on the land, or a party boss may find a job for a party member, connecting them in a direct and reciprocal, yet unequal exchange relationship. But corporations, especially global corporations, are large institutional actors, most often in relationships with large groups of stakeholders, sometimes organized and represented. A city, township, or county council, a development association, a school corporation, an NGO, an arts guild, and a labour union may each be in the role of client and this seems not to fit with the personal exchange property that Graziano presents. Yet perceived differently, each of these is an individual group with its own relationship to the corporation as patron, just as individual clients would in the traditional patron-client connection.

Mauss also noted how giving and creating obligations thereby need not be individual; in the societies where exchange is marked by such giving, he claimed, 'it is groups, and not individuals, which carry on exchange, make contracts, and are bound by obligations; the persons represented in the contracts are moral persons – clans, tribes, and families; the groups, or the chiefs as intermediaries for the groups, confront and oppose each other' (Mauss, 1954: 3). Furthermore, those relations are not generalizable; a corporation may assist with a direct financial grant to the arts guild while offering accounting assistance to the local school board in one community while at the same time discounting the costs of vaccines in a different community; some of these may be one-time benefits, and others annual or long-term assistance. Finally, at least one more possible similarity exists. A feature of the patron-client relation Graziani observed is that the relationship ends when a member of the dyad quits it. Similarly, an on-going difficulty with using corporations to supplement government or to act as governors is that as market creatures they may not only succeed with their primary business, but also fail or significantly alter their business model based on market conditions. If a large corporation closes a manufacturing site, or a firm is bought out or goes bankrupt and that site closes, the relation is ended. The client may no longer be a client, but similarly has been left bereft of the needed benefits or protections in want of a new patron.

This leads to the second property of clientelism: asymmetries of power. It becomes a common trope in writing about CC and CSR to make some passing allusion to the comic book phrasing 'with great power comes great responsibility'. While seeming to offer the moral basis of 'noblesse oblige' for CC and CSR in exactly those areas where they have governing functions, this likewise highlights that the basis is an unequal distribution of power. Further, the relationships between a corporation and its many stakeholders are not reciprocal or contractual. While exchanges with suppliers, stockholders and customers are either based upon or reflect contracts, in many of their governing functions, corporations provide benefits and protections that are offered with no expectation of equivalent or immediate returns. Of course the corporation may benefit by securing a stable community, a community that thinks well of the corporation, that provides benefits and protections, and one that supports the corporation in its political demands to the state; thus such a stakeholder client may support its corporate patron's needs at some future date. But this is not a contract or simple quid pro quo. This 'instrumental friendship' is not symmetrical, and the more a community of stakeholders becomes dependent upon a corporation for those benefits and protections, the less able it is to oppose it without threatening those very provisions. Graziano's discussion turns almost sinister as when he noted earlier how a patron 'gives ... to crush clients and rivals with onerous obligations sanctioned by personal submission of the defaulting debtor'; and this may not and need not reflect the character of activities that corporations undertake when practicing CC or CSR. Yet if seen through the experience of company towns in which corporations actually do serve as governments, the description is not entirely inapt.

The mention of company towns leads to the third property of client-elism that Graziano points to: the effect on political development. Company towns have been premier examples where corporations do act as governments; traditionally these have also offered poor working/living conditions and have also been notoriously brutal in their repression of dissent and opposition.[12] There may be analytical promise in applying this third property to corporations' relations to society, but some difficulty as well. The significance in the clientelism framework comes from the limitation that direct exchanges of the personal relation have upon establishing broad based norms that can be reflected in legitimate institutions of governance. Put differently, the rule of law can only develop when individual personal relations have been de-centred from power relations. Further, those broader values and shared norms offer the basis by which to criticize and hold power to account. While corporations do not fit neatly into the personal relationship characteristics suggested by the framework, it is possible to understand the particular and different relations that corporations have with different stakeholders in this manner. Can a diverse range of stakeholders create horizontal connections to each other, based upon common interests and values, so as to break the individual patterns and relations with various corporations? Graziano suggests that it is through horizontal connections between clients that the limiting dynamics of the traditional patron-client relationship can be overcome. 'It is such [horizontal] linkages based on identification of common interests that has permitted, for instance, the organization of workers through trade unions. Such linkages are impossible to realize within dyadically organized associations' (Graziano, 1976: 169). Scherer and Palazzo point to a complication with advocating a movement to an ethical view of CC and CSR based on shared norms and values: 'the question remains of how the legitimacy of corporate activities can be normatively accessed when no universal criteria of ethical behaviour are available in a post-modern and post-national world' (Scherer and Palazzo, 2011: 906). But here more contextually specific analyses and alliances that can allow for common identification and norms – not universal are what matters. It would be through such identification that procedures of accountability to those over whom power is exercised, and practices of dispute and opposition can be established. The framework then helps to identify a question regarding whether such horizontal linkages between stakeholders can be established in a form equivalent to something like trade unions is possible in order to overcome the narrowing position of the client.

Here the United Nations Global Compact offers an interesting possibility. The Global Compact seeks to institutionalize some part of corporate governance activities, moving these from the particular commitments of some corporations to particular communities to a shared set of norms of the community of transnational corporations. Graziano observes that the importance of such institutionalization is that 'norms come to be observed as a matter of principle and not for the social advantages that compliance carries with it' (Graziano, 1976: 169). This demonstrates the importance of moving beyond the language that endorses CC or CSR activities because 'it is good for business', rather such practices become necessary to reflect common norms, expectations and values. Yet this also suggests a possible limitation of the Global Compact: while it reserves a place for NGOs to speak on behalf of affected communities, it focuses primarily upon generating participation among the 'patrons'; conversely, Graziano emphasizes the importance for 'clients' to generate solidarity of interests and norms in order to push back against their position as client. Looking to corporations to provide such public goods may actually serve to empower the patron, limiting the growth of democratically accountable states which could develop the institutional mechanisms to provide for their citizens. Joshi and Mason identify such a pattern in which 'existing networks of patron-client ties alter the electoral preferences of peasant voters and create incentives for candidates to focus on the provision of private goods to patrons instead of public good for peasant voters' (Joshi and Mason, 2011: 171). While their focus is upon peasant and rural economies, they suggest a basic pattern in which state support ensconces the patron, making the capacity to challenge and surpass patron–client relations even more difficult.

Finally, in assessing the possibility of moving beyond patron-client relationships, the place of opposition is central. This is not based upon an assumption of conflicting interests with powers that govern; rather it is a means by which those over whom power is exercised can express difference, disagreement, alternate views of direction that then can hold those who govern accountable. This then identifies one other limitation of the Global Compact and similar institutions such as the Social Accountability International: the primary form of accountability is not to those over whom power is exercised but to the external constituencies. Not only Graziano and the framework of clientelism, but the basic forms of liberal democracy propose that the legitimacy of those claiming governing authority rests on the judgment of those over whom that governing power is exercised. Citizenship is centred not exclusively or primarily on who receives what benefits, but upon those who are governed exercising deliberation, judgment and power back to those who exercise power over them. Palazzo and Scherer make a similar argument in advocating for a view of 'Corporate Legitimacy as Deliberation' (Palazzo and Scherer, 2006; see also Scherer and Palazzo, 2007; 2011). Yet in adopting a constrained Habermasian view of deliberation exclude the sort of strategic action necessary to establish procedures of political accountability. Examining whether corporations as governments can or cannot move in the direction toward accountability will identify the significant challenges to how well this form of governance can become legitimately authoritative to those over whom it is exercised.

Conclusion

Pierre-Yves Néron and Wayne Norman in a provocative essay titled 'Corporate Citizenship, Inc.' ask the question 'Do we really want businesses to be good citizens?' (Néron and Norman, 2008: 1). It is tempting to ask the same about corporations and governance: 'Do we really want businesses to be good governments?' Yet theorists of the corporation such as Scherer, Palazzo, Crane, Chappel, Matten and Moon have done a significant service in proposing that the relationship of corporations to citizenship should be understood not primarily by viewing corporations as citizens, but also as political and governing institutions that already are providing and administering citizenship. The language of citizenship has always offered a paradox when viewing corporations. On the one hand, it offers a well-established discourse of rights and responsibilities that may offer an effective means to engage and enrol corporations as more complete members in the polities where they practice. On the other hand, the presumption of some basic equality that undergirds most conceptions of citizenship causes at least some unease when trying to bring corporations and human citizens into the same fundamental categories. The global scope and extraordinary resources that corporations are able to generate raise issues beyond individual citizens. By drawing attention to the power that corporations possess and exert beyond the market and into society and politics, Crane et al. reveal their role as governing institutions. The theoretical advantage of this move is not only its potentially greater accuracy, but in how it opens avenues for pursuing a broader set of analytical, empirical, and normative questions regarding the social and political roles of corporations. This chapter points to questions about the legitimacy of corporations in their governance capacities and to suggest a framework that can highlight the political problems that can develop when corporations play a role of provider and administrator of goods we associate with citizenship. This is not to imply that corporations cannot or should not do so, although some may reasonably pursue those positions, rather it is to recognize that it introduces new political relationships that create opportunities and problems, both for practitioners and researchers. A central feature of the struggle for democratic practices in the modern liberal state has been to create avenues by which citizens can question their government, hold it accountable, challenge it to reflect their interests, and criticize it when it does not. At least one central challenge in considering corporations' roles as governors will be to examine what practices and can lead to (or might prevent) a similar movement toward citizen empowerment and accountability.

Notes

1. See for instance 'Business and Human Rights: A Progress Report,' http://www.ohchr.org/Documents/Publications/BusinessHRen.pdf.

2. Thus John Ruggie, the Special Representative of the Secretary-General on the issue of human rights and transnational corporations and other business enterprises, in the report *Business and Human Rights: Further steps toward the operationalization of the 'protect, respect and remedy' framework* writes 'respecting rights is not an obligation that current international human rights law generally imposes directly on companies, although elements may be reflected in domestic laws' Section IV; para 55. (A/HRC/14/27).

3. I do not intend any fresh interpretation of Rousseau here and rely almost entirely on Book I, Chapter 6 of *On the Social Contract.*

4. Many histories of the corporate form exist. One brief but helpful review that stands well over time can be found in Part I of Stone (1975: 1–25).

5. The literature on corporate social responsibility and corporate citizenship is wide-ranging, filled with compelling theoretical and practical controversies, and too extensive to review here. Crane., McWilliams, Matten, Moon, and Siegel, (2009) and Scherer and Palazzo (2011) provide insightful and useful reviews.

6. This set of writers, Wendy Chapple, Andrew Crane, Dirk Matten, and Donald Moon, have collaborated on a number essays that develop, re-enforce but do not perfectly overlap each other. I will often refer to them as Crane et al. since three of the authors, Crane, Matten and Moon, have collaborated on the longest work, *Corporations and Citizens* (2008), yet I will also note the particular works I draw upon.

7. Debates regarding the state's incapacity, governance and globalization are extensive. Pierre (2000) provides a useful overview.

8. The response to this ruling has been voluminous; an excellent example of the concerns it raises for democracy and citizenship can be found in Youn (2011).

9. So also Scherer and Palazzo, while emphasizing the decline of the state and the new governance role for corporations in what they call "political CSR," undervalue the already existing strategic and rhetorical political activities of corporations (2011: 901).

10. While much attention has been given to *Citizens United v FEC*, it is worth noting that over 30 years earlier the court had established a corporation's right to political activity through advertising in a state level referendum. The political activity which the corporation had been undertaking that was upheld in *First National Bank of Boston v. Bellotti* (435 U.S. 765, 2010) was actually the actions of a bank in public advertising and advocacy against the adoption of a progressive state income tax.

11. Hilgers conversely argues 'In sum, the issue of clientelism is complex. Although it has a series of corrosive effects on society, it cannot be roundly dismissed as negative: the socio-economically marginalised perceive clientelism to be a useful strategy for fulfilling basic needs and, in some cases, clientelism actually has positive effects on collective action and political involvement by giving poor citizens organisational and participatory skills (2009: 52).' Yet, even Hilgers acknowledges that her 'evidence confirms the findings of researchers highly critical of clientelism: patron-client relationships are exclusionary and they can, and do, sometimes undermine grassroots organisation and mobilisation (2009: 70)'. Hilgers does also suggest that in certain situations 'clientelism is a highly dynamic form of exchanging

goods and services that also performs well in competitive political contexts' (2009: 70). While not disagreeing with her cases, I note that those she studies already take place 'in competitive political contexts'.

12. See for instance John Gaventa (1982).

References

Bernhagen, P., and N. Mitchell (2010). 'The Private Provision of Public Goods: Corporate Commitments and the United Nations Global Compact', *International Studies Quarterly*, 654, 4: 1175–1187.

Citizens United v. FEC, 494 U.S. 652 (2010).

Crane, A., D. Matten, J., and Moon (2008) *Corporations and Citizens*, Cambridge, UK: Cambridge University Press.

Crane, A., A. McWilliams, D. Matten, J. Moon, and D. S. Siegel (eds) (2009) *The Oxford Handbook of Corporate Social Responsibility*, Oxford: Oxford University Press.

First National Bank of Boston v. Bellotti, 435 U.S. 765 (1978).

Gaventa, J. (1982) *Power and Powerlessness: Quiescence & Rebellion in an Appalachian Valley*, Champaign: University of Illinois Press.

Graziano, L. (1976) A Conceptual Framework for the Study of Clientelistic Behavior, *European Journal of Political Research*, 4, 2: 149–174.

Hilgers, T. (2009) 'Who Is Using Whom? Clientelism from the Client's Perspective', *Journal of Iberian and Latin American Research*, 15, 1: 51–75.

Hilgers, T. (2011) 'Clientelism and Conceptual Stretching: Differentiating among Concepts and among Analytical Levels', *Theory and Society*, 40, 5: 567–588.

Joshi, M., and D. Mason (2011) 'Peasants, Patrons, and Parties: The Tension between Clientelism and Democracy in Nepal', *International Studies Quarterly*, 55, 1: 151–175.

Matten, D., and A. Crane (2005) 'Corporate Citizenship: Toward an Extended Theoretical Conceptualization', *Academy of Management Review*, 30, 1: 166–179.

Matten, D., A. Crane, and W. Chapple (2003) 'Behind the Mask: Revealing the True Face of Corporate Citizenship', *Journal of Business Ethics*, 45, 109–120.

Mauss, M. (1954) *The Gift* (Trans. Ian Cunnison), Glencoe IL: The Free Press.

Moon, J., A. Crane, and D. Matten (2005) 'Can Corporations Be Citizens? Corporate Citizenship as a Metaphor for Business Participation in Society', *Business Ethics Quarterly*, 15, 3: 429–453.

Palazzo, G., and A. G. Scherer (2006) 'Corporate Legitimacy as Deliberation: A Communicative Framework', *Journal of Business Ethics* 66: 71–88.

Pierre, J. (ed.) (2000) *Debating Governance: Authority, Steering, and Democracy*, Oxford: Oxford University Press.

Ruggie, J. G. (2010) *Business and Human Rights: Further Steps Toward the Operationalization of the 'Protect, Respect and Remedy'* (UN Doc. A/HRC/11/13/), http://198.170.85.29/Ruggie-report-2010.pdf, date accessed April 4, 2012.

Scherer, A. G. and G. Palazzo (2007) 'Toward a Political Conception of Corporate Responsibility: Business and Society Seen from a Habermasian Perspective', *Academy of Management Review*, 32, 4: 1096–1120.

Scherer, A. G., and G. Palazzo (eds) (2008) *Handbook of Research on Global Corporate Citizenship*, Northampton, MA: Edward Elgar Publishing.

Scherer, A. G. and G. Palazzo (2011) 'The New Political Role of Business in a Globalized World: A Review of a New Perspective on CSR and Its Implications for the Firm, Governance, and Democracy', *Journal of Management Studies*, 48, 4: 899–931.

Stone, C. D. (1975) *Where the Law Ends: The Social Control of Corporate Behavior*, New York: Harper Torchbooks.

Sundaram, A. K., and A. C. Inkpen (2004) 'The Corporate Objective Revisited', *Organization Science*, 15, 3: 350–363.

United Nations (1948) *United Nations Declaration of Human Rights*, http://www.un.org/en/documents/udhr/, date accessed April 4, 2012.

Van Oosterhout, J. (2005) 'Corporate Citizenship: An Idea Whose Time Has Not Yet Come', *Academy of Management Review*, 30, 4: 677–684.

Youn, M. (ed.) (2011) *Money, Politics, and the Constitution: Beyond Citizens United*, New York: Century Foundation Press.

3
Citizenship, Identity and the Corporation: Exploring New Avenues of Political Mediation

Andrew Crane, Dirk Matten and Jeremy Moon

Introduction

The questions of whether corporations can or should be regarded as citizens, and in which communities such citizenship should be acknowledged or contested, have received growing attention (Gerencser, 2005; Moon, Crane and Matten, 2005; Norman and Néron, 2008). A parallel debate on the role of corporations in governing the citizenship of individuals, through the transfer of authority from government to business in the privatization of public services, public-private partnerships, market-based regulation, and corporate social responsibility initiatives has also emerged as a major research theme across the social sciences (Cashore, 2002; Hall and Biersteker, 2002; Knill and Lehmkuhl, 2002; Matten and Crane, 2005; Ronit, 2001; Rosenau and Czempiel, 1992; Scherer and Palazzo, 2011). In both cases, however, the conceptualizations of citizenship deployed to make sense of these changing social, political and economic dynamics have relied heavily on notions of formal citizenship status (should corporations be granted the status of citizens?) and concomitant rights and duties (if so, what are their entitlements and responsibilities?). To date, the major shifts evident in the citizenship literature towards claims based on identity and difference (e.g. Isin and Turner, 2003; Isin and Wood, 1999) have made little or no impact on the study of business citizenship.

A citizenship of identity offers a challenge to conventional understandings of citizenship based primarily on formal legal status and entitlement. Whether based on gender, race, ethnicity, sexual orientation, disability, culture or other bases of identification, the politics of identity-based citizenship foreground new actors, issues and arenas of contestation and struggle, among which market based actors might be expected to feature strongly. Thus far, however, the literature on citizenship generally, and on identity and citizenship specifically, has paid scant attention to the corporation as a political actor. Whilst capitalism has been recognized as an important structural force shaping transformations of contemporary citizenship (e.g. Turner, 1990), and particular market phenomena such as consumption and employment have been identified among the contexts informing the identity politics of belonging, solidarity and recognition (Isin and Wood, 1999), the individual corporation has remained largely unexamined.

In our view, this represents a major lacuna in the citizenship literature since the corporation, despite its narrowly circumscribed economic role, has become increasingly wrapped up in identity politics. In this chapter, we seek to establish a multi-faceted role for the corporation in mediating the nature, meaning and significance of particular citizenship identities. Corporations can reflect citizenship identities, they can enable certain identities to find expression and flourish, or they can inhibit the expression and flourishing of these identities. In recognizing these roles, we suggest that we need to focus renewed attention on the effects of corporations, and business more generally, on the propagation and maintenance of distinct identity claims and representations within the political realm, as well as to analysing the important evaluative issues this raises. Here, we will first sketch out how corporations fit into the conceptual landscape of the citizenship and identity literature, before identifying and explaining their various roles, and then finally exploring the implications of our analysis.

Citizenship, identity, markets, and actors

Citizenship identities are premised on social identities which their advocates seek to politicize. Although the translation from social to political identity faces a number of conceptual obstacles (Huddy, 2001), the terrain of citizenship identity essentially captures the way groups understand and project themselves as internally integrated and distinct from others in the polity. These characteristics are then used as a basis for making claims, whether to share the wider citizenship status, entitlements or recognition from which they have been excluded, to win special citizenship advantages or exemptions, or to maintain distinct cultural lifestyles. This is because although 'formal citizenship in Western democratic societies is presumed to confer a universal set of rights and duties ... citizenship on the books and citizenship in action are not coterminous' (Calavita, 2005: 407). One can possess formal status as a citizen yet be excluded (in law or in fact) from certain civil, political, or social rights or from forms of political participation that are available to others. As Iris Marion Young observed: 'the attempt to realize the universal citizenship ... will tend to exclude or put at a disadvantage some groups, even when they have equal citizenship status ... insisting that as citizens persons should leave behind their particular affiliations and experiences to adopt a general point of view serves only to reinforce that privilege; for the perspectives and interests of the privileged will tend to dominate this unified public marginalizing or silencing of other groups' (Young, 1994: 391).

Citizen identity characteristics are usually: based on some long-term, often inherited, attributes; combined with activities and practices which reinforce the inherent characteristics; and that require internal affirmation as well as external recognition of the distinctive identity. The specific bases for social, and in turn, political citizenship identity vary – and indeed there has been a proliferation of such identities emerging in political realms across the globe (Heater, 2004; Isin and Wood, 1999; Tilly, 1995). In the emergence of liberal democratic politics, religion and gender were prominent citizenship identities. In the nineteenth- and twentieth-century struggles against empire and colonialism, nationalism was a key basis for identity. Subsequently, bases for identity-based citizenship claims have included ethnicity, sexual orientation, disability and age. Identity has become yet more kaleidoscopic as people assume multiple identities. This may reflect the increase in people with multiple nationalities and ethnicities resulting from migration but also from the recognition of people's multiple, shifting, and constructed identities when they remain in one social place (Heater, 2004). The key point is not *what* the basis for identification is, but rather *that* individuals in groups are constituted in some distinctive context and that this can be a basis for inclusion in, or exclusion from, a polity as a citizen, or a basis for claiming that this distinctiveness requires special recognition or remedy in order to enable one to enact citizenship.

The appreciation of citizenship identities contrasts with more universal conceptions of individuals and of citizenship which are sometimes implicit in politics. As a result, citizenship studies has evolved to examine a wide range of citizenship forms and domains where identity claims might be made, including economic citizenship (Kessler-Harris, 2001, 2003), cultural citizenship (Kalberg, 1993; Ong, 1999a; Rosaldo, 1997; Stephenson, 2001, 2003), sexual citizenship (Evans, 1993; Richardson, 2000), consumer citizenship (Banet-Weiser, 2007) and ecological citizenship (Curtin, 1999; Dean, 2001; Dobson, 2003). Although these approaches are diverse in their focus, purpose and assumptions, they share a broadened conception of the terrain of citizenship. This broadening has embraced cultural and commercial forms and expressions of citizenship, and markets as sites of political struggle.

Attention to markets has been prompted by two developments. First, over the past few decades government provision of social rights has been increasingly marketized, through various forms of privatization, contracting out, and the deployment of market mechanisms in the public sector. This has meant that those groups seeking to advance political identity claims have needed to incorporate attention to market dynamics in addition to traditional political processes. For instance, in the wake of privatization in health services and health insurance, the availability and affordability of sex reassignment surgery for transgender identifiers becomes a political struggle to be waged in the private as well as the public sector. Second, identity groups have increasingly taken their struggles for representation and recognition to the marketplace as well as to the more traditional public sphere. Claims for equality have tended to look towards labour markets (for example in women's claims for economic citizenship (Kessler-Harris, 2001)), whilst struggles for cultural representation typically engage with the media and advertising markets. Understanding the politics of identity within the context of market relations is therefore crucial, yet it also raises a number of conceptual and empirical complexities, not least of which is untangling the political from the economic.

The significance of identity politics for economics is that it challenges the assumption that business owners, managers, consumers, employees or investors, for example, make market calculations on the basis of commonly-held motivational frameworks. Instead, identities bring different value – or interest-based vantage points into economic transactions. Conversely, the significance of economics for identity politics is that it challenges the assumption that political struggle can be understood mainly in terms of solidarity and public interests since private interests and commercialism are inherent to market interactions. Economics also brings new actors such as consumers and corporations into the realm of politics (Micheletti, Follesdal and Stolle, 2004).

Extant research on citizenship identities and markets has tended to focus either on the role of markets in preventing or constraining access to citizenship entitlements (e.g. Solinger, 1999), or on the way that markets have reshaped citizenship, for instance towards a more fluid, transnational identity (Ong, 1999b). However, an overemphasis on market institutions has obscured the importance of powerful market actors in using or shaping markets to pursue particular ends. We need to go beyond the assumption that markets are blind with respect to race or gender, for instance, but in fact are an amalgamation of the strategies and preferences of actors, some of which may have more influence than others. Therefore, in this chapter, we seek to extend this literature by exploring the specific roles of corporations in identity politics.

Corporations are important actors in this domain because they are frequently the nodes around and through which identities are constructed. Wittingly or otherwise corporations have become significant actors in the politics of citizenship and identity. However, it is evident that the literature of citizenship has developed with little specific attention to the corporation as an institution, or to specific corporations active within the domain of citizenship. To the extent that corporations have been acknowledged, the main argument has been that they are a threat to existing notions of citizenship and their influence is conceptualized as incompatible with a rich enactment of status, rights and responsibilities of civic actors (e.g. Ikeda, 2004).

In this chapter we trace a different path, and examine how companies either place themselves or find themselves in positions which are critical to the ability of people of different identities to fulfil aspects of their citizenship. This is notwithstanding the assumption that some managers might hold the view either that market decisions are based on universal and abstract criteria or that it is the responsibility of governments to define and provide for citizenship possibilities of different social identities. In our view, corporations play a role in identity politics that cannot be reduced to merely passive recipients of market signals, nor however can they simply be passed off as simply another special interest. Corporations represent a critical terrain in which citizenship identities are contested – and corporate actions can shape how this terrain influences the enactment or otherwise of a fuller citizenship for identity groups. Before we examine this, though, we will first explore the essential nature of citizenship identities.

Social identities as a basis for citizenship identity

In this section we explore the sorts of social and citizenship identities that have emerged with which corporations may need to deal. We consider, first, identity as consisting of attributes; second, identity as a resource; and third, we examine responses to proliferating social and political identities.

Identity is usually understood as some basis for associating with one group of other humans on the basis of some attribute which also differentiates this group from others, be they the majority or minority (Jenkins, 2008). Thus, from Aristotle until the late nineteenth century it was frequently taken as axiomatic that citizenship should be accorded to male members of society. Over the last two centuries, in particular, women's suffrage movements have challenged this view and have offered an idea of citizenship which embraces women. However, feminist claims have developed such that equal citizenship is not simply regarded as a question of an equal vote or right to stand for election. It has addressed a whole range of issues concerning both the conditions of continuing inequality, which can and should be addressed, as well as the condition of gender difference which needs to be taken account of in advancing citizenship. These include the projection of women in media, employment conditions and remuneration, and the role of women in reproduction and care.

Other biological forms of identity include race, ethnicity, some forms of disability, and sexual orientation. In many countries, citizenship has been defined either by law or practice in racial or ethnic terms. Civil rights groups in numerous countries initially campaigned for equal political rights assuming that this was the key to citizenship. But, having won these rights, on finding that aspects of their lives were still slow to change, such groups broadened their conceptions of citizenship to focus on, for example, employment and remuneration conditions which have, as with gender, brought corporations into the reckoning. In the case of disability and sexual orientation, whilst citizenship has not usually been proscribed on this basis, those identifying as disabled or gay, lesbian, bisexual or transgendered (LGBT) have focused on such issues of recognition, and legal equality concerning their practices, and the resources and conditions for them to function fully as citizens. Again, corporations in their roles as employers and providers of retail and employment environments have been asked to accommodate such agendas.

Some bases for identity may not be biological but social. Thus, religion, nationalism and ethnicity reflect membership of social groupings which, respectively, heavily or even exclusively, reflect inherited affiliations but which individuals can choose to adopt or discard. These social bases for citizenship identity can either characterize dominant groups in society who wish to maintain their religion, nationalism or ethnicity as the basis for citizenship or groups at the margins (be it numerically or in terms of access to power) who wish to challenge the dominant basis for citizenship identity. This could either be to substitute one basis for identity for another or to amend or supplement the dominant basis in order to better establish and legitimize their own identity. Again, this can extend beyond the formal concomitants of citizenship to include employment rights, rules about investment and trade, consumption and representation in marketing. These issues have confronted business in such societies as Northern Ireland, Belgium and Canada as well as more dramatically in the Middle East and pre-democratic South Africa, for example.

Identity is not only an attribute, but also a resource. As a result, identity is something which is mobilized for political purposes, be it by groups seeking to win greater autonomy and power (e.g. European nineteenth-century nationalist movements) or by groups seeking to defend their status or other resources from other claimants (e.g. the Afrikaans National Party in the Republic of South Africa). Identity is therefore not only a basis for mutual recognition and association of the group in question but also a basis for differentiation from and mobilization against either another group or simply those not sharing the same attributes.

Identity politics is not unambiguously either a good or a bad thing. On the one hand it can be associated with greater social autonomy and flourishing. This is captured in the word 'liberation' that has been widely used by women's, gay and nationalist movements. It has been associated with the achievement of status and respect with established systems for women, LGBT and adherents to minority religions, for example. Conversely it can be associated from the outside, at least, as associated with the absence of toleration and mutual distrust as in the sectarian politics of Northern Ireland, Palestine and the former Yugoslavia, for example. It can also be associated with excessive pressure for conformity as the group strives to maintain its differentiation – the resource for those who wish to mobilize identity politics.[1]

Modern societies have responded to the claims of identity politics in a variety of ways. Some, like France, have tended to impose a form of national and secular identity in order to deter national break-up (e.g. in the suppression of the Breton and Languedoc languages and culture) and to preserve a strong sense of the modern French identity (e.g. in the laws concerning foreign language films, legislation on the wearing of religious symbols at school). Other conceptions of citizenship have effectively, rather than formally, excluded groups from citizenship as experienced by native and black Americans who suffered fundamental restrictions on their citizenship even in the twentieth century, notwithstanding constitutional assumptions about their political equality. More recently, the United States has shifted from its 'melting pot' approach to immigration in which distinctive citizenship resources were discouraged to the elevation of Spanish to the status of an official language following the wave of Latin American immigration.

Notwithstanding the fact that some forms of identity are more readily inherited than others it is certainly true that there is an element of choice about which identity or identities people assume. The attachment to identities is therefore complicated by the fact that many people, especially in post-industrial societies have multiple identities and that these are in flux. Research across the humanities and social sciences has increasingly acknowledged the importance of acquired, self-defined, and chosen identities (Giddens, 1991; Taylor, 1989). This applies even to characteristics such as nationality, race, ethnicity, or sexual orientation which we might usually consider to be relatively fixed (Huddy, 2001). That is, one's identification as British Asian, Jewish, lesbian, or Quebecois reflects an element of choice from among a repertoire of potential identity markers which may become more or less salient or meaningful for different people, at different times, and in different contexts. Corporations, we suggest, have become critical actors in these identifications and their mobilization as we shall now discuss.

Corporations and citizenship identity

Corporations have played a significant role in the development and articulation of many different citizenship identities. However, it is clear that the nature of this role will vary in different contexts. Three types of role are evident: corporations *reflecting* citizen identity; corporations *enabling* citizen identity; and corporations *inhibiting* citizen identity.

Corporations reflecting citizen identity

Corporations that identify with a particular citizenship identity (or are identified with it by others) can be said to reflect citizenship identity. This reflection may be achieved by branding or targeting of specific market segments (such as firms that target the gay market), through employment practices (e.g. by hiring a disproportionate number of a particular identity group), or through associations with a founder or owner (such as the designation of 'minority businesses' in the United States).

This reflection of citizenship identity is perhaps most obvious in the case of companies that seek to reflect a national identity as part of their explicit branding, as we see in the case of multinational companies such as American Apparel, Deutsche Bank or France Telecom. This is particularly true of publicly owned companies which operate under national or regional company names. But this often extends to formerly or partly publicly-owned companies such as 'flag carrier' airlines (e.g. Air France, British Airways, or Singapore Airlines). It is also true of other companies that extol their national identity through branding and promotion. For instance, IKEA actively promotes itself as a Swedish company whilst the clothing company Canada Goose uses its national identity to promote the 'authenticity' of its extreme weather gear.

Claims by corporations of a distinct national citizenship identity might be seen as more credible or persuasive by some. Indeed, governments often undertake significant efforts to prevent takeover of corporations by foreign companies in order to protect their national identity (Norman and Néron, 2007: 17). Over time, however, national identity may be seen as less attractive to companies who may want to vary these associations in order to appeal to other constituencies in other ways. It has also become increasingly untenable in a world of globalized production and marketing. Thus, globally oriented brands have increasingly severed their connection with a national identity in preference for a cosmopolitan global identity more suited to their target markets (Cao, 2002). This is most starkly illustrated by corporate name changes such as ANZ Bank rather than Australia and New Zealand Bank, HSBC rather than the Hong Kong and Shanghai Banking Corporation, BP in place of British Petroleum, and various other similar transformations away from a nationally-oriented corporate identity.

Just as we have seen a broadening of the basis of individual political identity from the nation state to a more variegated set of identity bases, so too have we witnessed a shift in the identities reflected by corporations. Companies may reflect a range of alternative, subnational, or minority identities based on race, religion, gender, sexual orientation, or other form of social identity. Hence, just as a company may once have been seen as an American or Japanese company, so may it now be also regarded as a Jewish, African-American, Mormon or gay company, because it shares something with these types of citizen identities. Moreover, individuals that patronize such firms (or who boycott them) may interpret their engagement with the company as an act of identification with and solidarity towards their fellow citizens (Micheletti et al., 2004).

The point is that sometimes, rather than reflecting a national citizen identity, business can reflect a minority citizenship identity and/or one in adversity. This is not new. Thus Ellis Marsalis Senior, the grandfather of the famous Marsalis jazz brothers, came to prominence in New Orleans because he founded and ran a hotel business which catered for black commercial travellers who otherwise experienced impediments to their citizenship rights of free movement and equal treatment. Since this time, there has been a significant growth in 'minority-owned businesses' that reflect the racial citizenship of their owners, especially in countries like the United States where the population of such enterprises grew dramatically over the 1980s and 1990s, more than doubling their share of US firms from less than 7 per cent in 1982 to almost 15 per cent by 1997 (US Small Business Administration Office of Advocacy, 2001). Indeed, minority owned businesses are evident in many countries and in many industries, often supplying products and services specific to their citizenship (such as kosher or halal food), but perhaps more frequently simply reflecting the broader racial mix of the countries in which they are formed.

A similar phenomenon is the emergence of 'the pink economy', in which LGBT people establish businesses that enable them to reflect their identity of sexual preference, and around which grow supply chains and customer networks which multiply this basis of identity. Regional clusters can be found in the US cities of San Francisco, New York and Boston, and the UK cities of Brighton and Manchester. By some accounts, the pink economy is worth some US$250 billion per year in the United States.[2] Moreover, there is plenty of evidence that mainstream corporations see this as an important business niche and are also reinforcing LGBT citizenship through business. Indeed, for many years, Boston has had an official LGBT chamber of commerce, the Greater Boston Business Council, which organizes networking events, group health insurance benefits, an annual business expo, and a directory of members and their businesses.

As some of these examples suggest, there may be immediate commercial benefits for firms that seek to reflect particular citizen identities with their brands. Consumers who perceive a brand as being a meaningful part of their community may be likely to exhibit significant loyalty and commitment to the brand. This is particularly the case when a brand goes further and appears to profess a political agenda associated with the community. For example, the vodka brand Absolut and the automotive brand Subaru have experienced tremendous loyalty from the gay community in the United States because of their persistent willingness to advertise in gay media and appeal to gay consumers, even when other brands sought to downplay or resist their connection to gay identity due to concerns about maintaining their mainstream appeal (Sender, 2005). Such brands may also be actively promoted by 'their' community, enjoying the status of a privileged citizen, for example when governments work on behalf of companies to secure export deals 'in the national interest', or when minority business associations promote their members' interests. Examples of the latter include the

Asian Women in Business Association, the National Black Chamber of Commerce, the Latin Business Association, and the National Minority Supplier Development Council, as well as the above mentioned Greater Boston Business Council for LGBT business professionals – all based in the United States.

Clearly though, corporate reflections of citizenship identity are unstable ones. They not only vary with the shifting branding strategies of marketing departments, but are also vulnerable to the market for corporate control. In the former instance, marketers may feel that an association with 'minority' interests of gay, environmental, or Latin consumers no longer serves corporate interests, and so may seek to lose their affinity with such a citizen identity. Alternatively, where the niche is attractive, faux citizen identities may be adopted by firms to capitalize on a growing market. For instance, as more mainstream businesses buy into the pink economy, an issue arises for those who want to make consumer choices strictly to support those who bear a genuine LGBT identity. It is harder for these consumers to distinguish those which 'really' share the identity from those which identify with it purely for marketing purposes.

In the case of the market for corporate control, firms may be bought by other companies that do not share the same identity. In the automotive industry, for example, takeovers led to the 'Swedish' automotive brand Volvo and the 'British' brand Jaguar falling under the ownership of the American company Ford, and more recently being sold to Chinese and Indian companies respectively. Acquisitions of 'environmentalist' companies such as Body Shop, Ben & Jerry's, Seeds of Change, and Green and Blacks (by the mainstream corporations L'Oreal, Unilever, Mars, and Cadbury's respectively) can also threaten their connections with alternative environmentalist citizen identities. The fact is that just as individuals may develop a range of citizenship identities, so too is it increasingly difficult to assign to corporations a unique citizenship status (and all the entitlements and duties that go with it), especially in the case of large multinational actors that produce a multitude of product lines to various target markets in hundreds of countries across the globe. This is clearly a challenge for corporations seeking to appeal on the basis of their citizenship identity, as well as for governments or consumers seeking to connect with, or reward, companies that share their identity (Cao, 2002). The allocation of citizenship status based on identity to corporations is highly precarious especially if it offers support to marginalized or at-risk identities. However, corporations can take a more active role in enabling the citizenship of different social identities, as we shall now discuss.

Corporations enabling citizenship identity

Corporations can go further than simply reflecting citizen identities in their corporate identities. There is also plenty of evidence that companies can actually enable marginalized social identities to acquire or develop their citizenship. They can do this in several ways: (i) by *enabling de facto citizenship status*; (ii) by *providing citizenship entitlements through employment and business opportunities*; (iii) by *providing products and services* used to enhance citizenship status, entitlements, and/or involvement in the political process.

The *enabling of de facto citizenship status* can occur when a company provides employment to non-citizen immigrant or migrant workers, and in doing so provides them with a status that enables them to gain certain entitlements of citizenship. The offer of a job, whether to legal or illegal non-citizens, is often the first step to securing citizenship status for those whose identity would not normally provide them with such rights. This has been particularly pertinent in the employment of illegal or poorly documented immigrants and migrant workers, for example in the southern and western states of the United States, and in Southern Europe. Here, a job, albeit one that is usually poorly paid, insecure, and lacking social benefits, can provide some degree of de facto citizenship status whilst in the country. Although the illegal Mexican worker in Texas may be exploited, some benefits of American citizenship may be available to him or her, such as schooling for their children, participation in markets, and the ability to enjoy a degree of security and public order. In well-developed immigrant communities, there may even be the potential for legal representation and protections as well as political participation.

The role of corporations here in facilitating this granting of de facto citizenship status is on the face it limited, but at the same time, it is clear that if corporations refused to break the law (or take advantage of poor enforcement) by employing illegal workers, there would be fewer incentives for illegal immigrants to enter the country to find work. Moreover, in doing so, corporations themselves, either explicitly or implicitly, are ascribing some level of de facto citizenship status (albeit usually of a second class, and economic variety) to legal non-citizens.

At times though, the corporate role is even more pronounced. For example, the sheer number of Mexican workers in the United States has led to periodic amnesties for illegal immigrants who have acquired employment. Thus, companies are providing what in retrospect can be regarded as a passport to legal citizenship status. Hence, as Tancredo (2004: 13) suggests, 'our political and legal institutions are subtly encouraged to follow the economic institutions in treating the illegal resident the same as the legal resident. The United States is thus moving toward de facto citizenship as a replacement for traditional citizenship. This movement is slow and subtle, but its signs are unmistakable.'

Most corporate involvement in enabling citizenship identity through de facto status is arguably more subtle, but no less profound, than the granting of status to non-residents and illegals. The granting of employment opportunities to women, racial minorities, LGBT, and disabled identifying people is widely seen as an important step on the path to more equal citizen status and entitlements to such groups. At one level, simply the ability to participate freely in labour markets is an essential constituent of contemporary citizenship. Beyond this, employment provides opportunities for subsequent participation in other (consumer) markets, and helps develop the type of cultural capital necessary for progressing into certain other arenas of citizenship such as running for political office. Quite simply, jobs – and, in particular, good quality jobs – help prevent disadvantaged groups from becoming 'second class citizens'. This, of course, relies to a large extent on the corporation being able to provide, through employment, appropriate citizen entitlements to those with non-dominant identities, as we shall now discuss.

Providing citizenship entitlements through employment and business opportunities is a significant issue on the diversity and equal opportunity agenda. Firms have long been involved in the provision of citizenship entitlements in the workplace. For citizenship based specifically on identity, corporations can clearly have a significant role to play in providing a richer experience of entitlements such as equality, freedom from discrimination, freedom of expression (as well as various others) by ensuring that their racial minority, LGBT, disabled, female, or religiously identified employees enjoy such freedoms in the workplace.

Whilst legislation may typically provide the baseline for such entitlements, firms can both go beyond legislation in this arena, as well as actively supporting legislation and living up to the spirit rather than the letter of regulation. Turning, for example, to the case of women at work, there is evidence that many western companies are seeking to recognize the gendered character of work experience and opportunity and are introducing policies to better enable women to fulfil their employment potential. They thereby contribute to a richer experience of women's employment rights beyond those required by government legislation. Such a situation can be envisaged for various other citizenship identities, notwithstanding the numerous counter examples of corporations inhibiting the expression of citizenship identity in other instances, as we will see below. The point here is that the emergence of citizenship identity movements may often take place outside the traditional state-citizen duality. The battle for equality, for instance, is just as likely to take place at the workplace, in the realm of the corporation, as it is the realm of state politics.

Beyond the direct provision of entitlements in the workplace and markets, it is also striking how the reinforcement of citizenship identity through business has also enabled constituencies to engage more fully in citizenship outside their business in broader identity politics. For example, it should also be noted that the elevation of women in business can also feed into their more effective formal political participation, as evidenced by the career paths of numerous female politicians that have crossed-over from the corporate sector. In the area of business associations based on identity grounds (e.g. gay or Hispanic business associations), the battle for entitlements in the workplace has also at times led to deeper political engagement through the association.

For example, the Boston LGBT chamber of commerce started in the 1990s with a group of Boston gay and lesbian professionals meeting to form a network and to discuss LGBT issues in the workplace. The network has since grown to include not only 700 individual business people but also corporate members which sponsor gay pride events and annual awards ceremonies. This citizenship identity has therefore now developed as the LGBT business community sees that leveraging its economic power 'can do more to change corporate America than holding rallies. ... You have to work at changing the power structure ... We've evolved from simply viewing big business as the enemy to thinking that we need to work with big business. We're being seen as important constituents'.[3] Now such political figures as the Mayor of Boston and gubernatorial candidates speak at network meetings. This represents a threshold change, first from when gay and lesbian people felt excluded from business because of their citizenship identity, second from when business became a means by which they could reflect their citizenship identity, and third when business could be leveraged to engage in political activity.

Providing *products and services* used to enhance citizenship opportunities, can happen quite innocuously, for example by simply providing certain opportunities as part of the firm's normal business. Some of the seventeenth- and eighteenth-century English coffee houses were identified by Habermas (1989) as critical in the emergence of 'the public sphere' by allowing a space for free talking (see also Sennett, 1996). That these businesses were often threatened by closure by governments illustrates some of their significance for the most basic form of citizenship participation, free exchange. More recently, media and technology companies have provided the products and services necessary for a wide range of minority communities to meet, organize and articulate their political values and aspirations in ways that would have been impossible a few decades ago.

These enabling environments for the expression of citizenship identities often will be developed in a self-conscious way by the corporations that we identified above as those reflecting the identities of 'their' community. Hence, gay entrepreneurs may start-up gay websites and magazines, Jewish butchers may provide kosher meat to Jewish consumers, and so on. A particularly striking example is provided by the case of Islamic banking which has operated for some time in Pakistan, Malaysia and Dubai but is now spreading and attracting western banks. This obviously allows a citizenship identity to be reflected, since the banking products must be approved by scholars who issue religious rulings that a product is Sharia compliant. The availability of these products is described precisely in terms of enabling a form of citizenship by identity as illustrated by lawyers working in the industry: 'These days even a Muslim who is not very devout will choose a Sharia-compliant product because it enhances his status in the community. ... Most Muslims don't want to live in an Islamic state. But if you offer them ways to assert their identity today that are not too hazardous, like with Islamic banking, there is a lot of demand.'[4]

Beyond simply providing products and services though, corporations also play a broader role in articulating the existence of, and empowering communities based on identity, or what Banet-Wiser (2007) refers to as 'consumer citizenship'. Marketers and journalists actively construct the existence, for example, of a 'gay market' or a 'Hispanic market' through press releases, magazine articles, or even directories of products, services or publications. As Sender (2004: 5) suggests in relation to the gay market:

> The gay community ... is not a pre-existing entity that marketers simply need to appeal to, but is a construction, an imagined community formed not only through political activism but through an increasingly sophisticated, commercially supported, national media. Marketing has thus been instrumental in the very formation of groups, including politically inflected groups.

Marketing activities aimed at identity-based groups provide visibility and, under some conditions, legitimacy to them. So when publications such as the *Hispanic/Latino Market Advertising Guide* proclaim that the Hispanic market is 'the fastest growing segment of the U.S. Market', they help to suggest that there is an identifiable, relatively homogenous community of Hispanics that represents a viable marketing niche. Such communities can then potentially gain political and other types of status and power through their perceived economic significance: 'in a capitalist society, market incorporation is of the utmost importance because it summons a social legitimation approaching that of citizen' (Peñaloza, 1996: 33). Beyond legitimacy, others argue that some forms of market incorporation also offer the possibility of citizen empowerment. Banet-Wiser (2007: 12) for instance has explored how the youth-oriented media company Nickelodeon makes 'claims about the cultural enfranchisement of children, contributing to sets of meanings that form a contemporary form of citizenship – meanings that evoke a sense of membership, community and individual agency'.

Of course, the causality here is difficult to disentangle – recognition as a defined market will often follow the creation of a politically constituted community as has been suggested for both the gay and African-American markets in the United States (Peñaloza, 1996; Sender, 2005). However, further civil and political gains can be made by communities through enhanced market visibility and attention from corporations, suggesting that the two are intrinsically intertwined. As Sender (2005: 242) argues in relation to the gay market, 'the distinction between business and politics is bogus: marketing images of and to GLBT people must necessarily involve both'. This intimate connection between business and identity politics also of course brings with it a downside to those seeking to articulate and validate certain identities. Just as corporations can enable citizenship identity so too can they inhibit it.

Corporations inhibiting citizenship identity

Corporations have often been associated with inhibiting citizenship, in that people's self-identifications with a citizenship based on religious, racial, gender, or sexuality types has been hampered by the actions of corporations. This can happen in four ways: (i) by *excluding* those with certain identities from employment in the corporation or from accessing the corporation's products and services; (ii) by ensuring that such identifications do not *prosper* within the organization; (iii) by failing to acknowledge and *represent* citizen identities in corporate communications or *misrepresenting* them; (iv) or even producing products and services that are actively used to *suppress* certain citizenship identities. Let us look at each of these in turn.

The process of *excluding* those with certain social identities from employment in corporations is illustrated by the rather familiar cases of companies in the southern states of the United States, Northern Ireland and apartheid South Africa conforming to the expectations of dominant social identities, be they white or Protestant, and disadvantaging those with other identities. However, there is evidence of such exclusion, or its more subtle manifestations, in many other contexts. In numerous countries and industries LGBT employees have suppressed their sexuality at work out of fear of reprisals. In some organizations, the outward expression of certain religious affiliations has been outlawed, e.g. by prohibiting the wearing of turbans, hijab, or kippah head coverings. Similar exclusions can affect customers with non-dominant identities, such as LGBT people who have found it necessary to obfuscate their domestic arrangements in order to obtain mortgages, women or people of colour who have been refused entry to golf clubs and restaurants, or Muslims that have been denied permission to board aeroplanes. Sometimes companies find themselves having to make choices among identities as the UK Co-operative Bank found when it told Christian Voice to close its account because 'its discriminatory pronouncements' concerning gay rights were deemed incompatible with the bank's ethos.[5]

At one level, these experiences could just be viewed in terms of discrimination, but in a wider political view, corporations here are potentially involved in a more fundamental inhibition of citizenship identities. When those who self-identity as black, lesbian, or Christian experience inequality, unfair treatment, or obstructions to accessing employment or services, their entitlement to some of the basic rights of citizenship are threatened. Whilst corporations may well argue that this is a problem for governments to deal with through equal opportunities legislation, it cannot be denied that business sometimes has a role to play in preventing certain citizenship identities from achieving free expression and participation in the workforce and in markets.

A more subtle sort of complaint that is made against companies is that whilst they may formally and behaviourally be prepared to employ people with a diversity of social identities, they do not create working conditions that enable them to *prosper* and, more specifically, to enjoy their full citizenship rights to equal consumption, employment, autonomy and recognition. A good example of this is the case of gender which has been a prominent instance of identity politics, particularly since the advent of liberal feminism of Mary Wollstonecraft and of John Stuart Mill and Harriet Taylor in the eighteenth and nineteenth centuries respectively. A recurring complaint among feminists is that even despite their achievement of the status of citizenship in democratic countries, women have not fared well at the workplace. This is often presented in terms of the corporations being male dominated and therefore unsympathetic to women's claims, and of governments being unwilling to legislate to require companies to improve women's lot at work.

Feminists demonstrate that corporations are hostile to women's issues by comparing women's inferior experiences of the workplace with those of men and by comparing women's inferior experiences of the private sector with those of their counterparts in the public sector. This includes the complaint that women have tended to receive lower wages for performing the same jobs as men, and that they do not enjoy similar levels of career development, as manifested in the very small proportion of chief executives and board members who are women, and the relatively small number of female senior executives (Singh and Vinnicombe, 2005).

Although corporations are therefore often regarded as unresponsive to female identity, most liberal feminists would regard this as simply reflective of the mores and practices of the wider family. Central, therefore, to women's workplace experiences are their roles in reproduction and childcare which have not been sufficiently recognized, rewarded and compensated for. Hence the perception that '[t]he equality of women and the institution of the family have long been at odds with each other' (Somerville, 2000: 2). Corporations simply reflect these wider mores not simply by exploiting women but also by failing to build their wider roles into the rewards and conditions of the workplace. Marxist feminists, however, would regard the corporation not as reflective of social phenomena but as their creator and maintainer. Both perspectives, however, share the view that companies' practices have tended not to reflect the social realities of gender identity and thereby compound (for liberals) or structure (for Marxists) deficiencies in women's citizenship experience.

A third way in which corporations may inhibit citizenship identities is by failing to *represent* citizen identities, or *misrepresenting* them, in corporate communications of one sort or another. As we discussed above, the exposure of certain identities in advertising and other forms of corporate communications is often presented as a way in which those identifying as such become normalized and accepted in society – and thus more able to enjoy the kinds of citizenship entitlements enjoyed by more dominant groups. Thus, for example, the portrayal of African American people in US television adverts, or gay men in British television adverts has been identified by some as a major milestone in their achieving equal political status in society. However, just as corporations can choose to include such identities, so too can they exclude or distort them in their communications. The latter can happen when corporations are seen to rely on 'negative' identity stereotypes, such as persistently portraying women as housewives, or racial minorities as low-status workers. Even ostensibly 'positive' stereotypes used in adverts, such as the affluent white gay man, the athletic black sportsman, or the multitasking executive mother can be argued to render others who identify as gay, black or female invisible or under-represented. Marketing can 'minoritize' among identity-based communities and privilege an 'ideal' version of the identity over others (Sender, 2005).

As with the processes identified in the previous sub-section, a major theme here is the question of whether advertisers create social identities and social attitudes towards them or merely reflect pre-existing identities and attitudes. This is a theme that has been taken up in a range of literatures, summarized by Richard Pollay (1986: 33) as one manifestation of the 'distorted mirror' idea of advertising – namely that 'some of our cultural values are reinforced far more frequently than others. Hence, while it may be true that advertising reflects cultural values, it does so on a very selective basis, echoing and reinforcing certain attitudes, behaviors and values far more frequently than others.' For many proponents of various forms of identity politics, then, the involvement of corporations in creating and reflecting citizen identities through markets and through marketing is a double-edged sword. Whilst it can offer some degree of mainstream recognition and acceptance, it can also lead to problems of misrepresentation, and the potential replacement of the political goals of identity movements with simple consumerism. There is understandably a degree of caution about the problems of assimilation and the relative benefits and drawbacks of becoming a target market, whereby political values and aspirations are reduced to consumer preferences.

Finally, another way in which citizenship identity can be compromised by companies is when they support or supply products and services to repressive regimes that *suppress* particular citizenship identities. This has been widely discussed in relation to companies involved in supplying products to the Nazis, for example in Edwin Black's (2001) controversial study of IBM's involvement in the Holocaust:

> IBM, primarily through its German subsidiary, made Hitler's program of Jewish destruction a technologic mission the company pursued with chilling success. IBM Germany, using its own staff

and equipment, designed, executed, and supplied the indispensable technologic assistance Hitler's Third Reich needed to accomplish what had never been done before – the automation of human destruction. ... IBM's subsidiary, with the knowledge of its New York headquarters, enthusiastically custom-designed the complex devices and specialized applications as an official corporate undertaking.

This suppression of citizenship identity by corporations typically falls into the category of complicity. That is, the company itself may not be directly suppressing a political identity, but in providing certain products and services to governments and other political actors, may be enabling the suppression to take place. This phenomenon has been illustrated recently in the case of Google accepting (and then rejecting) state censorship rules for their operations in China, which rendered the company potentially complicit in the suppression of rights to free expression for groups such as human rights advocates and the Fulan Gong. The global construction equipment company Caterpillar has similarly been accused of complicity in the suppression of Palestinian identity through the supply of bulldozers used by the Israeli military to tear down Palestinian homes, roads and farms in controversial land clearing operations. Of course, there are always questions about the rights and wrongs of the identity claims involved, as well as about whether corporations as economic entities should take a stand on such political questions. Can firms be responsible for what their governmental customers do with their products, and to what extent are they obliged to obey the law in the countries in which they operate if this goes against the laws and expectations of their home country? These are the types of underlying questions that prevail in assessing the role of corporations in suppressing citizenship identities through their products and services. Our point here is not to answer such questions, but simply to highlight the ease with which firms can become complicit in the suppression of political identity in a global economy.

Conclusion

In this chapter we have explored the way that citizenship has been transformed by the politics of identity, and how citizenship identities have been reflected, enabled, and inhibited by the corporation in various ways. We have observed a range of different roles and processes inhabited by the corporation in identity politics. In enacting these roles, corporations have been critical actors in the mediation of identity across business and politics. They also provide new sites for the articulation of identity claims.

The role of the corporation as a mediator of political identity is often implicit and has typically gone either unrecognized or has been downplayed by those in the business community. It has also gone largely unexamined in the research communities across politics, sociology and business studies. On the other hand, some of those seeking to understand or advance the position of different identity communities have recognized that corporations can potentially play a role in this process, but this is to date little understood or explored. What is clear though is that in a capitalist society, corporations are inevitably involved in the reconfiguration of citizenship along various constellations of identity, even if their actual role and responsibility here remains a matter of debate. The politics of identity cannot be entirely severed from the manifestations of identity in product and labour markets however much corporations may claim their involvement is in business, not politics, and however much activists for identity groups claim their interests are in politics not business (Sender, 2005).

This mixing of identity politics with economics is inevitably messy. However, the corporate role is not one that should be simply written off as necessarily detrimental to the flourishing of new identities, but then nor indeed should we arbitrarily celebrate the corporation as a positive force for good in the proliferation of identity. Although we may be uneasy about the interpenetration of the business and the politics of identity, we need to refrain from such easy judgements. Corporations are essentially self-interested actors, yet economic self-interest is not in itself incompatible with any of the roles we have identified in this chapter. The question is how companies come to recognize (or ignore), accommodate (or reject), and legitimate (or de-legitimate) their role in identity politics given the context of their (and others') economic self-interest. Moreover we might usefully ask how those seeking to press their identity claims can make use of (or are limited by) the corporation's self-interest in developing appropriate political strategies. These critical questions on the collision of economic self-interest and political values are easily overlooked in focusing on the state, individuals, and capitalism in exploring identity politics. Ultimately then our analysis suggests that the corporation itself is not simply a passive object within the domain of citizenship, but acts to shape and construct relations of citizenship – sometimes actively or deliberately, at times accidentally or passively. Either way, and for better or for worse, corporations are transformative in the arena of political identity.

Notes

1. It should be noted that it can also be associated with fear within the group as illustrated by intra-group 'policing' as evidenced in Northern Ireland.
2. Boston Business Forward, 26 August 2006: http://www.bizforward.com/bos/issues/2001-12/pinkeconomy/.
3. Ibid.
4. 'Make money not war', *FT Magazine* 23/24 September 2006: 21.
5. See 'Faith News' *The Times* 25 June 2005, p.75.

References

Banet-Weiser, S. (2007) *Kids Rule: Nickelodeon and Consumer Citizenship*, Durham, NC: Duke University Press.

Black, E. (2001) *IBM and the Holocaust: The Strategic Alliance Between Nazi Germany and America's Most Powerful Corporation*, New York: Crown.

Calavita, K. (2005) 'Law, Citizenship, and the Construction of (Some) Immigrant "Others"', *Law and Social Inquiry*, 30, 401–420.

Cao, L. (2002) 'Corporate and Product Identity in the Postnational Economy: Rethinking U.S. Trade Laws', *California Law Review*, 90, 2, 401–484.

Cashore, B. (2002) 'Legitimacy and the Privatization of Environmental Governance: How Non-State Market-Driven (NSMD) Governance Systems Gain Rule-Making Authority', *Governance*, 15, 4, 503–529.

Curtin, D. (1999) *Chinnagounder's Challenge: The Question of Ecological Citizenship*, Bloomington: Indiana University Press.

Dean, H. (2001) 'Green Citizenship', *Social Policy & Administration*, 35, 5, 490–505.

Dobson, A. (2003) *Citizenship and the Environment*, Oxford: Oxford University Press.

Evans, D. (1993) *Sexual Citizenship: The Material Construction of Sexualities*, London: Routledge.

Gerencser, S. (2005) 'The Corporate Person and Democratic Politics', *Political Research Quarterly*, 58, 4, 625–635.

Giddens, A. (1991) *Modernity and Self-Identity: Self and Society in the Late Modern Age*, Cambridge: Polity.

Habermas, J. (1989) *The Structural Transformation of the Public Sphere: An Inquiry into a Category of Bourgeois Society*, Cambridge, MA: MIT Press.

Hall, R. B., and T. J. Biersteker (2002) *The Emergence of Private Authority in Global Governance*, Cambridge: Cambridge University Press.

Heater, D. (2004) *Citizenship: The Civic Ideal in World History, Politics and Education*, Manchester: Manchester University Press.

Huddy, L. (2001) 'From Social to Political Identity: A Critical Examination of Social Identity Theory', *Political Psychology*, 22, 1, 127–156.

Ikeda, S. (2004) 'Imperial Subjects, National Citizenship, and Corporate Subjects: Cycles of Political Participation/Exclusion in the Modern World-System', *Citizenship Studies*, 8, 4, 333–347.

Isin, E. F., and P. K. Wood (1999) *Citizenship and Identity*, Thousand Oaks, CA: Sage.

Isin, E. F., and B. S. Turner (eds) (2003) *Handbook of Citizenship Studies*, London: Sage.

Jenkins, R. (2008) *Social Identity*, London: Routledge.

Kalberg, S. (1993) 'Cultural Foundations of Modern Citizenship', in B. S. Turner (ed.) *Citizenship and Social Theory*, London: Sage.

Kessler-Harris, A. (2001) *In Pursuit of Equity: Women, Men, and the Quest for Economic Citizenship in 20th-Century America*, New York: Oxford University Press.

Kessler-Harris, A. (2003) 'In Pursuit of Economic Citizenship', *Social Politics*, 10, 2, 157–175.

Knill, C., and D. Lehmkuhl (2002). 'Private Actors and the State: Internationalization and Changing Patterns of Governance', *Governance: An International Journal of Policy, Administration, and Institutions*, 15, 1, 41–63.

Matten, D. and A. Crane (2005) 'Corporate Citizenship: Towards an Extended Theoretical Conceptualization', *Academy of Management Review*, 30, 1, 166–179.

Micheletti, M., A. Follesdal, and D. Stolle (eds) (2004) *Politics, Products, and Markets: Exploring Political Consumerism Past and Present*, New Brunswick, NJ: Transaction.

Moon, J., A. Crane, and D. Matten (2005) 'Can Corporations Be Citizens? Corporate Citizenship as a Metaphor for Business Participation in Society', *Business Ethics Quarterly*, 15, 3, 427–451.

Norman, W. and P. Y. Néron (2008) '*Citizenship Inc.* – Do We Really Want Businesses to Be Good Corporate Citizens?', *Business Ethics Quarterly*, 18, 1, 1–26.

Ong, A. (1999a) 'Cultural Citizenship as Subject Making: Immigrants Negotiate Racial and Cultural Boundaries in the United States', in R. D. Torres, L. F. Miron and J. X. Inda (eds), *Race, Identity, and Citizenship: A Reader*, Oxford: Blackwell.

Ong, A. (1999b) *Flexible Citizenship: The Cultural Logics of Transnationality*, Durham, NC: Duke University Press.

Peñaloza, L. (1996) 'We're Here, We're Queer, and We're Going Shopping! A Critical Perspective on the Accommodation of Gays and Lesbians in the U.S. Marketplace', *Journal of Homosexuality*, 31, 1–2, 9–41.

Pollay, W. (1986) 'The Distorted Mirror: Reflections on the Unintended Consequences of Advertising', *Journal of Marketing*, 50, April, 18–36.

Richardson, D. (2000) 'Constructing Sexual Citizenship: Theorizing Sexual Rights', *Critical Social Policy*, 20, 1, 105–135.

Ronit, K. (2001) 'Institutions of Private Authority in Global Governance', *Administration & Society*, 33, 5, 555–578.

Rosaldo, R. (1997) 'Cultural Citizenship, Inequality, and Multiculturalism', in W. V. Flores and R. Benmayor (eds), *Latino Cultural Citizenship: Claiming Identity, Space, and Rights*, Boston, MA: Beacon Press.

Rosenau, J. N. and E. O. Czempiel (eds) (1992) *Governance Without Government: Order and Change in World Politics*, Cambridge: Cambridge University Press.

Scherer, A. G. and G. Palazzo (2011) 'The New Political Role of Business in a Globalized World – A Review of a New Perspective on CSR and Its Implications for the Firm, Governance, and Democracy', *Journal of Management Studies*, 48, 4, 899–931.

Sender, K. (2005) *Business, Not Politics: The Making of the Gay Market*, New York: Columbia University Press.

Sennett, R. (1996) *The Fall of Public Man*, New York; London: W.W. Norton.

Singh, V. and S. Vinnicombe (2005) *The Female FTSE100 Index*, Cranfield: Centre for Developing Women Business Leaders, Cranfield School of Management.

Solinger, D. J. (1999) *Contesting Citizenship in Urban China: Peasant Migrants, the State, and the Logic of the Market*, Berkeley, CA: University of California Press.

Somerville, J. (2000) *Feminism and the Family: Politics and Society in the UK and the USA*, Basingstoke: Palgrave.

Stephenson, N. (ed.) (2001) *Culture and Citizenship*, London: Sage.

Stephenson, N. (2003) *Cultural Citizenship. Cosmopolitan Questions*, Maidenhead: Open University Press.

Tancredo, T. (2004) 'Immigration, Citizenship, and National Security: The Silent Invasion', *Mediterranean Quarterly*, 15, 4, 4–15.

Taylor, C. (1989) *Sources of the Self: The Making of the Modern Identity*, Cambridge, MA: Harvard University Press.

Tilly, C. (1995) *Citizenship, Identity and Social History*, Cambridge: Cambridge University Press.

Turner, B. S. (1990) 'Outline of a Theory of Citizenship', *Sociology*, 24, 189–217.

US Small Business Administration Office of Advocacy (2001) 'Minorities in Business,' http://www.sba.gov/advo/stats/min01.pdf.

Young, I. M. (1994) 'Polity and Group Difference', in B. Turner and P. Hamilton (eds) *Citizenship: Critical Concepts*, London: Routledge.

4
Inadvertent Citizens: Corporate Citizenship and Moral Actorhood

Boris Holzer

Introduction

The notion of citizenship is bound up with expectations about behaviour in public. In contrast to the 'bourgeois' focus on the private and economic realm, the 'citoyen' plays his social role in the public sphere. Citizenship refers to the conditions of membership in a political community and thus concerns publicly relevant and observable aspects of behaviour. Whether organizations – and business firms in particular – may be considered as 'citizens', depends on what aspects of their public role are highlighted.[1] On the one hand, most organizations cannot help but act in public and are therefore confronted with the expectations of various groups affected by their decision-making: 'Organizations in modern societies are public not only in the sense that their structures, processes and ideologies are open to observation, but also in their ultimate dependence on public acceptance, i.e. positioning themselves in relation to the perceptions and policies of society at large', summarizes Brunsson (1989: 216). On the other hand, liberals such as Milton Friedman (1970) argue that business decisions are essentially 'private' decisions made by or on behalf of the owners of a company. Yet those two perspectives can be easily reconciled: just as the individual is both a 'bourgeois' and a *citoyen* (depending on whether economic or political roles are concerned), organizational role-sets, too, include both private and public dimensions. Paradoxically though, it seems that economic decision-making is scrutinized and observed more than ever before and thus hardly private any more.

Large corporations in particular are regarded as 'public institutions' similar to governments (cf. Vogel, 1975). Business decisions affect a wider public and touch on public interests and, vice versa, they are themselves afflicted by measures taken in the name of public interest (Dyllick, 1989). The public has grown wary of side effects and long-term consequences of corporate decisions. The potential hazards and environmental impacts of the chemical industry, but also the human rights situation and labour standards in other industries are critically observed by an increasingly global public. Corporations are thus becoming 'public' due to their alleged impact on other people. The larger the company, the more likely it is to have such an impact. Therefore the 'price of successful economic growth for a company is that it gains increased public visibility. It is thus more subject to public scrutiny and public criticism than a small company' (Willetts, 1998: 225).

The public visibility of corporate decisions and their impact on society suggest a political role of large corporations – a view shared not only by CSR scholars (Scherer and Palazzo, 2007; Crane et al., 2008: Chapter 7; Scherer and Palazzo, 2011) but also by social movement activists and advocacy groups for whom the corporation serves as a convenient conduit for their claims-making. Transnational corporations (TNCs) are engaged in many projects across the world, some of which are environmentally harmful or based on the exploitation of low wages and insufficient labour standards; they are also indirectly involved in grievances and human rights violations in developing countries. Social movement activists therefore seek to influence particular decisions as well as corporate policies as a whole. As a result, corporations have become one of the primary targets of transnational activism. Social movement activists and other moral entrepreneurs have adopted 'lobbying the corporation' (Vogel, 1978) as a viable strategy to achieve their goals (Spar and La Mure, 2003; den Hond and de Bakker, 2007). In prominent cases involving major corporations such as Nestlé, Nike and Royal Dutch/Shell, transnational activists have successfully mobilized public opinion and consumers against alleged corporate misdemeanours. Although their campaigns focus on particular brands and corporations, the intended effects often go beyond the specific organization that serves as the representative target.

Like other varieties of transnational activism, the power of anti-corporate protest often derives from 'boomerang effects', i.e. local groups link up with allies from abroad to put pressure on a corporation or on their own government (cf. Keck and Sikkink, 1998). But it also employs 'outside-in' campaigns that seek to change conditions in other countries and 'dual target' campaigns that target a corporation both in a particular locale and in other countries (cf. Hertel, 2006). Furthermore, anti-corporate campaigns often focus on the place of consumption rather than on the place of production because that is where politically and ethically minded consumers can be mobilized most effectively (cf. Micheletti, 2003).

In this chapter I argue that corporations become 'inadvertent citizens' as they are exposed to constant moral and normative scrutiny by critical observers such as human rights advocacy groups that command a high degree of credibility and 'voluntaristic authority' in the world polity (2). By observing, judging and criticizing corporations, anti-corporate activism establishes a framework of responsibility that revolves around the 'moral actorhood' of corporations (3). As a result, corporations find themselves in the position to defend and justify their decisions, but they are also given the opportunity to present themselves as responsible corporate 'citizens' (4). From the perspective of normative theories of corporate social responsibility, such a development seems desirable. Yet 'moralizing the corporation' (Holzer, 2010) does not result in a higher degree of ethical rationality; although it makes it more likely that external demands are reflected in corporate decision-making, that reflexivity cannot guarantee that societal expectations and corporate interests will be in harmony (5).

Contending authorities: corporate goliaths vs activist davids

Conflicts between protest groups and corporations are public and therefore discursive. Rather than to take their opponents to court, anti-corporate activists usually rely on the 'moralization' of decisions to mobilize public support. Moral observation is based on normative expectations, and for the case of global anti-corporate protest it is an interesting question where these norms come from. In the absence of a global system of law, global norms cannot have the degree of formality and bindingness of legal norms. Rather, they are part of a rather loose system of 'soft law' that is produced and elaborated by means of public discourse (cf. Mörth, 2004; Scherer and Palazzo, 2011: 910ff.). The fact that world society remains a stateless (and thus, in some sense: a 'lawless') polity does not imply that there are no norms at all. Neo-institutionalist theory argues that there exists a 'broad world polity of shared rules and models' (Meyer, 2000: 236). But these rules cannot be enforced 'from above' since authority in the world polity is fragmented. And in the absence of a world state, world authority must be constructed 'from below' (Boli and Thomas, 1999: 37). The political system of nation-states constitutes an established if fragmented framework of authority in the world polity. Even in a stateless world polity the sovereign national sub-units maintain the formal legal authority within their borders. But at the same time transnational advocacy networks and non-governmental organizations (NGOs) can exercise their own kind of authority, a form of 'rational-voluntaristic' authority as opposed to the 'legal-rational authority' of nation-states (Boli, 1999: 277–87). Filling the gap between a highly developed transnational economy and a rudimentary set of transnational regimes, activists have a high degree of authority and legitimacy.

In order to form expectations about what is legitimate at a transnational level, decision-makers have to take public opinion into account. Yet the transnational public sphere is a contested terrain in which different discursive actors compete for influence on public opinion. From the viewpoint of transnational corporations societal demands appear increasingly contradictory and elusive. The globalization of communication systems has exacerbated this problem because activities in one locale are now scrutinized by a transnational public representing heterogeneous values. For the implementation of decisions this may lead to problems, as Phil Watts of Shell International observed:

> Communications technology has created a global goldfish bowl. All multinational companies operate in front of a hugely diverse worldwide audience. [...] (S)ince the ethical, social, cultural and economic priorities which underlie their demands are ... often local and personal, those demands will differ, will often conflict, and may be irreconcilable. (Watts, 1998: 24)

The crucial and often worrisome point for corporations is that the 'legality' of their operations cannot ensure their 'legitimacy'. While the legal constraints of a decision may be easily established, even in different national contexts, the fuzzier standards of what is acceptable and what is not remain contested and vary from place to place. If such standards are successfully propagated by advocacy groups rather than states, TNCs cannot benefit from the legitimacy which legal regulation should bestow on their decisions. Since there is no all-encompassing authority on a transnational level, norms and standards are often constructed 'from below' by various groups and actors that can claim the legitimacy to proclaim and proscribe norms and rules, for instance those who propagate and defend the accepted principles of a 'world culture' (Meyer et al., 1997; Boli and Thomas, 1999). Non-governmental organizations (NGOs) are more likely to be able to claim such a position than transnational corporations because they are deemed to act on behalf of others or on behalf of highly legitimate, abstract values. They do not act in their own self-interest but, as it were, as 'rationalized others' (Meyer, 1996; Werron and Holzer, 2009). Corporate actors, in contrast, appear to act as self-interested agents and to neglect the legitimate interests of others (Boli, 1999). Pitting economic self-interest against altruistic concerns, NGOs as the representatives of disinterested 'otherhood' have a strong moral position. It is difficult for corporations to dispel the impression that their actions are based on narrow economic motives and, ultimately, on mere self-interest and therefore they are in a defensive position in this kind of discursive struggle.

The institutionalized distrust of self-interested actorhood makes it difficult for economic agents to cast themselves as benevolent, rational actors. Consumers worldwide are willing to listen to and follow the advice given by transnational campaigns and thus provide the leverage for social movements' claims against corporations. Yet transnational activism, too, faces a challenge. It needs to establish not only the inferiority of corporate motives but also that the corporation is 'responsible' for alleged wrong-doings and grievances.

The controversy between the Royal Dutch/Shell Group and Greenpeace over the Brent Spar oil buoy in 1995 is a paradigmatic example of the challenges posed by corporate citizenship.[2] The oil storage buoy Brent Spar in the North Sea, operated by Shell Expro on behalf of Shell and Esso, had been out of service since October 1991. Shell UK initiated an extensive inquiry to find the 'best practicable environmental option' (BPEO). The final report (BPEO, 1994) concluded that the dumping at sea and the disposal on shore were ecologically equivalent options. But land disposal was regarded as more dangerous and expensive and sea dumping was therefore chosen as the BPEO. The British Energy Secretary, Tom Eggar, granted permission for deep-sea disposal in February 1995. All North Sea littoral states were informed in accordance with the Oslo-Paris Convention in order to give them the opportunity to raise objections against the plan within a 60-day period. However, none of these countries questioned the disposal plans.

Shell's decision came at a time when Greenpeace was looking for an opportunity to boost its North Sea campaign (Vorfelder, 1995: 47f.). The Brent Spar provided an appropriate symbol to make the problems of the North Sea more palpable (Scherler, 1996: 252; see also Hecker, 1997: 114). Greenpeace decided to launch a campaign to prevent the deep sea disposal that culminated in Greenpeace activists' occupying the Brent Spar platform on 30 April 1995. They accused Shell of underestimating the amount of toxic waste on the platform. Initial media reports relied entirely on Greenpeace's account, portraying the seizure of Brent Spar as a 'dramatic bid to prevent a marine life disaster'[3] or at least citing Greenpeace's claims about hazardous waste on board.[4] Shell rejected the allegations that more than 5,000 tons of oil and toxic waste were to be sunk together with the Brent Spar (Shell UK 1995). An independent inquiry later showed that those numbers were wrong, but that was too late to dispel the impression that the Brent Spar disposal was a danger to marine life.

In addition to the factual claim that the Brent Spar contained toxic waste two other rhetoric devices play a role: that Shell behaved arrogantly in doing something that others were not allowed to do and that its motives were primarily of an economic nature – and therefore egoistic. In other words, the environmental group asserted its superior credibility and thus authority not only in terms of 'truth', but also in terms of 'justice' and 'motivation'.

Regarding standards of justice and equity, Shell was portrayed as taking liberties which are denied to 'ordinary people'. The attitude of Shell was pitted against the level of everyday environmentalism in many industrialized countries:

> A spokesman for Greenpeace said yesterday: 'Our general point is about environmental responsibility. Why should Government and local authorities be getting us to recycle bottles, cans and other waste when Shell is allowed to dump its litter in the sea? It goes against common morality'. (*Daily Telegraph*, Seabed must not become rubbish tip, 20 June 1995)

Shell's controversial plan was portrayed as a 'moral' problem of setting a good example. Shell could not be allowed to proceed because this would have resulted in an intolerable gap between the corporation's behaviour and what is expected of an ordinary citizen. It would have also damaged the authority of general calls for environmentally sound behaviour:

> How can you tell 90 million Germans religiously to sort their rubbish and not expect them to cry foul when they see a global company fly-tipping its rubbish into the sea, or have a government committed to integrating ecology into all policy areas without people beginning to take personal responsibility? (*Guardian*, Agenda benders, 22 June 1995)

Standards of social justice, not only physical facts discredited Shell's behaviour. The discrepancy between universally accepted norms of behaviour, e.g. not to carelessly dispose of waste, and Shell's plans, caused moral outrage. Against this backdrop, even a supposedly minor case of pollution constitutes a violation of universal principles. It cannot be allowed 'in principle' – because it violates a social norm that needs to be reasserted.

Of course, no one would actually expect a corporation to decide according to moral principles alone. On the contrary, most observers suspected that Shell's choice was motivated by economic interest. Although Shell had commissioned reports considering and weighing several criteria, the notion of a 'best practicable environmental option' did not succeed. The Shell Group was and still is a wealthy and powerful TNC. In PR campaigns such as the German 'We care about more than cars' campaign, the corporation itself sought to convey this image. Being powerful and wealthy, however, does not go well together with the impression that Shell basically had chosen the cheapest and most simple solution to the disposal problem. Considering the profits Shell had made out of its North Sea operations, Shell should have been able to afford a better option:

> Greenpeace campaigner Tim Birch told the Daily Mirror: '[...] They have raked in millions from North Sea oil and now they won't pay the bill to clean up'. [...] Greenpeace argue that the oil companies' massive profits mean they have a moral responsibility to clean up properly. Tim said: 'They cannot just take the profit and run'. (*Daily Mirror*, Murder at sea, 1 May 1995)

Against this background, the plan of Shell could only be regarded as driven by economic rather than environmental concern. The BPEO process appeared as a fig leaf for the 'real' motive of the corporation: to avoid the cost of cleaning up. The imputation of crass economic motives stood in contrast to Greenpeace's representing the public interest. By depicting Shell as an adversary with inferior motives Greenpeace managed to 'moralize' the conflict in terms of a struggle between good and bad. The activists claimed the position to speak on behalf of both the environment and the public, while Shell was merely representing its own narrow interests.

Located in UK waters and subject to international agreements, the Brent Spar was turned into a symbol of cross-border importance. The basic claim of Greenpeace – concerning the amount of toxic waste on board Brent Spar – was flawed. Yet 'it is clear enough that under certain conditions men respond as powerfully to fictions as they do to realities' (Lippmann, 1922: 14). Those conditions were created by invoking moral standards of justice and motivation. Thus depicted as an environmental villain, Shell provided an obvious target for Greenpeace precisely because of its previous endeavours to foster a social and environmental image and because of the relatively uniform and well-known corporate identity of the Royal Dutch/Shell Group. These two factors made Shell a 'sure target for environmental campaigning' (Yearley and Forrester, 2000); and it made the 'judo politics' (Beck 1995) that Greenpeace employed more likely to succeed. That transnational pressure from all over Europe that finally led to Shell's U-turn seemed to prove that the activist David's may prevail over a corporate Goliath (Tsoukas, 1999). At least, it shows that challenging corporate responsibility is a considerable source of power in the world polity.

Constructing corporate responsibility

In the Brent Spar controversy the corporation's responsibility was evident. The activists thus merely had to point out (and scandalize) the potential hazards of a corporate decision. In other situations, however, TNCs are entangled in more complicated situations in which their operations contribute to, but by no means are the only cause of, grievances for others. In such cases – such as the anti-sweatshop campaign against Nike (Stolle, Hooghe and Micheletti, 2005; Locke, 2003; Schipper and Bojé, 2008) – corporations and their opponents get involved in public, often transnational debates over the core of responsibility itself: to what extent the corporation can be regarded as a responsible and accountable 'actor' at all.

At first glance, the actorhood of corporations appears to be a moot question: Organizations are routinely regarded as 'actors' because they produce effects that can and must be attributed to them.[5] Such attributions may take the form of informal discourse but also of legal definitions of (corporate) liability. A corporation is a legal 'person' in the sense of a 'right-and-duty bearing unit' (see Dewey, 1926). Yet the mechanisms of constructing corporate actorhood go beyond a narrowly defined legal liability. The actorhood of corporations implies that they are treated as social – or even political – actors (Gerencser, 2005; Scherer and Palazzo, 2011) and it is this broader understanding of corporate actorhood that is particularly relevant for establishing a social basis for corporate citizenship. Its starting point is the simple fact that organizations that are faced with accusations and public criticism need to provide explanations and excuses. Or put differently, they need to give *accounts* of their actions. In such accounts, corporations justify, defend or even apologize for their actions (cf. Basu and Palazzo, 2008: 127). And it is precisely that ability to give accounts that is a distinctive feature of 'actors', be they individuals or corporations (Scott and Lyman, 1968; Blum and McHugh, 1971). For instance, the Brent Spar conflict shows how standards of human moral conduct are applied to organizations and how even the rules for deciding upon appropriate behaviour are basically derived from human models. Evidently, those rules presuppose that the corporation may be regarded as a motivated, goal-directed actor rather than as a non-social entity.

Considering their purposeful and strategic behaviour one might argue that 'corporations are much more like persons than not only automobiles but even animals' (Goodpaster, 1983: 313). Yet critics of corporate decisions do not need philosophical foundations to successfully direct their claims at corporations as actors liable to moral evaluation. They only need to trust that the public will be receptive to such claims. The construction of actorhood is a question of public discourse rather than one of philosophical or legal reasoning. Protest and advocacy groups merely grasp those strategic opportunities that the corporations themselves create by building global brands and images susceptible to anti-corporate campaigns.[6] Using the brand, its image and visibility as anchoring points, anti-corporate activists have been quite successful in 'framing' corporations for alleged misdemeanours. Even if such campaigns do not result in fundamental changes of corporate policies, they have a lasting effect in constructing it as a moral actor.

Treating corporations as actors necessarily implies some simplifications. More obviously than individuals corporations and other complex organizations pursue multiple, sometimes conflicting, goals over time and in different places (Luhmann, 1968). Despite their implied responsibility, corporations' capacities to control their environments often fall short of the perception that they are wealthy and powerful compared with governments. It is therefore difficult to pin down their motives and the effects of their decisions in an unambiguous manner. In other words, organizations are fundamentally different from individuals. Yet they possess 'actorhood' just like them (Meyer and Jepperson, 2000). At least, that is the result of a discourse that talks about organizations as actors and therefore makes them liable to behave like actors. Or to put it differently, corporate actorhood must be understood in terms of the 'Thomas theorem'[7]: If observers define corporations as actors, they 'are' actors because they are treated as if they 'were' actors.[8] And the ability and necessity to account for one's behaviour – both causally and morally – is a defining feature of actorhood. The struggle between corporations and their critics therefore takes the form of a (re-)negotiation of 'actor-hood'. Since TNCs have cast themselves as responsible 'actors' in the past, they are now haunted by the problem that actorhood is always inextricably linked to the moral evaluation by others.

Being a good citizen: accountability and hypocrisy

Corporate social responsibility (CSR) and corporate accountability poli-cies may be regarded as reactions to the risks and responsibilities attached to corporate actorhood (Garsten, 2003; Schepers, 2006). According to Carroll's (1991) 'pyramid' of CSR, to make profit and to obey the law are required of business in society, while ethical business practice is expected and philanthropic engagement desired. In so far as these expectations towards business are understood as moral obligations, they conceive of the corporation as a member of a community, similar to any other person. In other words, a political understanding of CSR implies that corporations should behave as responsible 'corporate citizens' (Zadek, 2001; Matten and Crane, 2005; Crane et al., 2008; Carroll, 1998). Yet the 'moralized' corporation is not necessarily an ethical business resulting from value-driven entrepreneurial spirit or ethical conviction. The moral conscience of responsible managers alone does not result in responsible behaviour at the organizational level: 'having a conscience in the run-ning of a large corporation does not translate automatically into running a conscientious corporation' (Goodpaster, 1983: 305). It is to a large degree due to others applying moral standards to corporate behaviour and forcing corporations to anticipate that. Corporations are not indif-ferent to the claims of stakeholders because they know (or have to learn) that those demands also reflect consumer preferences. It is therefore rational for organizations to take their social environment seriously.

For some companies, it is possible to embrace values with a high degree of legitimacy in their social environment, e.g. the supply of clean, healthy and organic food. For others, only the fear of being 'branded' and 'framed', i.e. a potential loss of reputation, leads to the internaliza-tion of external demands. Some corporations only surrender to those standards in specific conflict situations or seek to avoid 'actorhood' and the concomitant obligations altogether. For instance, they may refuse to accept responsibility for the operations of subsidiaries like the mul-tinational Mitsubishi did when it became the target of environmental groups for its involvement in rainforest logging (Holzer, 2001). One might speculate that other corporations achieve a similar result by hid-ing their global brand like, for instance, Nestlé, which uses a variety of different brand names, perhaps as a reaction to its being targeted by an international campaign against its marketing of infant formula products in developing countries (Sethi and Post, 1979). Yet most corporations cannot deny corporate actorhood completely and they actively nurture and present their global brand, accepting the resulting calls for corporate accountability and responsibility (Garsten, 2003).

In terms of relationships with specific stakeholders on the one hand, and with the public at large on the other, the focus of CSR has shifted from giving accounts only when asked or pressured to do so to the voluntary and verifiable disclosure of information (cf. Visser, 2011). That indicates a move towards a broader notion of accountability that goes beyond routine 'accounting' catering to specific audiences such as regulators or investors (Holzer, 2008a). Drawing on the above mentioned broad notion of 'giving accounts', one can observe an increasing prominence of a form of nonfinancial 'accounting' – explanations, justifications or excuses – that must be regarded as a response to (and anticipation of) public criticism and lobbying by social movements and NGOs. Those external observers are not primarily interested in economic performance but in evaluating corporations according to a moralized notion of corporate actorhood. If corporations accept their role as actors at all, they need to respond to such broad and ultimately moral assessments of their behaviour. Accounting for the motives, effects and side effects of decisions therefore becomes an important dimension of their corporate activities.

Corporations may go one step further and not only anticipate but actually embrace societal values and expectations. Despite some successes with a truly ethical and principled business practice, such an approach is of limited applicability since it does not really confront the problem of necessarily diverging and sometimes conflicting rationalities in a differentiated and complex society.[9] Instead, corporate 'reflexivity' – i.e. the explicit acknowledgement of, and respect for, diverging rationalities – is a more viable response. Embodied in policies of stakeholder engagement and corporate accountability and often based on 'long-term politicized collaboration with governments and civil society' (Scherer and Palazzo, 2007: 1111), it seeks to avoid manifest conflict by anticipating and incorporating external expectations and it uses the corporate self-presentation as a switchboard for translating between societal constraints and organizational goals.

There are two bases for corporate reflexivity: First, 'inside' the corporation. The organization itself is a sounding board for external demands: Members of the organization are aware of political and environmental issues in their roles as citizens, family members and so on (Holzer, 2008b).

They often strive to accommodate those interests and affiliations with their membership. Thus movement topics and agendas permeate organizational boundaries – even if they are not the subject of official corporate policy. Although the corporate organization is a 'closed system' that can only react to outside pressure according to its own structures, those structures provide anchoring points for external demands that support efforts to align corporate policies with societal expectations.

Second, the social 'environment' enforces a certain degree of corporate reflexivity. Societal expectations lead to demands for accountability and justification. But public scrutiny also gives corporations the opportunity to present themselves in a favourable light: as responsible and accountable corporate citizens who subscribe to the very norms and values propagated by the activists. Thus, many corporations have adopted the CSR discourse and put a lot of effort into portraying themselves as good 'corporate citizens'. Although the discourses of CSR and 'corporate citizenship' do of course serve marketing purposes, too, they hint at a transformation of corporate self-presentation and self-management: Under the threat of public pressure and moral outrage corporations seek to anticipate areas of conflict and to avoid them. As their behaviour is 'moralized' by their critics, TNCs have to deal with the consequences of being moral actors. That requires them to anticipate how their actions are evaluated by the public and to make themselves accountable to external observers; but it also includes managing or manipulating the kind of impressions they make on others.

However, if accountability becomes a matter of routine it inevitably involves a component of 'organizational hypocrisy' (Brunsson, 1989). Organizations, just like individuals, cannot live up to the high standards of their own self-presentations and therefore need to decouple the way they present themselves from what is actually going on. Given the fact that fully ethical behaviour is difficult to realize, hypocrisy has the advantage that moral standards can be upheld and celebrated despite limited chances of actually realizing them. Talk also is a substitute for control (Brunsson, 1993). That does not mean, of course, that they can then commit whatever misdeeds they fancy. On the contrary, the high expectations raised by elaborate corporate accountability give critics excellent starting points for challenging the corporation.

Moralization and rationality

The public role of the corporation, which is the basis for corporate citizenship, is not an entirely new phenomenon. The fact that large corporations separate between ownership and control opens the door for stakeholders' claims because it makes it impossible to restrict the responsibility of management to shareholders alone. Therefore it becomes plausible and legitimate to add more and more demands and constraints to the list of corporate goals:

> Because the corporation has been perceived as responsible to none, suddenly it becomes responsible to everyone. ... Once there were only the owners' goals to attend to, later the systems goals. Today the corporation is being asked to respond to a confusing host of public goals, social as well as economic. (Mintzberg, 1983: 464)

The globalization of production and consumption, resulting in the decreasing effectiveness of regulation on a nation-state level has highlighted the resulting dilemmas. While the nation-state context has long been able to contain the possible and legitimate demands, in a global environment the diverging and conflicting expectations claims of stakeholders multiply. Given the difficulty of reconciling the interests of various groups, it seems unlikely that any kind of solid and straightforward rationality would result from business simply acceding to all those demands.

Whilst advocacy groups and protest groups can put pressure on corporations and influence their policies, there are some limitations regarding the rationality of the results of such forms of regulation 'from below'. First, the issues and targets addressed are necessarily 'selective'. Campaigns seldom challenge the worst corporate practices or villains. In the Brent Spar case, for instance, the evidence suggests that the argument against deep-sea disposal was not quite as straightforward as Greenpeace claimed. More importantly, Greenpeace's campaign was triggered by exogenous and fairly contingent factors, i.e. the fact that Greenpeace was looking for a way to make its North Sea campaign more visible. Transnational advocacy campaigns need to be properly 'marketed' in a competitive environment of issues seeking public attention (Bob, 2005). It is difficult to predict or even to assess the success or failure of a campaign. Transnational activism thus can hardly guarantee meaningful and systematic regulation. Second, it is important to keep in mind that the responsibility of business that is at stake is 'constructed' in such campaigns – and not given right from the beginning. Transnational activism has to make an unambiguous and selective judgement about who is responsible and therefore has to reduce the complexities involved in questions of agency, cause and effect. Due to their visibility and global reach, corporations are often chosen as campaign targets (Lenox and Eesley, 2009) – and therefore they are more likely to be 'framed' for complex grievances even if their contribution to the problem and a potential solution is relatively small.

One should therefore refrain from equating the authority of advocacy groups with an increased rationality of regulation and business practice. That would be naïve considering that the public attention to issues, which is the backbone of any successful challenge raised by activism, is of a random and contingent nature. For the same reason it is also difficult to regard the 'moralizing' or 'politicization' of corporations as an element of a 'deliberative democracy', as Scherer and Palazzo (2007, 2011: 917ff.) argue. Conflicts between corporations and their critics involve public debates and therefore some sort of deliberation, but they lack institutionalized criteria and procedures for participation in those conflicts and the binding authority and scope of the results remains unclear.

Yet, if not the place of rationality and ideal discourse, the transnational public sphere is nevertheless an important source of legitimacy in the world polity. Conflicts between TNCs and protest groups contribute to the elaboration of rules of appropriate behaviour that all actors in the field come to regard as models of appropriate actorhood. These models are more than mere semantic phenomena. They involve sets of rules that – given corresponding public pressure – corporations and other organizations perceive as behavioural constraints. World society cannot rely on a world state to enforce standards of behaviour. But world society, a society 'filled with rationalized others' (Meyer, 1994: 48), can rely on a multitude of observers to ensure that the violation of standards will not go unnoticed. Drawing on Goffman's (1990 [1956]) useful distinction, the significance of protest groups and the mass media particularly lies in their ability to constantly scrutinize the 'front' appearances of actors, be they individuals or corporations, with regard to their 'backstage' performances.

Even if they do not result in a coherent system of regulation, conflicts and their resolutions establish 'precedents' of appropriate behaviour. Such precedents are important substitutes for legitimate and collectively binding decisions in the world polity. For instance, although there is no general ban on deep-sea disposal it would be difficult to find an oil company which would embark on a similar project like the Brent Spar in the future. Similarly, Nike's sweatshop debacle and Shell's troubles in Nigeria have changed corporate perception of what is appropriate and acceptable business practice. The outcomes of those conflicts thus were more or less equivalent to political decisions at a transnational level. Given the lack of global enforcement of rules and standards, such proto-political mechanisms may well be indispensable to hold otherwise unfettered economic power in check. The 'moralized' corporation is not necessarily an ethical business resulting from value-driven entrepreneurial spirit or ethical conviction. It is to a large degree due to others applying moral standards to corporate behaviour and forcing corporations to anticipate that.

Conclusion

A critical discourse which only emphasizes the apparent power of corporations without taking into account the new challenges arising from the globalization of business and the negotiation of actorhood must remain incomplete. It neglects that the lack of a unified global political and legal framework is not only a feature that corporations can exploit – for instance by adopting double standards in their operations – but also a source of new uncertainties (Scherer and Palazzo, 2007: 1108). The decisions and operations of corporations have border-crossing consequences whose acceptability and legitimacy cannot be taken for granted. They are increasingly scrutinized by individuals and protest groups across the world.

In case of perceived misdemeanours, corporations are confronted with campaigning efforts to 'frame' them for their wrongdoings. The fact that corporations are forced to defend and justify their decisions constitutes them as 'moral' actors. Even if corporations do not intend to be 'good' corporate citizens at all, they may be turned into citizens inadvertently – through others defining and treating them as such. Corporate morality, however, is not necessarily an expression of business ethics. It is less an instrument of control than a matter of self-presentation. Public scrutiny is a thorn in the side of corporations but it also gives them the opportunity to present themselves in a favourable light: as responsible and accountable corporate citizens who subscribe to the very norms and values propagated by the activists. Thus, many corporations have adopted the CSR discourse and put a lot of effort into portraying themselves as good 'corporate citizens'. One may deplore the fact that the reality of such corporate citizenship often falls short of its aspirations. Yet the 'moralization' of the corporation is first of all a regime of attributing actorhood and distributing responsibility. Therefore it cannot rule out misdemeanours but only make it more likely that corporations will be interested in avoiding them.

Notes

1. See Crane et al. (2008: Chapter 2) and Gerencser (this volume) for overviews of the classical notion of citizenship and its application to corporations.

2. For in-depth analyses of the Brent Spar conflict and its consequences see Grolin (1998), Hansen (2000), Jordan (2001), Livesey (2001), Neale (1997), Tsoukas (1999), and Wätzold (1996).
3. *Daily Mirror*, Murder at sea, 1 May 1995.
4. *Guardian*, 'Hazardous' oil platform seized, 2 May; *taz*, Inseln versenken, 2 May 1995.
5. In the following paragraphs I summarize an argument that I have developed in more detail elsewhere (Holzer, 2008a).
6. One could see this as a particular dialectic of the patron-client relationship created by corporations (see Gerencser, this volume) in which the image of the corporate benefactor strikes back.
7. 'If men define situations as real, they are real in their consequences' (Thomas and Thomas, 1928: 572).
8. Of course scientists are sceptical in case of both the individual and the organization: 'The individual is often not a particularly true description of people, and it appears to be an even less satisfactory description of organizations' (Brunsson and Olsen, 1993: 67).
9. See also Crane et al. (this volume) on the temporal fragility of such corporate reflections of particular values and citizen identities.

References

Basu, K. and P. Palazzo (2008) 'Corporate Social Responsibility: A Process Model of Sensemaking', *Academy of Management Review*, 33, 1: 122–136.

Beck, U. (1995) 'Judo-Politik', *Die Tageszeitung*, 1 July, 13–14.

Blum, A. F. and P. McHugh (1971) 'The Social Ascription of Motives', *American Sociological Review*, 36, 1: 98–109.

Bob, C. (2005) *The Marketing of Rebellion: Insurgents, Media and International Activism*, Cambridge: Cambridge University Press.

Boli, J. (1999) 'Conclusion: World Authority Structures and Legitimations', in J. Boli and G. M. Thomas (eds) *Constructing World Culture: International Nongovernmental Organizations since 1875*, Stanford, CA: Stanford University Press, pp. 267–300.

Boli, J. and G. M. Thomas (1999) 'INGOs and the Organization of World Culture', in J. Boli and G. M. Thomas (eds) *Constructing World Culture: International Nongovernmental Organizations since 1875*, Stanford, CA: Stanford University Press, pp. 13–49.

BPEO (1994) *Brent Spar – Best Practicable Environmental Option Assessment (Rudall Blanchard)*, London: Shell UK (http://www.shellexpro.brentspar.com).

Brunsson, N. (1989) *The Organization of Hypocrisy. Talk, Decisions and Actions in Organizations*, Chichester: John Wiley & Sons.

Brunsson, N. (1993) 'Ideas and Actions: Justification and Hypocrisy as Alternatives to Control', *Accounting, Organizations and Society*, 18, 489–506.

Brunsson, N. and J. P. Olsen (1993) *The Reforming Organization*, London/New York: Routledge.

Carroll, A. B. (1991) 'The Pyramid of Corporate Social Responsibility: Toward the Moral Management of Organizational Stakeholders', *Business Horizons*, 34, 4: 39–48.

Crane, A., D. Matten and J. Moon (2008) *Corporations and Citizenship*, Cambridge: Cambridge University Press.

den Hond, F. and F. G. A. de Bakker (2007) 'Ideologically Motivated Activism: How Activist Groups Influence Corporate Social Change', *Academy of Management Review*, 32, 3: 901–924.

Dewey, J. (1926) 'The Historic Background of Corporate Legal Personality', *Yale Law Journal*, 35, 6: 655–673.

Dyllick, T. (1989) *Management der Umweltbeziehungen. Öffentliche Auseinandersetzungen als Herausforderung*, Wiesbaden: Gabler.

Friedman, M. (1970) 'The Social Responsibility of Business Is to Increase Its Profits', *New York Times Magazine*, 13 September 1970, 32–33 and 122, 124, 126.

Garsten, C. (2003) 'The Cosmopolitan Organization – An Essay on Corporate Accountability', *Global Networks*, 3, 3: 355–370.

Gerencser, S. (2005) 'The Corporate Person and Democratic Politics', *Political Research Quarterly*, 58, 4, 625–635.

Goffman, E. (1990 [1956]) *The Presentation of Self in Everyday Life*, London: Penguin.

Goodpaster, K. E. (1983) 'The Concept of Corporate Responsibility', in T. Regan (ed.) *Just Business. New Introductory Essays in Business Ethics*, Philadelphia: Temple University Press, pp. 292–323.

Grolin, J. (1998) 'Corporate Legitimacy in Risk Society: The Case of Brent Spar', *Business Strategy and the Environment*, 7, 4: 213–222.

Hansen, A. (2000) 'Claims-Making and Framing in British Newspaper Coverage of the "Brent Spar" Controversy', in S. Allan, B. Adam and C. Carter (eds) *Environmental Risks and the Media*, London/New York: Routledge, pp. 55–72.

Hecker, S. (1997) *Kommunikation in ökologischen Unternehmenskrisen*, Wiesbaden: Deutscher Universitätsverlag.

Hertel, S. (2006) *Unexpected Power: Conflict and Change among Transnational Activists*, Ithaca, NY: Cornell University Press.

Holzer, B. (2001) 'Transnational Protest and the Corporate Planet – The Case of Mitsubishi Corporation vs. the Rainforest Action Network', *Asian Journal of Social Science*, 29, 1: 73–86.

Holzer, B. (2008a) 'From Accounts to Accountability: The Corporate Response to Public Criticism and Social Movement Activism', in M. Boström and C. Garsten (eds) *Organizing Transnational Accountability*, Cheltenham: Edward Elgar, pp. 80–97.

Holzer, B. (2008b) 'Turning Stakeseekers into Stakeholders: A Political Coalition Perspective on the Politics of Stakeholder Influence', *Business & Society*, 47, 1: 50–67.

Holzer, B. (2010) *Moralizing the Corporation: Transnational Activism and Corporate Accountability*, Cheltenham: Edward Elgar.

Jordan, G. (2001) *Shell, Greenpeace and the Brent Spar*, Houndmills/New York: Palgrave.

Keck, M. E. and K. Sikkink (1998) 'Transnational Advocacy Networks in International Politics: Introduction', in M. E. Keck and K. Sikkink (eds) *Activists Beyond Borders: Advocacy Networks in International Politics*, Ithaca, NY: Cornell University Press, pp. 1–36.

Lenox, M. J. and C. E. Eesley (2009) 'Private Environmental Activism and the Selection and Response of Firm Targets', *Journal of Economics & Management Strategy*, 18, 1: 45–73.

Lippmann, W. (1922) *Public Opinion*, London: George Allen & Unwin.

Livesey, S. M. (2001) 'Eco-Identity as Discursive Struggle: Royal Dutch/Shell, Brent Spar, and Nigeria', *Journal of Business Communication*, 38, 1: 58–91.

Luhmann, N. (1968) *Zweckbegriff und Systemrationalität. Über die Funktion von Zwecken in sozialen Systemen*, Tübingen: J.C.B. Mohr (Paul Siebeck).

Meyer, J. W. (1994) 'Rationalized Environments', in W. R. Scott and J.W. Meyer (eds) *Institutional Environments and Organizations: Structural Complexity and Individualism*, Thousand Oaks, CA: Sage, pp. 28–54.

Meyer, J. W. (1996) 'Otherhood: The Promulgation and Transmission of Ideas in the Modern Organizational Environment', in B. Czarniawska and G. Sevón (eds) *Translating Organizational Change*, Berlin/New York: de Gruyter, pp. 241–252.

Meyer, J. W. (2000) 'Globalization: Sources and Effects on National States and Societies', *International Sociology*, 15, 2: 233–248.

Meyer, J. W., J. Boli, G. M. Thomas and F. O. Ramirez (1997) 'World Society and the Nation-State', *American Journal of Sociology*, 103, 1: 144–181.

Meyer, J. W. and R. L. Jepperson (2000) 'The "Actors" of Modern Society: The Cultural Construction of Social Agency', *Sociological Theory*, 18, 1: 100–120.

Micheletti, M. (2003) *Political Virtue and Shopping. Individuals, Consumerism, and Collective Action*, New York: Palgrave Macmillan.

Mintzberg, H. (1983) *Power In and Around Organizations*, Englewood Cliffs, NJ: Prentice-Hall.

Mörth, U. (ed.) (2004) *Soft Law in Governance and Regulation: An Interdisciplinary Analysis*, Cheltenham: Edward Elgar.

Neale, A. (1997) 'Organisational Learning in Contested Environments: Lessons from Brent Spar', *Business Strategy and the Environment*, 6, 93–103.

Schepers, D. H. (2006) 'The Impact of NGO Network Conflict on the Corporate Social Responsibility Strategies of Multinational Corporations', *Business & Society*, 45, 3: 282–299.

Scherer, A. G. and G. Palazzo (2007) 'Toward a Political Conception of Corporate Responsibility: Business and Society Seen from a Habermasian Perspective', *Academy of Management Review*, 32, 4: 1096–1120.

Scherer, A. G. and G. Palazzo (2011) 'The New Political Role of Business in a Globalized World: A Review of a New Perspective on CSR and Its Implications for the Firm, Governance, and Democracy', *Journal of Management Studies*, 48, 4: 899–931.

Scherler, P. (1996) *Kommunikation mit externen Anspruchsgruppen als Erfolgsfaktor im Krisenmanagement eines Konzerns. Erfahrungen aus dem Fall Brent Spar (Greenpeace vs. Shell)*, Basel/Frankfurt: Helbing & Lichtenhahn.

Scott, M. B. and S. M. Lyman (1968) 'Accounts', *American Sociological Review*, 33, 1: 46–62.

Sethi, S. P. and J. E. Post (1979) 'Public Consequences of Private Action: The Marketing of Infant Formula in Less Developed Countries', *California Management Review*, 21, 4: 35–48.

Shell, U. K. (1995) 'Press Release: Shell Refutes Greenpeace Allegations (17 June 1995)', http://www.shellexpro.brentspar.com.

Spar, D. L. and L. T. La Mure (2003) 'The Power of Activism: Assessing the Impact of NGOs on Global Business', *California Management Review*, 45, 3: 78–101.

Stolle, D, M. Hooghe and M. Micheletti (2005) 'Politics in the Supermarket: Political Consumerism as a Form of Political Participation', *International Political Science Review*, 26, 3:245–269.

Thomas, W. I. and D. S. Thomas (1928) *The Child in America. Behavior Problems and Programs*, New York: Alfred A. Knopf.

Tsoukas, H. (1999) 'David and Goliath in the Risk Society: Making Sense of the Conflict between Shell and Greenpeace in the North Sea', *Organization*, 6, 3: 499–528.

Visser, W. (2011) *The Age of Responsibility: CSR 2.0 and the New DNA of Business*, Chichester: John Wiley & Sons.

Vogel, D. (1975) 'The Corporation as Government: Challenges & Dilemmas', *Polity*, 8, 1: 5–37.

Vogel, D. (1978) *Lobbying the Corporation: Citizen Challenges to Business Authority*, New York: Basic Books.

Vorfelder, J. (1995) *Brent Spar oder die Zukunft der Meere*, München: Beck.

Watts, P. (1998) 'The International Petroleum Industry: Economic Actor or Social Activist?' in J. V. Mitchell (ed.) *Companies in a World of Conflict: NGOs, Sanctions and Corporate Responsibility*, London: Royal Institute of International Affairs/ Earthscan, pp. 23–31.

Wätzold, F. (1996) 'When Environmentalists Have Power: The Case of the Brent Spar', in H. Madsen and J. P. Ulhoi (eds) *Industry and the Environment. Practical Applications of Environmental Management Approaches in Business*, Gylling: Naryana Press, pp. 327–338.

Werron, T. and B. Holzer (2009) *'Public Otherhood'. World Society, Theorization and Global Systems Dynamics (Working Paper 02/2009)*, Bielefeld: Institut für Weltgesellschaft, http://www.uni-bielefeld.de/soz/iw/publikationen/ workingpaper_gk/WP-2009-02_Werron-Holzer_Public-Otherhood.pdf.

Willetts, P. (1998) 'Political Globalization and the Impact of NGOs Upon Transnational Companies', in J. V. Mitchell (ed.), *Companies in a World of Conflict: NGOs, Sanctions and Corporate Responsibility*, London: Royal Institute of International Affairs/Earthscan, pp. 195–226.

Yearley, S. and J. Forrester (2000) 'Shell, a Sure Target for Global Environmental Campaigning?' in R. Cohen and S. M. Rai (eds), *Global Social Movements*, London: Athlone Press, pp. 134–145.

5
Standards, Triple Bottom Lines and Balanced Scorecards: Shaping the Metaphor of Corporate Citizenship with Calculative Infrastructures

Fabrizio Panozzo

Corporate citizenship as a metaphor

It was never easy, and will probably never be, for capitalist corporations to state precisely and officially what they are, whom they serve and what they do to society. Of course reliable solutions have been found over time. Legal systems have had to provide stable definitions of the corporation as an economic and legal entity with specific aims, rights, duties and obligations to fulfil. But this was, and still is, an exercise that mainly responds to the need of assuring varying degrees of economic freedom – and set limits to it – within a more or less regulated market systems. The 'laws of the market' are not really enforceable until they are expressed in proper legal terms and stabilized across time and space. But it is precisely such stabilization provided by the legal language that causes its inadequacy to fully grasp the complex identity of the corporation, its variations over time, its adaptations to changing conditions, and its capacity to evolve into something that better 'fits' with the environment. On the contrary, management has always been concerned, probably due to its double nature of professional skill and academic discipline, by the need to mediate between abstractions and practice and thus capture the nature of the corporation as it unfolds. Such conciliation has historically been made possible by the intercession of one of the most notorious and celebrated rhetorical devices: the metaphor. The need to synthetically express the nature of the modern corporation finds an ideal answer in the metaphorical device that concentrates in powerful, vibrant, incisive and sometimes dramatic images, complex bundles of relationships, values, hope, rights and duties. In both managerial literature and practice, metaphors have been proposed as powerful ways to synthesize, evoke and diffuse certain ideas of management and visions of corporate identity (Morgan, 1980). They have also been used to draw the boundary and define the relationship of the capitalist corporation with the political systems and society at large. Morgan (1980; 1986) has notoriously offered the most extensive analysis of metaphorical thinking in management studies. From his contribution we learnt that corporations have been represented first as 'machines', later as 'organisms' and more recently as 'cultures'. Such sequence of metaphors (that includes also slightly less celebrated ones like 'political systems' or 'theatres') shows an inexorable shift from the need to use the metaphor to synthetically represent corporation to a more active attempt to construct a better or improved image of them.

The necessity to call on metaphorical reasoning to illuminate/create the nature of the corporation thus appear like a never-ending process that constantly renovates itself and ventures into new domains where new, more effective, images could be borrowed. The key element in this exercise seems to be the detection of the right image for the right time, one that is more attuned with the relevant economic and political debates of the day, which better captures the Zeitgeist. After machines, bodies, cultures, arenas and brains it is now seems to be the turn of citizenship (Maignan et al., 1999; Moon et al., 2005). As highlighted throughout this book, in a globalized, post-national context corporations aspire to the role that was once limited to the individual in its relationships with the collective entity of the city or the state. Talking of corporations as 'citizens' represents as Moon et al. (2005) aptly state yet another 'move to the metaphorical' and basically evokes the idea that the actions of corporations could be understood as being in some meaningful way similar to that of citizens or citizenship. Citizenship thus adds up to the numerous metaphors used to portray business but it becomes particularly relevant if seen as the expression of sophisticated corporate branding implemented as a key strategic response to critical environmental conditions (Hatch and Schultz, 2008). The metaphor indeed emerges when the legitimacy of the corporation comes under attack because corporate scandals reveal their anti-social behaviour. Such a socially and politically dysfunctional role of corporations promises to be repaired by reference to images of community membership, participation and accountability. New roles and identities for the corporation come to life in the name of citizenship: corporations start to herald the awareness that they are social and political actors deriving their legitimacy from the contexts in which they operate. As new – born public entities they proclaim the understanding of their full social and environmental impacts and responsibilities. This is turn leads to the need to present them as more informed and enlightened members of society which are able to better articulate their role, scope and purpose (Mirvis and Googins, 2006). Of course, such awareness (and with it the full expression of the metaphor) is itself the result of a progressive enlightenment. Corporation may well be established and registered in a place but they become 'good citizens' only when they start embracing a notion of 'civic good' that is more than the simple sum of individual or private goods (Moon et al., 2005).

Authors from different perspectives agree on the fact that the metaphor of corporate citizenship is inherently evolutionary. From a strictly normative point of view Mirvis and Googins (2006) see it evolving from an 'elementary' form (focused mainly on jobs and profits) to a 'transforming' version of corporate citizenship fuelled by ambitions to 'change the game'. Adopting Stokes's (2002) conceptual framework, Moon et al. (2005), suggest that the metaphor of corporate citizenship could acquire radically different meanings depending on its adherence to one of the models along a spectrum that goes from 'liberal minimalist' to 'deliberative' views of democracy. Corporations could express their basic 'civic virtues' either by taking part in those multi-stakeholder governance settings that have so widely been promoted in the last decades or by sharing in the administration of individual citizens' rights, both within and outside the corporation (Moon et al., 2005). A further step would be to incorporate in the notion of corporate citizenship the issue of human and societal improvement. Fulfilment of formal obligations and participation in good governance would not be enough to express the virtues of the corporation: it would rather have to engage in forms of dialogue aimed at generating simultaneous positive developments for both the corporations and its stakeholders. Finally, a 'radical' view of corporate citizenship envisages the metamorphosis of the corporation itself into an object of contestation and a terrain for 'deliberative democracy'. By openly constituting a political arena in which issues of complexity, pluralism, and inequality in corporate life can be deliberated upon in a democratic manner rather than imposed by the authority of management, the corporation would become both an actor and the arena in which citizenship's rights are exercised (Moon et al., 2005).

A metaphor in search for a language

Confronted with such a potential variety of meanings the metaphor of corporate citizenship is somehow at risk. To succeed and endure a metaphor needs to be rhetorically articulated and possibly generate an original discourse. As with other metaphorical exercises the power of the image that is evoked has to be supported by a corresponding vocabulary, a new syntax that complements the imaginary and the visual with a constant supply of re-presentations and narratives of a consistent type. The role that contemporary corporations want to enact in the theatre of global governance requires, as any other, a language that can be understood, a script that makes some sense and certain ability in reciting the lines. With the previous metaphors used by the corporation to construct its identity all that was readily available was provided by other domains. For instance, engineering and physics provided the language to talk of the corporation as a machine. Anthropology did the same for 'corporate culture'. Biology and demographics wrote the script for corporations to behave like organisms or ecosystems and cybernetics and later neurosciences have always been very active in trying to convince us that corporations are complex cognitive systems that think, make mistakes, take risks and learn.

But what about the corporation as a citizen? Where is it going borrow the language, the script and the lines to recite at the right time to sound like a plausible citizen? The mobilization of the notion of citizenship undoubtedly involves the vocabulary of political values such as rights, duties, participation, democracy, representation, and allegiance. But all these elements bear the impression of the primordial relationship between the individual, active and concerned citizen with the public/political entity. What thus becomes necessary in the case of corporate citizenship is a semantic shift that relocates those traditional values into new subjectivities, new relationships, new notions of right and duty. In order to be visible and comprehensible as a citizen the corporation has to first position itself and its interlocutors into a new realm of citizenship that mimics the political/democratic one and thus makes a new discourse possible. In fact, the first linguistic innovation that is brought about by the discourse of corporate citizenship is, not surprisingly, the one of 'stakeholder ship'. The invention of the stakeholder responds to the fundamental discursive precondition of having somebody with whom to exchange narratives and, ultimately, accountabilities. It is indeed the notion and language of accountability and its ability to mobilize concepts of legitimacy and identity the one that makes much of the discourse of corporate citizenship possible. In fact accountability has to do with the giving and taking of accounts on the activity conducted by economic and social agents (Mouritsen and Munro, 1996). The construction, re-construction and maintenance of a relationship of accountability require the use of a language that allows for communication between those that produce the account and its recipients. Discussions and discourses can develop once such language is made available and its rules shared by the interested parties. There is therefore a linguistic issue at the hearth of the transformation of private firms into public actors: the managerial discourse of corporate citizenship is to a significant extent dependent on the possibility of representing the firm as capable of expressing the ways in which it contributes to society and the environment (Sahlin Andersson, 2006). Thanks to these specific types of representations, the firm is in the position of enhancing its social and political legitimacy (Meyer, 1994). But the availability of such language and the development of a discursive potential for corporate citizenship is in itself problematic. It is not only a question of inventing a new language but also to come to terms with the one that firms normally use to account for their results. The private firm has indeed traditionally used a language – the financial one – to affirm its identity and communicate its performances to interested parties. In doing so the corporation has established a specific type of legitimacy on purely economic grounds and constructed a relationship of accountability with those parties that are solely interested in the financial returns it generates. Throughout the history of capitalism these characteristics of the language of business have rarely been seen as fundamental limitations and the role of the firm within society was seen as accurately represented by its ability to generate financial profits. This attitude has been radically challenged by the advent of corporate social responsibility, which has invited a fundamental redefinition in the language of business. The discourse of corporate citizenship has drawn attention to the limits of the mainstream business language and evoked the existence of more appropriate ways of narrating the identity and the functioning of the private enterprise. Corporate citizenship is to a significant extent constituted by the demand and supply of new forms of corporate accountability that should supplement the existing mainstream ones. But what does this call for new, improved accountability imply? What is it precisely that has to be redefined in order for private firms to be made more 'transparent' to the public scrutiny? The critique of traditional forms of accountability invites us to take into consideration the role of the accounting language. Although in an indirect manner, discourses of corporate citizenship criticize accounting for its inability to account for those aspects that manifest the identity and action of the firm as a good citizen. What is seen a problematic is the technical language that is conventionally used to report on the functioning and performance of the corporation. It comes therefore as no surprise that the development of new forms of corporate accountability is parallel by corresponding calls for transformation of the tools and principles of accounting.

During the last decades the field of accounting has been characterized by a constant attempt to redefine its margin in the search for more 'relevant' representations of economic, social and political phenomena. More recently corporate social responsibility and corporate citizenship have indeed played a key role in driving such a transformation of the domain of accounting. But even before contemporary calls for 'improvement', the theory and practice of accounting had been faced with the need to take into consideration and attribute values to the 'truly relevant' functioning of the firm or to its wider societal impacts. It can be argued that developments in accounting take place in continuous attempts to rectify, improve, integrate or expand the representations that are produced by its conventional concentration of monetary values. Those seeking to extend the boundaries of accounting contend that by confining itself to information that can be assigned monetary value, traditional financial accounting and reporting is unable to account for the complexities associated with various issues of concern to the public (Gray, 2002; Yongvanich and Guthrie, 2006). Therefore existing and traditional accounting practices are criticized, gaps are identified and systems of accountability are questioned. Such a problematizing attitude paves the way for the preparation and proposal of new frameworks and techniques that promise to fill the gaps redress relationships of accountability and ultimately produce more accurate representations, more fine-grained pictures. Accounting, both as professional practice and field of academic inquiry, appears to be permanently involved in the exploration of its margins: 'It is at the margins that accounting intersects with, and comes into conflict with, other bodies of expertise. And it is at the margins that accounting comes to be linked up to the demands, expectations, and ideals of diverse social and institutional agencies' (Miller, 1998). Those margins are indeed populated by a vast array of phenomena that for various reasons are labelled as new, relevant or strategic and as such in search for an appropriate representation in the official language of the firm. The visibility in the official accounting documents or in specially created reports is indeed what attributes legitimacy and allows certain episodes or dimensions to be 'taken seriously' both inside the firm and in the context in which it operates. For instance, knowledge is one of those dimensions that have been identified as strategic for organizations that operate in 'knowledge intensive' industries or more in general in a 'knowledge-driven economy' (Carroll and Tansey,

2000). To face such type of competition conditions the source of a firm's value which is to be found in strategic, internally generated, intangible resources (Guthrie, 2001). Forms of accountability that take knowledge into consideration see the value created by corporations as stemming from the management of intellectual capital, rather than from the management of traditional physical assets. As a consequence, models for reporting immaterial assets in general and Intellectual Capital in particular have been developed (Brooking, 1996; Edvinsson and Malone, 1997) thus expanding the boundaries of accounting into the territories of what was previously considered immeasurable.

Calculative infrastructures for corporate citizenship

Changes in competitive conditions thus represent one fundamental driver of change for accounting theory and practice. One other important source of pressure can be identified in a broad category: that of the 'interest of the public'. Under this generic label various perspectives on the activity of the private firm are kept together by their difference from those of the traditional recipients of financial reporting. It is in this broad territory that demands for greater social responsibility of the firms have met accounting to give origin to 'new' and 'improved' forms of accountability. The expansion of accounting into the realm of corporate responsibility took place primarily through the identification of items that would:

(a) express the wider responsibility of the firm beyond its legal obligations and financial objectives;
(b) speak to a wider audience than the one conventionally and historically interested in accounting reports.

The domains of the social and the environmental have been originally identified as the two in which greater corporate accountability was needed and accounting had therefore to expand. Furthermore, by reporting on social and environmental issues, new audiences would have been involved in the cycle of corporate accountability. In fact, this expansion corresponded to the emergence of the category of the stakeholder in opposition to the one of the shareholder. The latter was conventionally conceived as interested solely by the maximization of its returns as owner of the firms and therefore the traditional recipient of financial reports. The notion of stakeholder, on the other side, would encompass 'all those individuals, groups of individuals or organizations that affect and/or could be affected by an organization's activities, products or services and associated performance' (Accountability, 2008). These developments constitute an antecedent and a precondition to the explosion of the corporate responsibility/citizenship discourse. Building upon the identification of new areas and new audiences, companies have increasingly been reporting social and environmental information as a response to pressures broadly defined as 'public' (Deegan et al., 2002; Gray et al., 1995; Guthrie and Parker, 1989; Hogner, 1982; Neu et al., 1998; Patten, 2002). The one of 'social and environmental accounting' has been conceptualized as a 'project' generally concerned with examining and encouraging the emergence of new 'accountings' broadly aimed at reconceptualizing the notions of 'business and society' (Gray, 2002). The early experiments of the project date back to the late 1970s when the first explorations into corporate social responsibility were conducted and a new vocabulary of social audit, social performance, social disclosure and accountability initially developed. For a period, the social and environmental accounting literature was dominated by labour concerns such as information disclosure to employees and their consequent decision-making, collective bargaining, the role of trade unions and only later, during the 1990s, environmental issues emerged and even became dominant. It was in that decade that the project of social and environmental accounting started to abandon its fragmented state and became somehow disciplined and, partially, globalized by a number of initiatives that sought to provide some kind of technical framework for the reporting, benchmarking and ultimately management of social and environmental performance. It was during those same years that the discourses of corporate responsibility and sustainable development gained ground and found a fertile terrain for growth in the parallel evolution of social and environmental reporting.

A distinctive convergence brought together early experiments on new accountings with emergent discourses and sustainability and corporate responsibility and was progressively shaped by the development of a distinctive (albeit not necessarily coherent) calculative infrastructure. A number of initiatives sought to stabilize the field by offering technical guidance and proposing practical tools that would allow for the rigorous reporting of social and environmental information and thus enable discourses of corporate citizenship. This is what stimulated, over the last two decades, the proliferation of principles and tools for measuring and visualizing corporate social responsibility intended to offer ways of measuring, shaping and communicating corporate citizenship. Despite their growing popularity in practice, these instruments only recently became the target of a more specific research focus (Williams, 2004; Rasche and Esser, 2006; Bernstein and Cashore, 2007; Gilbert and Rasche, 2007; Jamali, 2010; Waddock, 2008). Most of these contributions suggest that such a calculative infrastructure took shape to fill the 'governance voids' generated by the lack of transnational regulation on corporate citizenship and the imbalance in global rulemaking (Ruggie, 2002, Gilbert et al., 2010). In a recent contribution Gilbert et al. (2010) systematize the calculative infrastructure of corporate social responsibility in four categories:

1. Principle-based standards. They are mainly used as general guidelines for action, learning and the exchange of best practices. These sets of principles aim at helping to shape corporate behaviours by providing a baseline of foundational values and principles that are prominent and focus broadly on a wide range of corporate responsibilities.
2. Certification standards. They involve verification and monitoring against predefined criteria to provide external observers with a degree of assurance that stated standards are actually being met. Many of these certification schemes include both a set of principles that corporations are expected to live up to and a process for both implementing the standards and verifying compliance on the part of the corporation.
3. Reporting standards. They provide comprehensive and standardized frameworks for economic, social and environmental reporting. They define indicators and guidelines that corporations can use to standardize non-financial reporting practices and to communicate their social and environmental impact to interested stakeholders.
4. Process standards. They only define methods and processes that can be used by corporations to develop an organizational framework around corporate accountability. Process standards offer essential managerial guidance on how to manage towards corporate accountability in a firm. Without an explicit focus on high-quality implementation processes, improvements in social and environmental performance cannot be achieved.

It is thus pretty evident that accountability as the language of corporate citizenship is significantly affected by the practices that are imported from other domains of management and financial accounting. Calculative infrastructure dictate what should be understood as 'appropriate' accountability by articulating a system of rights and duties that shapes the notion of corporate citizenship but which is also very much dependent on the logic of quantification, commensuration and certification. In is thus of some interest to conduct a further exploration of some of the tools that compose such an infrastructure in order to shed some light on the ways in which certain ideas of corporate citizenship have been constructed, operationalized and acted upon. The following paragraphs are thus devoted to a short presentation of three of the most significant attempt to provide technical solutions to the problems of comparable non-financial reporting, the management of social and environmental performance and the need to scrutinize the claims of corporate citizenship.

Triple bottom lines

There can be little doubt that one of the most successful attempts to shape the agenda of corporate accountability has been the proposal of an analogy between the indicator of the financial results of the firm and its social and environmental impacts. Responsible firms, argued business consultant John Elkington in 1994, have more than one 'bottom line', they actually have to have three: the conventional financial one has to be supplemented by a social bottom and environmental bottom line. The notion of 'Triple Bottom Line' (TBL) thus came to light and immediately started to gain currency in the emerging field of corporate responsibility. The triple bottom line statement purports to render corporate actions more understandable and transparent in areas not covered under current reporting conventions. TBL reporting has been generally presented in the accounting and reporting literature as a significant step forward in the search for enhanced social and environmental corporate responsibility. Advocates of the triple bottom line argue that since an organization's long-term viability is dependent on sustaining 'profitability' over all three dimensions, they should be measured, reported, and even audited on a periodic basis, in a manner conceptually similar to the current financial reporting model (Brown et al., 2006).

The growth of TBL inspired reports marked a clear turning point in the 'social and environmental accounting project' that had been active for more than a decade then. With the advent of TBL concerns for a more extended corporate accountability moved beyond the boundaries of academic circles, social and environmental activists and enlightened businesses. The ambition was quite clearly the one of mainstreaming social and environmental reporting first of all by adopting a language that would 'resonate with business brains' (Elkington, 2004). Not surprisingly, many consultancies and big accounting firms in particular began using the concept and offering services to help firms that want to measure, report or audit their two additional 'bottom lines'. TBL promotional literature is highly evocative, couched in the jargon of business consultancies and only marginally preoccupied with the accurate illustration of how the three bottom lines should actually be calculated (Gray and Milne, 2004). Nevertheless, it has been argued that the whole idea of TBL reporting rests on a series of pretty strong claims (Norman and MacDonald, 2003):

- Measurement Claim: the components of 'social performance' or 'social impact' can be measured in relatively objective ways on the basis of standard indicators. These data can then be audited and reported.
- Aggregation Claim: A social 'bottom line' – that is, something analogous to a net social 'profit/loss' – can be calculated using data from these indicators and a relatively uncontroversial formula that could be used for any firm.
- Convergence Claim: measuring social performance helps improve social performance, and firms with better social performance tend to be more profitable in the long-run.
- Strong Social-Obligation Claim: firms have an obligation to improve their social bottom line – their net positive social impact – and accurate measurement is necessary to judge how well they have fulfilled this obligation.
- Transparency Claim: the firm has obligations to stakeholders to disclose information about how well it performs with respect to all stakeholders.

Such claims have been taken up and further operationalized on a global scale by other relevant actors that saw in the TBL approach the most promising way to mainstream the cause of corporate responsibility and reporting. TBL ideas have in fact progressively evolved to embrace the notion of sustainability in partnership with the United Nations Environment Programme (UNEP) who, at the end of the 1990s, was instrumental in promoting the Global Reporting Initiative (GRI). Among the initiatives to adopt a TBL approach to non-financial reporting, the GRI represents the predominant development; the GRI is both an independent institution and what is claimed to be the world's first standardized approach to social and environmental reporting (Milne et al., 2008). More precisely, the GRI identifies 'sustainability reporting' as its object of interest but explicitly interprets it a synonym for other types of social and environmental reporting. Sustainability thus becomes the notion that qualifies the type of reporting that is produced to demonstrate corporate accountability and construct corporate citizenship. The GRI Reporting Framework is intended to serve as a generally accepted framework for reporting on an organization's economic, environmental, and social performance. It is designed for use by organizations of any size, sector, or location. It takes into account the practical considerations faced by a diverse range of organizations – from small enterprises to those with extensive and geographically dispersed operations. The GRI Reporting Framework contains general and sector-specific content that has been agreed by a wide range of stakeholders to be generally applicable for reporting an organization's sustainability performance.

The Sustainability Reporting Guidelines consist of principles for defining report content and ensuring the quality of reported information. It also includes Standard Disclosures made up of Performance Indicators and other disclosure items, as well as guidance on specific technical topics in reporting. Indicator Protocols exist for each of the Performance Indicators contained in the Guidelines. These Protocols provide definitions, compilation guidance, and other information to assist preparers of reports and to ensure consistency in the interpretation of the Performance Indicators.

Balanced scorecards

The Balanced Scorecard (BSC) is a managerial tool that was developed by Kaplan and Norton and described in their 1996 book 'The Balanced Scorecard'. Both the book and the tool immediately gained a widespread success among practitioners while at the same time fuelling an intense debate among academics (Nörreklit, 2003). The BSC developed out of dissatisfaction with the ways in which companies were identifying their targets, measuring the performance and reporting their results both within and outside the corporation. The main target of critique, also in this case, was the almost exclusive reliance on financial measures as indicators of performance and information base for the development of corporate strategies. Conventional accounting measures are seen as 'irrelevant' for the inherently historical nature and their inability to capture the essence of the 'real' phenomena affecting the competitiveness of firms (Johnson and Kaplan, 1987). Once again, the development occurs at the margins of accounting and is based on a problematization of existing practices. The critique is directed at hard, material investment capital whose efficient use is no longer seen as the sole determinant for competitive advantages, but increasingly immaterial factors such as intellectual capital, knowledge creation or excellent customer orientation become more important. In this way the BSC aims to solve the problem related to the historical nature of the financial measures of accounting systems. It does so by integrating financial and non-financial strategic measures in a cause and effect relationship, which assumes a logical connection between

- measures of organizational learning and growth;
- measures of internal business processes;
- measures from the perspective of the customer;
- financial measures.

The measurements in non-financial areas make the performance measurement system a feed-forward control system that solves the problem of the historical nature of accounting data (Nörreklit, 2003). 'Scores' and indicators of performance are therefore measured at different moments in time, at different levels within and outside the corporation and from different perspectives. The combination of these diverse views into one single scorecard makes it a 'balanced' tool that takes into consideration values deriving from the measurement of physical and organizational phenomena. The promise of the BSC is the one of embedding traditional financial measurement in a more balanced management system that links short-term operational performance with long-term strategic objectives (Kaplan and Norton, 1996). The BSC involves choosing the market, identifying the critical internal processes at which an organization must excel and selecting internal capabilities required for meeting the firm's internal, customer and financial objectives (Kaplan and Norton, 1996). The use of the BSC moves attention ways from the short-termism of financial accounting measures to focus companies on strategies for long-term success. By identifying the most important objectives on which an organization should focus its attention and resources, the BSC provides a framework for a strategic management system that organizes issues, information, and a variety of vital management processes.

The very nature of the BSC, namely its criticism of financial measures of performance, its search for multiple perspective and metrics and its focus on those elements that directly impact of the competitive advantage of the firm, make it an ideal candidate for an adaptation in the domain of social and environmental measurement. The focus in this case shifts from mere reporting to a more strategic vision that sees the identification and measurement of core dimension as fundamental elements of organizational decision-making.

The BSC has indeed been suggested as a management tool that integrates the management of social and environmental issues into mainstream business activities (Figge et al., 2002; Schaltegger and Wagner, 2006; Van der Woerd and Van den Brink, 2004). Several of these relatively recent contributions suggest that the BSC would be beneficial in determining the main content for sustainability reporting and provide the sort of information that should enable stakeholders to envisage how the company conducts its activities (Schaltegger and Wagner, 2006; Yongvanich and Guthrie, 2006). According to Figge et al. (2002) the BSC 'helps to overcome the shortcomings of conventional approaches to environmental and social management systems by integrating the three pillars of sustainability into a single and overarching strategic management tool'. Epstein and Wisner (2001) as well argue that the incorporation of social and environmental metrics into the Balanced Scorecard can also help managers reposition their organizations toward improved corporate responsibility. The process of developing social and environmental BSC measures also helps managers identify the key performance measures that link to strategic objectives. The BSC framework is seen as highly flexible and able to accommodate strategic social and environmental goals with the work of the organization, to communicate the importance of these initiatives throughout the firm, and to measure the impact of these programmes on corporate profitability (Epstein and Wisner, 2001). Perrini and Tencati (2006) respond to the call for new metrics of corporate responsibility from a stakeholder perspective with the development of a 'sustainability evaluation and reporting system' (SERS) aimed at balancing financial and non-financial measures. The proposed framework aggregates other instruments of corporate responsibility in a broad range of measures that generates a 'dashboard of sustainability' featuring integrated performance indicators relating physical and technical quantities to financial ones.

A different type of 'Responsibility Balanced Scorecard' (RBS) has been proposed by Van der Woerd and Van den Brink (2004) that moves beyond the traditional BSC by adding new perspectives to the four that make up the original version. The emphasis is thus more clearly shifted towards sustainability aspects, therefore presupposing an adjusted set of cause-and-effect relations. While in the traditional Scorecard the emphasis is on Profit, with 'People' and 'Planet' play a supporting role at most. In a RBS, People and Planet become on equal footing with Profit. Adjusted relations will result in an adjusted set of strategic topics and may result in a new set of strategic perspectives. The 'Responsive Scorecard' should enable companies to score at Profit, People and Planet, at the same time to integrate stakeholder demands into internal programmes to improve performance.

The RBS includes five Perspectives: Customers and Suppliers, Financiers and Owners, Society and Planet, Internal Process and Employees and Learning (Van der Woerd and Van den Brink, 2004).

Standards of corporate accountability

One additional area of development for formal tools of corporate accountability is the one of standards. Standardization is a common and widespread process impacting on several domains of company's functioning, first and foremost on ideas of quality of processes and products. It comes therefore as little surprise that the mechanism of standardization has accompanied the expansion of the interest for social and environmental accountability. Two standards in particular – AA1000 and SA8000 – appear to have gained relevance and visibility and a record of adoption in many countries and for a variety of purposes (Göbbels and Jonker, 2003). A short illustration of the principle and mechanisms of the two standards will follow, based on the provisions of the official documentation issue by the standard-setting bodies.

The purpose of the AA1000APS (2008) is to provide organizations with an internationally accepted, set of principles to frame and structure the way in which they understand, govern, administer, implement, evaluate and communicate their accountability. The AA1000 AccountAbility Principles are primarily intended for use by organizations developing an accountable and strategic approach to sustainability. The standard was developed using a broad-based, multi-stakeholder process. All of the input received was considered by the AccountAbility Standards Technical Committee, which prepared a draft standard for public review. Between each of these periods of public review and following the final period, the AccountAbility Standards Technical Committee reviewed and revised the draft. The final draft was agreed by the AccountAbility Standards Technical Committee and submitted to the AccountAbility Operating Board which approved it for publication.

There are three AA1000 AccountAbility Principles, Inclusivity, Materiality and Responsiveness. The foundation principle of Inclusivity is necessary for the achievement of Materiality and Responsiveness. Inclusivity is the starting point for determining materiality. The materiality process determines the most relevant and significant issues for an organization and its stakeholders. Responsiveness is the decisions, actions and performance related to those material issues.

- Inclusivity requires a defined process of engagement and participation of stakeholders that provides comprehensive and balanced involvement and results in strategies, plans, actions and outcomes that address and respond to issues and impacts in an accountable way.

- Materiality involves the determination of the relevance and significance of an issue to an organization and its stakeholders. To determine what is material requires a process designed to ensure that comprehensive and balanced information is input and then analysed. Such inputs include information other than financial information: information on non-financial, sustainability drivers and their impact on stakeholders.

- The principle of responsiveness deals with the ways in which an organization responds to its stakeholders and is accountable to them. This may include: establishing policies, objectives and targets, governance structure, management systems and processes, action plans, stakeholder engagement, measurement and monitoring of performance or assurance. Stakeholders should participate in developing responses although an organization's responses may not agree with the views of all stakeholders.

Audits con be conducted and assurance engagements performed on the application of AA1000 standards. There are two types of sustainability assurance engagement. Type 1 focuses on AccountAbility Principles and is intended to give stakeholders assurance on the way an organization manages sustainability performance, and how it communicates this in its sustainability reporting, without verifying the reliability of the reported information. The assurance provider evaluates publicly disclosed information, the systems and processes the organization has in place to ensure adherence to the principles and the performance information that demonstrates adherence. For Type 1 assurance, the evaluation of performance information does not require the assurance provider to provide conclusions on the reliability of the performance information. In a Type 2 engagement, the assurance provider also evaluates the reliability of specified sustainability performance information that the reporting organization agrees to include in the scope of the assurance engagement. Specified information is selected based on the materiality determination and needs to be meaningful to the intended users of the assurance statement. The evaluation of the reliability of specified sustainability performance information is based on explicit management assertions about sustainability performance and includes a review of their completeness and accuracy. For assurance on specified sustainability performance information an assurance provider provides findings and conclusions relating to the reliability of the sustainability performance information.

An assurance engagement may be carried out to provide a high level of assurance or a moderate level of assurance. Since different subject matter may be addressed in one assurance engagement, a high level of assurance may be provided for some subject matter while a moderate level of assurance may be provided for other subject matter in the same assurance statement. Minimum evidence gathering for evaluating adherence to the AA1000 AccountAbility Principles at a moderate level of assurance include:

- understanding and testing on a sample basis the processes used to adhere to and evaluate adherence to the AccountAbility Principles;
- inquiring by management, including senior management at executive and functional levels, and by relevant management responsible for the day-to-day management of sustainability, about the effectiveness of processes used to adhere to the AA1000 AccountAbility Principles;
- observing and inspecting management practices, process testing and evidence gathering across the organization on a sample basis, and collecting and evaluating documentary evidence and management representations that support adherence to the principles.

For a high level of assurance the assurance provider shall also seek more extensive evidence in all areas as well as corroborative evidence where available, including direct engagement with stakeholders.

The second initiative, SA8000, is an international standard for improving working conditions globally. It is based on the principles of thirteen international human rights conventions, ten of which are conventions of the International Labour Organization (ILO). The SA8000 standard is intended to help apply these norms to practical work-life situations. SA8000 expands on the eight conventions of the ILO's Declaration of Fundamental Principles of Rights at Work which covers the following:

- child labour
- forced labour
- health and safety
- freedom of association and the right to collective bargaining
- discrimination
- disciplinary practices
- working hours
- remuneration

These eight core elements of SA8000 are essential to enabling auditors to crosscheck and verify compliance. All eight elements are interrelated and, to varying degrees, compliance with one is dependent on compliance with another. The final provision of management systems' requirements of SA8000 has been introduced to move beyond a checklist approach, encouraging managers to make sustainable systemic changes in how they run their business. The SA8000 management system is designed to protect workers' basic rights, to improve working conditions, and to enhance worker-manager communication. The SA8000 management system therefore has several unique features. For example, to be certified, a company must take responsibility for working conditions beyond its own facilities. Under SA8000, companies must monitor and control suppliers, subcontractors and suppliers to ensure they also comply with SA8000. Two other distinguishing feature of the SA8000 management system are the requirement of participation by non-management personnel to ensure that employees at all levels are served by the system and requirements that there be a system for outside communication with interested parties about the company's performance.

It is the workplace process, not the actual product or product quality, which is being certified. Once an organization has implemented the necessary improvements, it can earn a certificate attesting to its compliance with SA8000. The certificate provides a report of good practice to consumers, buyers, and other companies. Certification lasts for three years, with surveillance audits required every six months. Certified workplaces are required to make public their certification, maintain and improve the systems put in place to achieve certification. Companies that are certified can display their certificate in a store or factory or catalogue, in company advertising, and on company stationery.

Third-party assessment of compliance to SA8000 standards is available through independent organizations accredited by Social Accountability International (SAI). Third-party assessment includes documentation, site audits, and observation of auditors in the field. The assessment can be conducted by any SAI-accredited body which could be a certification agency, a management systems auditing firm, an NGO, or a trade union. The assessment addresses working conditions at specified locations and activities of the organization seeking certification. Company performance deemed to be in conformance with the standard is acknowledged by the granting of a certificate that can be displayed as specified and its contents communicated to relevant parties.

Certification under SA8000 can apply to companies, suppliers, and subcontractors. A company can fall into any or all of these three categories, depending on which party is asking to be certified or which party is requiring another party to be certified. The term 'company' is used to designate the production facility, farm, service provider or any other entity pursuing compliance.

The management system requirements of SA8000 require management to develop policies and track performance improvements resulting from those policies. To succeed in the implementation of social standards, a company must have documented proof of compliance and systems to ensure continued compliance with all elements of SA8000. The burden of proving compliance is on the audited company. The intent of these management system requirements is to institutionalize and substantiate the eight SA8000 performance requirements; that these requirements assume continuous improvement will be evident over time both prior to certification and following certification. Procedures to verify and sustain implementation of the eight SA8000 elements consistently over time are the key to the system. The company's records should substantiate that the required practices were followed in the past in order to give the auditor reasonable confidence that these same practices will be followed and can be verified in the future.

Conclusion: on corporate citizenship as commensuration

By providing a short description of three ways of expressing corporate social responsibility, I have sought to illustrate the relationship between corporate citizenship as a broad socio-economic programme and its practical dimension. It is indeed important to acknowledge that the grand aspirations of corporate citizenship and accountability depend on the availability of certain sets of techniques that make those aspirations visible and manageable. As Rose and Miller (1992) have pointed out discussing the modalities of advanced liberal government, there exists a fundamental relationship between programmes and technologies. Ambitions of reshaping the citizenship of corporations ultimately need to be expressed in forms that use mundane technologies of formal classification, measurement and calculation. Mainstream corporate citizenship literature displays faith the inclusiveness of standards as well as their capacity to ensure free and equal discourses among participants (Palazzo and Sherer, 2006; Gilbert et al., 2010). The discourse of corporate citizenship appears to be irresistibly geared towards forms of commensuration conducted in the name of an abstract, delocalized and mythical stakeholder, discursively constructed through the categories of financial reporting, standardization, certification and verification. Such modalities contribute with an essential ingredient to the mainstream discourse of corporate citizenship: they translate in a simple, common and supposedly objective language what would otherwise appear as the realm of peculiarity and subjectivity. Dense notions such as 'citizenship' are heavily dependent on the cultural and historical conditions that shaped them within specific institutional contexts. In much the same way the role of corporations within society is influenced by the ways in which national and local economic systems developed.

Furthermore moral values and notions of ethical behaviour that are conspicuously mobilized in the definition of responsibility, are highly subjective, rooted as they are in philosophical and religious beliefs. Should all these elements be captured in their specificity and singularity we would witness the developments of very localized dialogues at the expense of a general discourse of corporate citizenship. This is why the latter structures itself as governmental programme that establishes a fundamental alliance with technologies of classification, measurement, audit and certification that render its object uniform and manageable even 'at a distance' (Rose and Miller, 1992). With a growing use of quantitative indicators such technologies have come to characterize the mainstream discourse of corporate citizenship and contribute to the transformation of the meaning itself of accountability (Hoskin, 1996). Where accountability once included many different practices, making corporations accountable now usually means developing reporting standards and uniform indicators to classify and order their performance (Espeland and Sauder, 2007). Notions of 'bottom lines' and 'scorecards' create a symbolic and operational connection with both long-established and more innovative tools of accounting while the idea of 'standards' of accountability evokes the possibility of conducting audits similar to those performed on financial statements. Within standardization decisions are linked to professional and replicable methodologies of verification, which are seen to transcend individual subjectivity, and deemed universally applicable (Porter, 1992). In this sense, the calculative infrastructure of corporate citizenship can support the aspiration to 'escape from perspective' and obtain a 'view from nowhere' of what corporate accountability is about (Daston, 1992; Jasanoff, 2005; Samiolo, 2012). The notion of commensuration can be aptly mobilized here to indicate the process whereby different qualities are measured with a single standard or unit, to derive a common metric through a series of aggregations (Espeland and Stevens, 1998; Espeland, 2000). In this way new links are forged between things previously separated, but at the same time distance is created by the mediation and abstraction imposed by numbers (Espeland, 1998; Samiolo, 2012). A fundamental exercise of commensurability is what allows the making of corporate responsibility manageable: the vast array of qualities that make up the idea of corporate citizenship becomes expressed according to a common metric. A new aggregate is formed, and the meaning and value of the individual elements thus aggregated changes as a result (Samiolo, 2012). Commensuration 'changes the locus and form of attention, both creating and obscuring relations among entities' (Espeland and Sauder, 2007). The logic of accountancy is central in this process of commensuration as it provides the basic tools to quantify and calculate those aspects that are then added up to construct certain notions of responsibility and citizenship. The accounting language makes available the common metric that allows logically associating People, Planet and Profit in Triple Bottom Lines as requested, for instance, by the GRI framework. It is in this way that the social dimension is first unpacked by, among others, the 'Occupational Health and Safety' aspect and subsequently measured by indicator LA6 – percentage of total workforce represented in formal joint management-worker health and safety committees that help monitor and advise on occupational health and safety programs' (GRI, 2002). In the name of improved accounting calculation, space can be created on the business scorecard for phenomena such as child labour in much the same way in which 'learning' was computed when it was declared strategic for the corporation. As noticed earlier in the chapter, accounting has the capacity to extend its margins to respond to new stimuli for calculation that are generated by the encounter with different forms of expertise (Miller, 1998). In doing so accounting as a calculative practice fully expresses its double identity: it can gain and provide legitimacy as a technology that neutrally and objectively reflects reality while at the same time being engaged in the active construction of the objects it declares to represent (Hopwood, 1987). Numbers and calculative technologies like accounting have been shown to reconfigure and change the domains they make calculable, often in unintended ways. Numbers have the power to 'standardize' both the subject and the object of calculation (Porter, 1992). They make decisions appear to descend from a neutral logic of quantification rather than subjective judgement, thus making them virtually replicable and independent of the people taking these decisions.

Numerical representations condense and reduce information people have to process, which facilitates judgement and decision-making (Espeland and Stevens, 1998). The commensurability of corporate citizenship makes it appear a naturally calculable set of phenomena that is finally coherently packaged into triple bottom lines and balanced score-cards. But any intervention of a calculative practice is to be appreciated for what it makes visible as well as for what it dismisses or conceals. What these celebrations of neutrality and objectivity render virtu-ally invisible is the process through which certain qualities are made countable and specific aspects, rather than others, are made auditable. Precision and objectivity are obtained through progressive rounds of simplification that dissolve complex notions of responsibility and citi-zenship into manageable units. The three episodes analysed earlier show that instruments and processes for monitoring and reporting corporate responsibility emerge from what Ayres and Braithwaite (1992) term 'responsive regulation': the voluntary collaboration of corporations in developing forms of monitoring and regulation within setting that are often orchestrated by international organizations. Such forms of self-monitoring are by no means natural or spontaneous: they involve a great deal of political and administrative work (Shamir, 2010). Business associations, international organizations, trade unions, governmental representatives, non-governmental organizations, academics, and other groups are regularly brought together to present best practices and sug-gest guidelines (Sahlin Andersson, 2006).

Processes such as learning networks, policy dialogues and stakeholder forums are the primary generators of standards and frameworks for social and environmental accountability. In such dialogues between the regulator and the regulated, common norms and understandings are developed and notions of corporate citizenship evolve in the negotia-tions between corporations and their stakeholders (Sahlin Andersson, 2006). Within these policy networks, communities of practice are established that are highly receptive to the development of new tools and indicators and to measurement innovation in general. It is this combination of political power and technical expertise that favours the development of popular and seemingly democratic measures but most of all makes commensuration and measurement appear natural (Power, 2004). In this way the amount of work that is necessary to fabricate calculability and auditability becomes largely invisible and taken for granted. There is indeed a need to further investigate these forms of 'mechanical objectivity' that tend to conceal the amount of political work required to measure and calculate corporate citizenship and the assumptions that surround the use of triple bottom lines, standards and balanced scorecard. For instance, and given the centrality of com-mensuration in the corporate citizenship discourse, greater attention could be devoted to areas of 'incommensurability' which eventually emerge at the margin between different institutional domains where rights, duties and identities are contested (Samiolo, 2012). This would bring the attention back to communal relationships, personal interactions and local knowledge, i.e. some of the elements that constitute the essence of social and political citizenship. Yet, as pointed out by both Espeland and Stevens (1998) and Porter (1992) commensuration tends to develop in opposition to communitarian cultures based on personal ties and rather tries to reform them in the name of impersonality and universality and the pursuit of the 'common interest'. It is indeed around the idea of what is to be constructed and considered as 'common' that the discourse of corporate citizenship displays a fundamental contradiction. Traditional values of citizenship such as participation, involvement, democracy and collective choice would lead to the expression of the common good as a view emerging from the multiplicity of individual dialogues and local knowledge (Samiolo, 2012). In spite of this, one single shared view inspired by impersonality and universality and obtained through standards, calculative practices, financial reports and certification is that 'commensurate' is ultimately preferred as the expression of the 'common good'. The paradox that demands further critical investigation lies in the fact that although stakeholder involvement would support a multi-voiced approach expressing a 'view from everywhere', dialogue, let alone conflict, can hardly develop when the preference is given for a search for 'mechanical objectivity' (Porter, 1992) generated from a global 'view from nowhere' (Jasanoff, 2005). An improved understanding of the relationship between metrics of corporate citizenship asks from a more systematic investigation of whether and how stakeholders are actually willing and able to resist commensuration and of how they develop capabilities of attributing different 'orders of worth' (Boltanski and Thévenot, 2006) to the elements that compose the virtues of corporate citizenship.

References

Bernstein, S. and B. Cashore (2007) 'Can Non-State Global Governance Be Legitimate? An Analytical Framework', *Regulation and Governance*, 1: 347–371.

Boltanski, L. and L. Thévenot (2006) *On Justification: Economies of Worth*. Princeton: Princeton University Press.

Brown, D., Dillard, J. and R. S. Marshall (2006) 'Triple Bottom Line. A Business Metaphor for a Social Construct', Document de Treball, Universidad Autonoma de Barcelona, 06/2.

Carroll, R. F. and R. R. Tansey (2000) 'Intellectual Capital in the New Internet Economy: Its Meaning, Measurement and Management for Enhancing Quality', *Journal of Intellectual Capital*, 1, 4: 296–311.

Daston, L. (1992) 'Objectivity and the Escape from Perspective', *Social Studies of Science*, 22, 4: 597–618.

Elkington, J. (2004) 'Enter the Triple Bottom Line', in A. Henriques and J. Richardson (eds) *The Triple Bottom Line: Does It All Add Up*, London: EarthScan.

Epstein, M. J. and P. S. Wisner (2001) 'Good Neighbors: Implementing Social and Environmental Strategies with the BSC', Balanced Scorecard Report.

Espeland, W. N. and M. Sauder (2007) 'Rankings and Reactivity: How Public Measures Recreate Social Worlds', *American Journal of Sociology*, 113: 1–40.

Espeland, J. and W. Nelson (2000) 'Bureaucratizing Democracy, Democratizing Bureaucracy', *Law & Social Inquiry*, 25, 4: 1077–1109.

Espeland, W. N. and Stevens, M. L. (1998) 'Commensuration as a Social Process', *Annual Review of Sociology*, 24: 313–343.

Figge, F., Hahn, T., Schaltegger, S. and M. Wagner (2002) 'The Sustainability Balanced Scorecard – Linking Sustainability Management to Business Strategy', *Business Strategy and the Environment*, 11: 269–284.

Gilbert, D. U., A. Rasche and S. Waddock (2010) 'Accountability in a Global Economy: The Emergence of International Accountability Standards', *Business Ethics Quarterly*, 21, 1: 23–44.

Gilbert, D. U. and A. Rasche (2008) 'Opportunities and Problems of Standardized Ethics Initiatives – A Stakeholder Theory Perspective', *Journal of Business Ethics*, 82: 755–773.

Global Reporting Initiative (GRI) (2002) *Sustainability Reporting Guidelines*. Boston, MA: GRI.

Göbbels, M. and J. Jonker (2003) 'AA1000 and SA8000 Compared: A Systematic Comparison of Contemporary Accountability Standards', *Managerial Auditing Journal*, 18, 1: 54–58.

Gray, R. (2002) 'The Social Accounting Project and AOS: Privileging Engagement, Imaginings, New Accounting and Pragmatism Over Critique?', *Accounting, Organisations and Society*, 27: 687–708.

Gray, R. and M. J. Milne (2004) 'Towards Reporting on The Triple Bottom Line: Mirages, Methods and Myths', in A Henriques and J. Richardson (eds), *The Triple Bottom Line: Does It All Add Up?* London: Earthscan.

Gray, R., R. Kouhy, and S. Lavers (1995) 'Corporate Social and Environmental Reporting: A Review of the Literature and a Longitudinal Study of UK Disclosure', *Accounting, Auditing & Accountability Journal*, 8, 2: 47–77.

Guthrie, J. (2001) 'The Management, Measurement and the Reporting of Intellectual Capital', *Journal of Intellectual Capital*, 2, 1: 27–41.

Guthrie, J. and L. D. Parker (1989) 'Corporate Social Reporting: A Rebuttal of Legitimacy Theory', *Accounting and Business Research*, 19, 76: 343–352.

Hatch, M. J. and M. Schultz (2008) *Taking Brand Initiative: How Companies Can Align Strategy, Culture, and Identity Through Corporate Branding*, Hoboken, NJ: Wiley Desktop.

Hoskin, K. (1996) 'The "Awful Idea of Accountability": Inscribing People Into the Measurement of Objects', in Munro, R. and J. Mouritsen (eds) *Power, Ethos and the Technologies of Managing*, London: International Thompson Business Press, pp. 265–281.

Jamali, D. (2010) 'MNCs and International Accountability Standards Through an Institutional Lens: Evidence of Symbolic Conformity or Decoupling', *Journal of Business Ethics*, 95: 617–640.

Jasanoff, S. (2005) 'Restoring Reason: Causal Narratives and Political Culture', in Hutter, B. and M. Power (eds) *Organizational Encounters with Risk*. Cambridge: Cambridge University Press.

Johnson, H. T., and R. S. Kaplan (1987) *Relevance Lost, the Rise and Fall of Management Accounting*, Boston, MA: Harvard Business School Press.

Kaplan, R. S. and D. P. Norton (1996) *The Balanced Scorecard – Translating Strategy into Action*, Boston, MA: Harvard Business School Press.

Maignan, I., O. C. Ferrell and G. T. M. Hult (1999) 'Corporate Citizenship: Cultural Antecedents and Business Benefits', *Journal of the Academy of Marketing Science*, 27, 4: 455–469.

Meyer, J. W. (1994) 'Rationalized Environments', in Scott, W. R. and J. W. Meyer (eds) *Institutional Environments and Organizations*, Thousand Oaks, CA: Sage, pp. 28–54.

Miller, P. (1998) 'The Margins of Accounting', *European Accounting Review*, 7, 4: 605–621.

Milne, M. J., A. Ball and R. Gray (2008) *Wither Ecology? The Triple Bottom Line, the Global Reporting Initiative, and the Institutionalization of Corporate Sustainability Reporting*. Paper presented at the American Accounting Association Annual Meeting in Anaheim, CA, August 3–6.

Mirvis, P. and B. K. Googins (2006) *Stages of Corporate Citizenship: A Developmental Framework*, Boston, Connecticut: The Center for Corporate Citizenship at Boston College.

Moon, J., A. Crane and D. Matten (2005) 'Can Corporations Be Citizens? Corporate Citizenship as a Metaphor for Business Participation in Society', *Business Ethics Quarterly*, 15, 3: 429–453.

Morgan, G. (1980) 'Paradigms, Metaphors and Problem Solving in Organization Theory', *Administrative Sciences Quarterly*, 25, 4: 605–622.

Norman, W. and C. MacDonald (2003) 'Getting to the Bottom of "Triple Bottom Line"', *Business Ethics Quarterly*, March, 14, 2: 243–262.

Palazzo, G., and A. G. Scherer (2006) 'Corporate Legitimacy as Deliberation: A Communicative Framework', *Journal of Business Ethics*, 66: 71–88.

Perrini, F. and A. Tencati (2006) 'Sustainability and Stakeholder Management: The Need for New Corporate Performance Evaluation and Reporting Systems', *Business Strategy and the Environment*, 15, 296–308.

Porter, T. M. (1992) 'Objectivity as Standardization: The Rhetoric of Impersonality in Measurement, Statistics, and Cost-Benefit Analysis', *Annals of Scholarship*, 9, 1/2: 19–59.

Power, M. (2004) 'Counting, Control and Calculation: Reflections on Measuring and Management', *Human Relations*, 57, 6: 765–783.

Rasche, A. (2009) 'Toward a Model to Compare and Analyze Accountability Standards – The Case of the UN Global Compact', *Corporate Social Responsibility and Environmental Management*, 16: 192–205.

Rose, N. and P. Miller (1992) 'Political Power Beyond the State: Problematics of Government', *The British Journal of Sociology*, 43, 2: 173–205.

Sahlin, K. (2006) 'Corporate Social Responsibility: A Trend and a Movement, but of What and for What?', *Corporate Governance*, 6, 5: 595–608.

Samiolo, R. (2012) 'Commensuration and Styles of Reasoning: Venice, Cost–Benefit, and the Defence of Place', *Accounting, Organizations and Society*, 37, 6: 382–402.

Shamir, R. (2010) 'Capitalism, Governance, and Authority: The Case of Corporate Social Responsibility', *Annual Review of Law and Social Science*, 6: 531–553.

Van der Woerd, F. and T. Van den Brink (2004) 'Feasibility of a Responsive Business Scorecard – A Pilot Study', *Journal of Business Ethics*, 55: 173–186.

Waddock, S. (2008) 'Building a New Institutional Infrastructure for Corporate Responsibility', *Academy of Management Perspectives*, 22: 87–108.

Yongvanich, K. and J. Guthrie (2006) 'An Extended Performance Reporting Framework for Social and Environmental Accounting', *Business Strategy and the Environment*, 15: 309–321.

6
Revisiting Corporate Citizenship Theory and Practice from the Perspective of Local Communities in Africa: Lessons from Nigeria

Uwafiokun Idemudia[1]

Introduction

The various efforts to better understand the challenges and opportunities that confront business-society interaction have seen the emergence and proliferation of a multitude of concepts (see Birch, 2001; Wood and Logsdon, 2001; Waddock, 2008; Ludescher et al., 2008). These concepts include but are not limited to Corporate Social Responsibility (CSR), triple bottom line, sustainable development, and Corporate Citizenship (CC), which are often either portrayed as complementary or competing concepts. However, some have also argued that these concepts especially CSR have engineered more analytical confusion than conceptual clarity and therefore should be abandoned (see Freeman and Liedtka, 1991; Freeman and Velamuri, 2006; Van Oosterhout, 2005, 2008). In response to such criticisms, considerable efforts have recently been directed at rethinking the concept of CC as way of addressing its analytical weakness and making it a useful framework for managerial decision-making (see Idemudia, 2008). This is partly because the concept of CC has in the past few decades emerged as the dominant discourse employed by academics, businesses and consultants to describe the changing socio-political role of business in society (Matten and Crane, 2005; Moon et al., 2005; Néron and Norman, 2008).

However, the notion of CC lacks a consensual definition and it is highly contested. This is due to both the multifaceted nature of the notion of 'citizenship' and the differences in the perception of the nature of the corporation (i.e. whether moral character is an essential property of corporate existence)[2] and the purpose of the corporation in society (i.e. to serve the public good or to maximize shareholder value).

Indeed, Windsor (2001) has argued that the difficulties with the concept of CC lie in the fact that it conflates citizen (which a firm cannot be) and person (which a firm can be but only as a legal fiction).

Similarly, there is also disagreement over whether the language of CC is useful for thinking and justifying the changing roles of business in society.[3] On one hand, many proponents of CC would agree that the corporation is not a person,[4] and that the lack of conceptual specificity hinders theoretical development. Besides, few would deny the fact that CC has traditionally been deployed in a manner that does often not define any new role for the corporation, and that the conception of the corporation as a 'citizen' has not necessarily led to a critical interrogation of the notion of 'citizenship' in a way that might enthuse new meanings for societal governance (Crane et al., 2008). On the other hand, the process of globalization driven by the information technology revolution and the predominance of the neo-liberal agenda in the past decade have meant that traditional binaries like the state versus the market or clearly delineated boundaries of responsibilities among the state, business and civil society are no longer sufficiently adequate to understand the evolving nature of societal governance. Hence, CC concerns have evolved from efforts to assess its usefulness for capturing the changing nature of the role of business in society to efforts that seek to rethink the concept of CC and consider its implication for societal governance. However, a key limitation of these recent efforts to rethink CC is that they continue to marginalize African voices and experiences in the theoretical debate on CC and are often based on limited empirical evidence. Against this background the specific objectives of this chapter[5] are to:

(a) critically examine the similarities and differences between contemporary conceptions of CC with local communities understanding their relationship with oil Transnational Corporations (TNCs) in the Niger Delta;
(b) critically explore community perceptions of the relationship between corporate community development efforts and governmental efforts;
(c) consider the implications of findings for CC theory and practice from a developing country perspective.

By addressing these objectives, this chapter begins to potentially bridge existing gaps in the literature, contextualize the emerging CC theory and offer insights about CC from a developing country perspective that is so far limited in CC discourse.

Revisiting the corporate citizenship debates: addressing existing gaps

The effort to re-theorize CC has evolved from the deliberate attempt to address the different understandings of what the notion of citizenship can mean for organizations (see Wood and Logsdon, 2001; Logsdon and Wood, 2002; Wood and Logsdon, 2002; Néron and Norman, 2008) to how the corporation can also be used to examine the theory and practice of citizenship (see Crane et al., 2008). In the absence of a common understanding of CC, three broad usages of the concept have so far been identified. These are the limited view of corporate citizenship that equates CC with philanthropy in local communities, the equivalent view of CC, that is said to conflate CC with the existing conception of CSR, and finally the extended view of CC that takes seriously the idea that citizenship can provide a political conceptualization of the corporation (Matten and Crane, 2005; Crane et al., 2008).[6] Building on the extended view of CC as way of addressing the weaknesses of the limited and equivalent view of CC, Crane et al. (2008a) have argued that analysing the corporation through the lens of citizenship should expose the political dimension to the many social and economic relationships of corporation within society. They suggested that citizenship offers a way of thinking about the roles and responsibilities among members of a polity (i.e. on a horizontal dimension), and between these members (i.e. on a vertical dimension) and their governing institutions. Following this logic and drawing on three principal themes that underpin the idea of citizenship (status, entitlement and process), Crane et al. (2008) suggested linking corporation and citizenship metaphorically in three ways.

The first linkage is to conceptualize the 'corporation as a citizen', which suggests a position in which corporations are examined on similar horizontal relationship with other corporate citizens and human citizens, and like human citizens, corporate citizens are also examined on a vertical relationship of power with government. Hence, the focus here tends to be on how the corporation shares the status, and the process elements of citizenship. The second view is to think of the corporation as government.[7] This refers to the manner in which corporations are taking up roles and responsibility previously assumed only by governments. As such, the corporation is conceptualized as sharing a horizontal dimension with government and vertically aligned with human citizens within a political community. The focus here is therefore on how the corporation informs the status, processes and entitlement of people as citizens. Matten and Crane (2005) suggest that the corporation can play any of three roles i.e. a providing role, an enabling role and a channelling role. Finally, we have the stakeholders as citizens model in which citizenship is used as a metaphor for understanding stakeholder relations within the arena of the corporation. This conception of the corporation and citizenship focuses not on governing the political community but on vertical relations between the governing body of the corporation and a variety of stakeholders.

Although this extended view of CC has been particularly helpful in enriching our understanding of CC by adding some analytical clarity and conceptual rigour to the use of the concept, it has also been heavily criticized.[8] First, the extended view of CC has been criticized for lacking strong empirical bases (Van Oosterhout, 2005; Jones and Haigh, 2007). According to Van Oosterhout (2005), the extended view of CC makes sweeping claims that are neither supported by facts nor references to empirical studies. Similarly, Amaeshi (2009) asserted that because the extended view of CC confronts the 'real' through metaphors, in its use of metaphor the reality only therefore becomes these metaphors. As such, its theorization of CC becomes more or less intellectual gymnastics that offers nothing more than some intellectual stimulation and satisfaction.

In response, Crane and Matten (2005) have often turned to developing countries to cite examples that shore up the empirical basis of their theory. However, the failure to sufficiently include the voices of the poor and marginalized people of developing countries as well as consider how their lived experiences might influence their own conception of CC means that the extended view inadvertently essentializes the firm and its behaviour while excluding a variety of actors in the shadow of theoretical debate. Indeed, Mir et al. (2008) have pointed to a long-standing tradition in which while egregious violation of CC behaviour occurs in developing countries, yet theoretical debates about these take place in metropolises. In essence, the theorization of CC has intrinsically been rooted in western expectations, values and ways, but it supposedly better captures the realities in developing countries. The implication therefore is that a critical challenging still facing CC theorization is how the debate can avoid the traps of imperialism on one hand, and the limitations of relativism on the other (Palazzo and Scherer, 2008).

Second, disagreements also persist with regard to the implications of the extended view of CC for society and business. For example, Van Oosterhout (2005) criticized the Matten and Crane (2005) for failing to consider corporate rights and what that might mean for society. Van Oosterhout noted that the extended view of CC fails to consider 'what

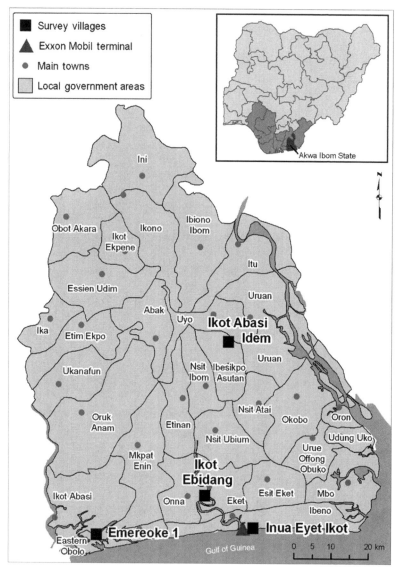

Figure 6.1   Map showing study area in of Akwa Ibom State, Niger Delta

the corporations want in return (i.e. for being considered corporate citizens), and are states and citizens willing and able to give what corporations demand?' While acknowledging the validity of this concern, Crane and Matten (2005) suggested that a more pertinent question lies in considering the reciprocal responsibilities of citizens. In a developing country context, this debate is manifested in disagreement over the ramifications of business taking up developmental roles previously assumed by government for government and society. For instance, while Ward and Fox (2002), Ite (2004) and Frynas (2005) fear that CC's contribution to development has or will allow governments of developing countries to abnegate their development responsibility, Ferguson (1998) and Matten et al. (2003) seem to hold a contrasting view and instead foresee a kind of complementary relationship between CC contributions to development and governments meeting their development responsibility. Remarkably, none of these positions is supported by systematically analysed empirical evidence.

Hence, addressing these two gaps in the literature is critical if the concept of CC is to move beyond just being a metaphor to become both relevant to stakeholders and a useful guide for managerial decision-making. A key step in that process requires a systematic attempt to better ground recent CC conceptualization in empirical data and to explore the extent to which such propositions are consistent with or diverge from the lived experience of key stakeholders. The next section begins to address these issues as it attempts to link the extended view of CC with the lived experience of local communities in the Niger Delta area of Nigeria. As a result, the strengths and limitations of the extended view of CC from a developing country context are revealed and their theoretical and practical implications considered.

Linking the local community's expectations to the CC obligations of oil TNCs

Communities near a project that exploits non-renewable resources normally have a wide range of expectations. These expectations from a limited CC view should define the responsibilities of oil TNCs in the Niger Delta, as corporate responsibilities are supposedly derived from societal expectations (Carroll, 1998). Hence, exploring community expectations offer an avenue for understanding local community views of what constitute oil TNCs' CC obligations. Table 6.1 shows that 98 per cent of the respondents expected oil TNCs to provide employment, and set up micro-credit and other poverty-alleviation schemes. A total of 94 per cent of the respondents expected oil TNCs to assist in training community members in new trades. Also 93 per cent believed it was imperative for oil TNCs to meet regularly with host communities to discuss issues of mutual interest as well as allow for a two-way communication between companies and communities. Table 6.1 also shows that 81 per cent

Table 6.1   Community expectations of oil TNCs (ranked)

Community expectations	Villages				Total
	Ikot Ebidang (*N* = 32)	Inua Eyet Ikot (*N* = 70)	Emeoroeke 1 (*N* = 43)	Ikot Abasi Idem (*N* = 15)	*N* = 160
Focus on poverty reduction in communities	31 (97%)	67 (96%)	43 (100%)	15 (100%)	156 (98%)
Local capacity building	30 (94%)	64 (91%)	42 (98%)	15 (100%)	151 (94%)
Community engagement	30 (94%)	63 (90%)	41 (95%)	15 (100%)	149 (93%)
Provide basic infrastructures	32 (100%)	40 (57%)	43 (100%)	15 (100%)	130 (81%)
Donates to fund to support community activities and projects	23 (72%)	40 (57%)	23 (54%)	15 (100%)	101 (63%)

Source: Questionnaire survey.

of the respondents expected oil TNCs to provide social infrastructure, like the construction and renovation of roads, schools and hospitals, thus addressing community needs. Only about 63 per cent of the respondents expected oil TNCs to donate funds to support community projects. Hence, there is relatively low support to fund donation to communities by oil TNCs among the survey villages. A chi-square test of data in Table 6.6 yielded insignificant results (chi-squared = 8.8, degrees of freedom = 12, $p = 0.71$). The implication is that there are no real differences in respondents' expectations across the survey villages. The similarities across the survey villages suggest that most respondents in the four survey villages seem to share a common expectation for human development, defined here largely in terms of capacity building and poverty reduction. For instance, all the respondents in Ikot Abasi Idem expect oil TNCs to help in training community members, and 98 per cent of the respondents in Emereoke 1 shared a similar view.

In the survey villages of Inua Eyet Ikot and Ikot Ebidang, 91 per cent and 96 per cent of the respondents respectively had similar expectations. A similar trend was also observed with regard to communities expecting oil TNCs to provide employment and the establishment of poverty alle-viation schemes. All respondents (100 per cent) in the survey villages of Ikot Abasi Idem and Emereoke 1 expected oil TNCs to provide employ-ment for community members and micro-credit schemes. Table 6.1 also shows that 96 per cent and 97 per cent of respondents in Inua Eyet Ikot and Ikot Ebidang respectively shared a similar expectation. The need for oil TNCs to meet regularly with communities was also widely shared in the survey villages. In Ikot Abasi Idem and Emereoke 1 respectively, 100 per cent and 95 per cent of the respondents expected oil TNCs to meet with them on a regular basis, while 93 per cent of respondents in Ikot Ebidang, and 91 per cent of respondents in Inua Eyet Ikot had similar expectations (see Table 6.1).

However, there was a disparity in community expectations across the different survey villages concerning the provision of social infrastructure and the donation of funds. While 100 per cent of the respondents in Ikot Abasi Idem, Emereoke 1, and Ikot Ebidang expected oil TNCs to provide social infrastructure, only 57 per cent of respondents in Inua Eyet Ikot shared a similar view. Similarly, while 100 per cent of the respondents in Ikot Abasi Idem and 72 per cent of the respondents in Ikot Ebidang expected oil TNCs to donate funds to support the community, only 53 per cent and 57 per cent of respondents in Emereoke 1 and Inua Eyet Ikot respectively shared this expectation. A further variation is that, whereas all respondents (100 per cent) in Ikot Abasi Idem a (non-host community) expected oil TNCs to meet all the categories of community expectations, this was not the case with the three other survey villages (host communities). The similarities and differences in expectations across the survey villages (see Table 6.1) can be best explained by the nature of the socio-economic context in the Niger Delta (locality) and the communities' geographical proximity to oil TNCs that has shaped community needs and its ideals, as well as differences in community experiences that influence their expectations. The unanimity across sur-vey villages in demanding or expecting poverty reduction programmes, employment and the development of human capacity has its roots in the shared problem of poverty that is endemic in the Niger Delta due to the historical, political and economic marginalization of the region.

Local community conception of their relationship with oil TNCs

Beneath community expectations are the various socio-cultural mores with which they make sense of their environment and therefore their relationship with oil TNCs. Indeed, Burke (1999) has suggested that community expectations are often informed by a psychological contract that exists between communities and companies. However, unlike a social contract that is explicit, the psychological contract is largely about implicit expectations that communities and companies have of each other. This subsection identifies the various socio-cultural mores used by members of the survey villages to understand their relationship with oil TNCs. These categories were identified from a combination of a careful reading of interview and focus group discussions notes, and how respondents during interviews and focus group discussions described themselves in relations to oil TNCs. These socio-cultural mores are by no means the only ones used by members of the survey villages to understand their relationship with oil TNCs. However, the discussion is limited to only three categories because these appear to be quite common.

Landlord-squatter relationship category

One of the common categories used by community members in their discussion of their relationship with oil TNCs during interviews and focus group discussions was one that defined them as the landlord and the oil TNCs as their squatters. Members of the survey villages see this framework as the basis for their relationship with oil TNCs. They see crude oil being prospected by oil TNCs, and the land upon which oil TNCs' infrastructures are located as their property. Hence, oil TNCs are their squatters and like all other squatters, oil TNCs would eventually leave if they no longer derived utility from the leased property. This category has two intimately related ramifications for corporate-community relations (CCR). First, as landlord, communities define how their properties are used, in this case how oil TNCs should operate. Second, the squatter is expected to meet the landlord's expectation; otherwise, the squatter is evicted. In other words, while the landlord has rights that persist as long as the squatter continues to derive utility from its properties, the squatters have rights and responsibilities as defined by the landlord. Members of the survey villages did not couch this landlord-squatter relationship in any legalistic tone. Rather, it was a tacit assumption of how they see things ought to be. For example, when the youth leader was asked that Exxon Mobil might be afraid that even if they meet all community expectations, they will still be asked to do more. He asserted that:

> Yes, we will continue to ask for more as long as Mobil is here in our land. If they (Mobil) do not want us to demand from them, then

they should leave our land. If they are not in our property, we will not go to America to go look for them to make demand.

A tacit assumption that underpins this category is that oil TNCs ought to respond to community demand because oil TNCs benefit from community resources. This argument is consistent with the equivalent view of CC that argues that business is part of society and benefits from society resources and therefore ought to contribute to solving societal problems. Here, community expectations in Table 6.1 are seen as considerations that should be received from oil TNCs for their exploitation of their resources. This partly supports and explains the provider role that Matten and Crane (2005) suggested that corporation can play as 'corporations as governments'.

Good neighbours category

The neighbourhood conceptualization of CCR stems largely from the geographic proximity of oil TNCs to host communities and the length of time oil TNCs have operated in the host communities. Members of the communities see oil TNCs as part of the host communities. Some even go as far as seeing oil TNCs as part of the family. The sense of good neighbourliness is therefore seen as a yardstick for measuring oil TNCs' social performance and a framework that ought to guide oil TNCs' operations and practices. Accordingly, the secretary to the village council of Inua Eyet Ikot said:

Oil TNCs operate, and their staffs live, in our communities. As a part of our communities, we are not supposed to tell them what to do. Our problems should automatically be a priority for them.

This understanding partly informs the channelling role that oil TNCs are also expected to play. According to a female respondent in Inua Eyet Ikot:

Exxon Mobil is very close to government in Abuja and Abuja is far from us here, if Exxon Mobil cannot provide what we need in the community, they should help us tell the government in Abuja to provide it for us.

The implication of this category is that community members expect oil TNCs to instinctively take into consideration community concerns in their decision-making and interaction with the Nigerian government as well as treat community issues as priority issues without community pressure to do so. The failure of oil companies to do so has invariably led to disappointment among communities and the proliferation of negative perceptions. Similarly, this category suggest that CC initiatives undertaken by oil TNCs out of community pressure invariably lose a substantial part of their value in the eyes of community members as such initiatives are seen as earned by the community rather than a product of oil TNCs' good will. For example, the youth leader in Inua Eyet Ikot referred to the free electricity from Exxon Mobil in the following way:

> We fought for the electricity, people lost their lives, if we did not fight, Mobil will never give us electricity. So it is our effort that is bearing fruit not because Exxon Mobil cares about us.

The ramification of this assertion is that Exxon Mobil is unable to derive maximum benefit from its CC initiatives in communities because Exxon Mobil's CC initiatives are seen as mere response to community pressure. This category therefore partly explains Frynas's (2005) assertion that despite significant increases in oil TNCs' community development spending they have been unable to secure their social licence to operate in the Delta.

Community partners category

Community members also see oil companies as partners to be worked with to achieve community objectives. However, this was largely a position shared by chiefs, local government councils and community elites during interviews. This is because CCR is seen as a forum for the development of such partnership between communities and oil TNCs. This position is how local government officials define their relationship with oil TNCs. For example, the former secretary to the council of Onna, asserted, 'We see oil companies as developmental partners'. Similarly, the Chief of Ikot Ebidang asserted that:

> Oil companies are very vital to the development of communities because they bring development if they can work with us. We see them as partners, but the problem is that they don't want anything to do with us.

The ramification of this category is that there is a willingness of community members to work with oil TNCs (see also Table 6.2) as they are aware of the potential benefits to be derived from oil MNC involvement in host communities development. This idea that collaboration with oil TNCs would yield better community development benefit is also consistent with the enabling role that corporation can play according to Matten and Crane (2005).

Reciprocal responsibility and community development

The rethinking of CC necessitates the need to focus on stakeholder responsibility because the notion of citizenship focuses on the rights and responsibilities of all stakeholders which are mutually interlinked and dependent upon each other (Waddell, 2000). Hence, addressing this issue of stakeholder reciprocal responsibility has been identified to be critical to any theoretical advancement in the field of business and society (Bowie, 1991; Crane and Matten, 2005; Idemudia, 2008). The discussion that follows is a preliminary exploration of this issue.

The survey data in Table 6.2 shows that while 86 per cent of the respondents accepted that the community has a reciprocal responsibility to assist oil TNCs to contribute to community development, 14 per cent of the respondents did not accept this view. A chi squared analysis of data yielded insignificant results (chi-squared = 7.55, degree of freedom = 3, $p = 0.056$). The implication of this test result is that there are no real differences in the acceptance of reciprocal responsibility across the survey villages.

All the respondents in Ikot Abasi Idem accepted that communities have a reciprocal responsibility for community development. Only 94 per cent, 88 per cent and 79 per cent of respondents in Ikot Ebidang, Emereoke 1 and Inua Eyet Ikot, respectively, accepted this view. This difference might be explained by the disparity in proximity between the survey villages and oil TNCs. The proximity of host communities

Table 6.2 Community response to idea of reciprocal responsibility

Acceptance of reciprocal responsibility	Village				Total ($N = 160$)
	Ikot Ebidang ($N = 32$)	Inua Eyet Ikot ($N = 70$)	Emereoke 1 ($N = 43$)	Ikot Abasi Idem ($N = 15$)	
Yes	30 (94%)	55 (79%)	38 (88%)	15 (100%)	138 (86%)
No	2 (6%)	15 (21%)	5 (12%)	0 (0%)	22 (14%)
Total	32 (100%)	70 (100%)	43 (100%)	15 (100%)	160 (100%)

Source: Questionnaire survey.

and associated contact with oil TNCs perhaps make them more likely to rely on oil TNCs to help meet their community development needs. This is opposed to non-host communities like Ikot Abasi Idem that have no contact with oil TNCs, and are therefore more likely to be inclined to pursue self-help community development or seek aid from government and are therefore more likely to accept reciprocal responsibility. For example, the majority of the respondents from this village asserted that government should have more responsibility for community development than oil TNCs, which is in contrast with the position expressed by members of the host communities (see also Table 6.7).

Overall, the implication of this finding is that it contradicts the ideas of Frynas (2005) and Ite (2004) that a 'dependency mentality' is widespread in the Niger Delta. This might be because the people are culturally accustomed to self-help strategies. For example, the problem of water shortage in the village of Ikot Abasi Idem was resolved by the community by coming together to plan and execute a borehole water project for the community, without the assistance of any external agent or the government (see Figure 6.2).

Indeed, Akinola's (2008) empirical research in the Niger Delta supports this position as it demonstrated that in the face of social deprivation, local communities had revived the local tradition of collective

Figure 6.2   Community water project in Ikot Abasi Idem

Table 6.3 Reciprocal responsibility by age distribution (ranked)

Reciprocal responsibility	Age						Total
	Below 19	20–29	30–39	40–49	50–59	60+	
Yes	3 (2%)	43 (27%)	32 (20%)	33 (21%)	17 (11%)	10 (6%)	138 (86%)
No	0 (0%)	10 (6%)	7 (4%)	1 (0.6%)	2 (1%)	2 (1%)	22 (14%)
Total	3 (2%)	53 (33%)	39 (24%)	34 (21%)	19 (12%)	12 (7%)	160 (100%)

Source: Questionnaire survey.

action to meet their developmental needs. Furthermore, the full support for reciprocal responsibilities in Ikot Abasi Idem also seems to suggest that if there is any kind of dependency mentality in local communities, it is likely to have arisen out of oil TNCs' strategy of implementing CC initiatives in such communities. This position is plausible given that a one-way analysis of variance (ANOVA) of Table 6.3 (ANOVA = 1.029, degree of freedom = 1, $p = 0.312$) suggests that there are no significant differences between the ages of respondents in the two groups (yes/no), suggesting that Table 6.2 is a realistic representation of community perceptions.

Community ideas of reciprocal responsibility practices

Besides ascertaining if local communities would accept the principles of reciprocal responsibility, it was also pertinent to explore what for them might constitute their reciprocal duties. A total of 138 respondents (86 per cent) accepted that the community has reciprocal responsibility to assist oil TNCs in contributing to community development (see Table 6.2). Of these 138 respondents, 59 per cent suggested that telling oil companies about communities' needs and giving oil companies feedback, while supplying free labour in support of community development projects being provided by the oil TNCs, is part of community reciprocal responsibility (see Table 6.4). Another 58 per cent asserted that taking responsibility for maintaining community development projects provided by oil companies was also a part of the community's reciprocal responsibility. This also contradicts Dobber and Halme's (2009) assertion that a victim mentality pervades communities like the ones in Niger Delta in developing countries. The need to provide a safe and conflict-free environment for oil TNCs to operate was identified by 48 per cent of the respondents as one of the ways communities can assist oil TNCs in contributing to community development. Respondents asserted that this was necessary given the incessant conflict in the region that often paralyses oil companies' operations. This assertion seems to suggest that respondents are well aware of the need for oil TNCs to meet their economic responsibility as a basis for continued community support.[9]

Table 6.4 shows that 21 per cent of the respondents felt that starting self-help community development projects that oil TNCs can then support is a way by which communities can meet their reciprocal responsibility for community development. This finding suggests that the survey villages are not only likely to be willing to take on reciprocal responsibility if and when they are encouraged to do so, but they also have a relatively clear idea of what can be expected of them. A chi-square test of data in Table 6.4 yielded significant results that implies that there are variations in the favoured reciprocal responsibility practices by respondents in the different survey villages (chi-square = 30, degrees of freedom = 9, p = .000). For instance, while facilitating communication and supplying free labour to support oil TNCs' development projects is widely shared in the survey villages, the support for the responsibility for the maintenance of CC projects or to start a project that can then be supported by oil TNCs varied across the survey villages.

In Emereoke 1 and Ikot Abasi Idem, 84 per cent and 73 per cent of respondents respectively agreed to support projects undertaken by oil TNCs, while only 47 per cent and 36 per cent of respondents in Inua Eyet Ikot and Ikot Ebidang shared a similar view. This trend is observed again with the idea that communities can start development projects, which can then be supported by oil TNCs. Table 6.4 shows that

Table 6.4   Reciprocal responsibility practices (ranked)

Reciprocal responsibility practices	Ikot Ebidang (N = 30)	Inua Eyet Ikot (N = 55)	Emereoke 1 (N = 38)	Ikot Abasi Idem (N = 15)	Total (N = 138)
Information sharing and free labour	10 (33%)	29 (53%)	31 (82%)	12 (80%)	82 (59%)
Maintain CSR projects	11 (36%)	26 (47%)	32 (84%)	11 (73%)	80 (58%)
Provide secure environment	13 (43%)	34 (62%)	14 (36.8%)	6 (40%)	67 (49%)
Start projects that oil TNCs can support	3 (10%)	2 (4%)	19 (50%)	5 (33%)	29 (21%)

Source: Questionnaire survey.

50 per cent and 33 per cent of respondents in Emereoke 1 and Ikot Abasi Idem, respectively, acquiesced to this form of reciprocal responsibility. In contrast, in Ikot Ebidang and Inua Eyet Ikot only 10 per cent and 4 per cent of respondents respectively shared this view. However, while 61 per cent of respondents in Inua Eyet Ikot took on the responsibility of creating a secure environment for oil TNCs' operations, only 36 per cent of the respondents in Emereoke 1 shared this view.

A possible explanation for these variations is the differences in proximity between these villages and oil TNCs and the nature of the CC strategy being employed by oil TNCs in these survey villages. Although oil production is largely offshore, Exxon Mobil has a huge terminal office in the village of Inua Eyet Ikot, and the people of Inua Eyet Ikot are well aware of their ability to enforce 'social licences to operate'. In contrast, such an office does not exist in Emereoke 1 (see Figure 6.1). This partly explains why respondents in Inua Eyet Ikot regard securing a peaceful working environment as a paramount concern, but this not so for respondents in Emereoke 1, where Total has no office or immediate oil infrastructure. Similarly, the CC strategy of corporate foundation employed by Total in Emereoke 1 seems to have built on the local culture of self-help in the village. Hence, respondents in Emereoke 1 were more open to accepting the responsibility for maintaining community development projects supplied by oil TNCs or starting such projects. In contrast, respondents in Inua Eyet Ikot have not been exposed to a similar CC strategy and are used to oil TNCs single-handedly providing social infrastructure.

Reasons for rejecting the idea of reciprocal responsibility

Out of 22 respondents who did not accept that communities have reciprocal responsibility, 63 per cent maintained that the community did not have the capacity to assist oil TNCs to contribute to community development (see Table 6.5). A possible explanation is that most respondents seem to interpret community capacity mostly in terms of financial capacity. Hence, they were reluctant to accept reciprocal responsibility. As one respondent in Emeroke1 puts it 'we do not have money to contribute'. The implication is that if an attempt is made to clarify for community members that reciprocal responsibility is not only about financial obligations, they might be persuaded to accept the idea of community reciprocal responsibility.

Table 6.5 also shows that 45 per cent of the respondents rejected the idea of the community's reciprocal responsibility, because they owned the oil and the land from which oil is being prospected. For these respondents, this ownership claim exempts communities from having reciprocal responsibility for development outside the provision of *free land* (a very scarce resource) for oil TNCs to operate and provide communities with social infrastructure. While these respondents explicitly rejected reciprocal responsibility, their willingness to donate land for free for which oil TNCs are at present expected to pay does suggest some form of willingness to reciprocate the goodwill extended by oil TNCs.

The negative impact of oil production on host communities was another reason cited by 27 per cent of the respondents for rejecting the idea that communities have reciprocal responsibility. These respondents argued that it would be unfair to expect communities to accept reciprocal responsibility for community development, after bearing the full brunt of the negative social and environmental externalities generated by the oil industry. Similarly, 18 per cent of the respondents rejected the idea of community reciprocal responsibility because the community was not getting its fair share of oil revenue. According to a resident of Ikot Ebidang:

> Government and oil companies are cheating us. If to say they are not cheating us, then you can talk of how we can help the oil companies contribute to the development of the community. As for now I don't think we should contribute.

A chi-square test of data in Table 6.5 yielded insignificant results (chi-square = 3.4, degrees of freedom = 6, p = 075). The result suggests that there is no difference in the reasons for rejecting reciprocal responsibility across the survey villages. Hence, any attempt to secure community acceptance of reciprocal responsibility in the survey villages would

Table 6.5   Reasons for rejecting reciprocal responsibility (ranked)

Rejection of reciprocal responsibility	Ikot Ebidang (N =2)	Inua Eyet Ikot (N = 15)	Emereoke 1 (N = 5)	Total (N = 22)
Lack of capacity	1 (50%)	10 (66%)	3 (60%)	14 (63%)
Land ownership	1 (50%)	7 (47%)	2 (40%)	10 (45%)
Negative effects of oil production	0 (0%)	3 (20%)	3 (60%)	6 (27%)
Lack of benefit from oil revenue	0 (0%)	2 (13%)	2 (40%)	4 (18%)

Source: Questionnaire survey.

benefit from addressing these common concerns for rejecting community reciprocal responsibility.

Community perceptions of stakeholder responsibility for community development

Existing literature suggests that businesses have a responsibility to contribute to development. However, the literature fails to address the issue of how much developmental responsibility business can be expected to assume or the balance of developmental responsibility between government and business in a partnership arrangement that is often promoted as the way forward to address developmental problems. In addition, the literature also fails to suggest what business should or can do when and if other stakeholders are not pursuing their responsibility (Wiig and Ramalho, 2005). Hence, exploring local communities' views would help shed some light on this conundrum.

The balance of responsibility: government and oil TNCs

Table 6.6 shows that 71 per cent of the respondents felt that government and oil TNCs should not have equal responsibility for community development. In contrast, 29 per cent of the respondents shared an opposing view. A chi-squared test of the data in Table 6.10 yielded insignificant result (chi-squared = 10.960, degree of freedom = 3, p = .012).

The implication of the test result is that there are no differences in respondents' perceptions of stakeholder development responsibility across the survey villages. For example, most respondents in the survey villages did not expect government and oil TNCs to have equal responsibility. Nonetheless, a close examination of Table 6.6 showed that

Table 6.6 The balance of responsibility for community development

Equal responsibility	Village				Total (N = 160)
	Ikot Ebidang (N = 32)	Inua Eyet Ikot (N = 70)	Emereoke 1 (N = 43)	Ikot Abasi Idem (N = 15)	
No	25 (78%)	42 (60%)	31 (72%)	15 (100%)	113 (71%)
Yes	7 (22%)	28 (40%)	12 (23%)	0 (0%)	47 (29%)
Total	32 (100%)	70 (100%)	43 (100%)	15 (100%)	160 (100%)

Source: Questionnaire survey.

while no respondent in the non-host communities (Ikot Abasi Idem) expected government and oil companies to have equal responsibility; some respondents did in the other three host communities. This deviation is similar to what was observed in Table 6.2. Available evidence presented in Table 6.8 suggests that the argument of proximity between host communities and oil companies explained a similar variation in Table 6.2 which is also applicable here.

Table 6.6 also shows that 100 per cent, 78 per cent, 72 per cent and 60 per cent of respondents in Ikot Abasi Idem, Ikot Ebidang, Emereoke 1 and Inua Eyet Ikot respectively shared the view that government and oil TNCs should not have equal responsibility for community development. Another 40 per cent, 23 per cent and 22 per cent of respondents in Inua Eyet Ikot, Emereoke 1 and Ikot Ebidang respectively shared an opposing view and instead felt both should have equal responsibility for community development. A possible explanation for the relatively high percentage of respondents in Inua Eyet Ikot who supported equal developmental responsibility for stakeholder appears to be due to the perception that a co-ordinated partnership between government and oil TNCs will provide better and faster community development than either government or oil TNCs working alone (see Table 6.7).

Arguments for balance of stakeholder developmental responsibility

Respondents identified a number of reasons for adopting their various positions regarding the distribution of responsibility for community development. Table 6.6 shows that 47 respondents (i.e. 29 per cent) felt that government and oil companies should share equal responsibility for community development. A total of 53 per cent of these respondents (see Table 6.7) made this choice because they believed that equal contributions from both government and oil companies would ensure that a wide range of community needs are addressed. According to secretary to the village council Inua Eyet Ikot:

> Only government or only oil companies cannot solve all our problems, but if both of them are contributing, our community will develop faster and most of our problems would be solved.

Another 34 per cent of the respondents felt it would not be fair for one stakeholder to have more responsibility for community development than the other, since both are benefiting from oil production. Table 6.7 also shows that 11 per cent of the respondents did not see any difference between government and oil companies because they

Table 6.7 Community perception of equal stakeholder developmental responsibility (ranked)

Reasons for equal stakeholder responsibility	Villages				Total (N = 47)
	Ikot Ebidang (N = 7)	Inua Eyet Ikot (N = 28)	Emereoke 1 (N = 12)	Ikot Abasi Idem (N = 0)	
Better development	4 (57%)	15 (54%)	6 (50%)	0 (0%)	25 (53%)
Both are benefiting	2 (29%)	10 (36%)	4 (33%)	0 (0%)	16 (34%)
Both are partners	1 (14%)	2 (7%)	2 (17%)	0 (0%)	5 (11%)

Source: Questionnaire survey.

are partners conniving together to cheat the communities. As such, both stakeholders should have equal responsibility for community development. However, out of a total of 113 respondents who felt that oil companies and government should not have equal responsibility for community development, 30 per cent thought that oil TNCs should have more responsibility for community development. This is because oil companies are in direct daily contact with communities more than the government in Abuja and that they are also responsible for a number of social and environmental problems facing communities. About 20 per cent of the respondents asserted that government should have more responsibility for community development because it is directly responsible for the welfare of the people (see Table 6.8). Similarly, 19 per cent of the respondents suggested that oil TNCs should have more responsibility for community development than government.

Not only do oil companies benefit more than government, respondents also fear that possible future negative effects of oil production would be borne by government alone, given that oil companies would leave as the oil wells dry up. A total of 13 per cent of the respondents also wanted oil companies to have more responsibility than government because government has so many communities to look after. According to the chief of Ikot Ebidang:

Akwa Ibom has 32 local government areas out of which Exxon Mobil has chosen 4 as its host communities, leaving 28 LGAs. Exxon Mobil should have more responsibility for the development of these four LGAs so that government can focus more on the other 28 LGAs.

Table 6.8   Reasons behind community perception of differential stakeholder developmental responsibility

Reasons for differential stakeholder responsibility	Villages				Total N = 113
	Ikot Ebidang (N = 25)	Inua Eyet Ikot (N = 42)	Emeoroeke 1 (N = 31)	Ikot Abasi Idem (N = 15)	
Proximity of oil TNCs	1 (4%)	16 (38%)	16 (52%)	2 (13%)	35 (30%)
Government's responsibility	4 (16%)	5 (12%)	5 (16%)	9 (60%)	23 (20%)
Oil TNCs benefit more	6 (24%)	10 (24%)	4 (13%)	1 (7%)	21 (19%)
Government has more responsibility	7 (28%)	8 (19%)	0 (0%)	0 (0%)	15 (13%)
Government inadequacies	4 (16%)	0 (0%)	4 (13%)	3 (20%)	11 (10%)
Government benefits more	2 (8%)	4 (10%)	4 (13%)	0 (0%)	10 (8%)

Source: Questionnaire survey.

This statement seems to corroborate the thinking of Ferguson (1998) and Matten et al. (2003) that business contribution to development could complement government efforts and allow the governments of developing countries to allocate their scarce resources to other important developmental needs of their people.

Table 6.8 shows that about 10 per cent of the respondents also felt that oil TNCs should have more responsibility than government because of government inadequacies. Only 8 per cent of the respondents felt that government should have more responsibility because government benefits more than oil companies do from oil production. A chi-square test of data in Table 6.8 yielded a significant result (chi-square = 49, degrees of freedom = 15, p = .000). The implication of this test result is that there are differences in the reasons behind how respondents see the balance of responsibility between oil TNCs and government in the survey villages. For example, while a majority (60 per cent) of respondents from Ikot Abasi Idem maintained that government should have more

Table 6.9 Perception of stakeholder developmental responsibility (ranked)

Stakeholder responsibility	Number of respondents (N = 113)	% of respondents
More responsibility for oil TNCs	81	72%
More responsibility for government	32	28%

Source: Questionnaire survey.

responsibility for community development, a majority of respondents in the host communities shared an opposing view.

Overall, 72 per cent of the respondents expected oil TNCs to have more responsibility for community development than the government, and about 28 per cent of the respondents expected government to have more developmental responsibility for the survey villages than oil TNCs (see Table 6.9). This finding provides some sort of empirical evidence to support the argument made by Wiig and Ramalho (2005). They argued from a utilitarian perspective that oil companies should take on more responsibility based on their capacity to do so, when government and other agents are failing or unable to address their responsibility.

According to Wiig and Ramalho (2005), utilitarianism only shows an interest in redistribution in far as it has an impact on the overall utility – in this case, for instance, when the loss of utility for the rich is much smaller than the gain of utility for the poor. Hence, it follows from a utilitarian perspective that, when government does not take its share of responsibility, the responsibility of the other agents has to increase insofar as the consequences of their acts increase overall utility. They concluded that such an increase in responsibility should be temporary and should eventually pave the way for public institutions to take over the responsibilities.

The impact of CSR on government efforts at community development

Table 6.10 shows that 55 per cent of the respondents felt oil TNCs' contribution to community development had no effect on government efforts to provide social infrastructures for them. The table also suggests that 30 per cent of the respondents asserted that government never provided any social infrastructure before oil TNCs provided social infrastructures. Another 9 per cent of the respondents asserted that infrastructures were not provided by oil TNCs before government provided such infrastructures. Only 6 per cent of the respondents asserted that oil TNCs' contribution to community development negatively affected government efforts to provide social infrastructure in the survey villages. A chi squared test (chi-squared = 203, df = 9, p =.000) and a one-way analysis variance (Anova = 58, df = 3, p = .000) yield significant results. This suggests that there is significant variation in respondents' perception of the effect of CC on government development effort in the survey villages. This variation can be explained by the difference in the distribution of governmental and oil MNC's social investments in the survey villages. In the surveyed villages of Ikot Ebidang, Emeoroke 1 and Ikot Abasi Idem where oil TNCs' social investment is relatively poor, most respondents asserted that oil TNCs' contribution did not affect government performance. In contrast, in Inua Eyet Ikot where an oil MNC has made significant investment in social infrastructures, they asserted that oil TNCs' efforts had an impact on government contribution to community development.

Table 6.10 seems to suggest that oil TNCs' efforts at community development have no real effect on governmental development efforts. However, where government did not provide social infrastructures, oil TNCs seem to have provided the needed infrastructures. Similarly, where oil TNCs did not provide social infrastructure, government either also fails to provide or does provide. There is therefore some support for the argument raised by Ferguson (1998) and Matten et al. (2003) that both government and business contributions to development can be complementary. This finding must nonetheless be treated with circumspection, because it was perception that was measured and not a one-to-one correlation relationship between government and oil TNCs' development efforts. Nonetheless, the finding remains plausible. This is because, as argued by Akwa Ibom State commissioner for Mineral and Environmental resource:

> Government cannot go and provide the same infrastructures that oil TNCs have already provided for the host communities. Instead when we get to a village like the host communities, we focus on what the oil TNCs have not provided.

Two observations were made in the assessment of the relationship between oil TNCs' community development efforts and government development efforts in the survey villages. The first is that the complementary nature of oil TNCs' and government efforts is largely based on chance, un-coordinated, and *ad hoc* in nature as opposed to being a carefully orchestrated plan.

Hence, there are still numerous incidences of project duplication and ineffective allocation of development resources as in the case of the teachers in Inua Eyet Ikot who were paid by the government and Exxon Mobil. Another example is the establishment of a rice farm in Mbiabet Ikot Ikpe by the NDDC, while the Ibom Rice Farm established by Exxon Mobil and the Akwa Ibom State government is yet to fully take off after five years. The result is likely to be that Akwa Ibom State would eventually end up with two inefficient and poorly funded rice farms that could have been avoided, if the efforts of the NDDC, state government and Exxon Mobil were co-ordinated to establish one vibrant and active rice farm that would make more difference to local development.

The second observation is that CC is a domain of political contestation, manifested in the buck-passing policies pursued by government and oil TNCs. While oil TNCs argue that community development is principally the responsibility of government, government in turn argues that oil TNCs are responsible for part of the problem in the region and therefore should be involved in ensuring the development of their host communities. In practice, this contestation is often manifested in the attempts by both parties to shift development responsibility to the other.

Table 6.10 CC impact on governmental community development efforts (ranked)

		Village				Total
		Ikot Ebidang	Inua Eyet Ikot	Emereoke 1	Ikot Abasi Idem	
Relationship between CC and government development efforts	No	29 (91%)	25 (36%)	34 (79%)	0 (0%)	88 (55%)
	Infrastructure not provided by government before oil MNC	1 (3.1%)	38 (54%)	9 (21%)	0 (0%)	48 (30%)
	Infrastructure not provided by oil MNC before government	0 (0%)	0 (0%)	0 (0%)	15 (100%)	15 (9.4%)
	Yes	2 (6.3%)	7 (10%)	0 (0%)	0 (0%)	9 (6%)
Total		32 (100%)	70 (100%)	43 (100%)	15 (100%)	160 (100%)

Source: Questionnaire survey.

For example, oil TNCs often use the concept of 'host communities' to delimit their social responsibility to specific geographical areas. In Akwa Ibom State, the state government has expanded the geographic boundary of Exxon Mobil's social responsibility by playing on this concept of host communities and identifying operational base, host communities, core communities, and catchments/oil bearing communities as the different geographic areas where Exxon Mobil should address its social responsibility. This new definition of host communities means that Exxon Mobil is expected to expand its corporate social investment that was initially only focused on its operational base (i.e. its immediate host community) to the four core communities. The consequences so far have been that local communities tend to lose potential social investments as Exxon Mobil is often unwilling to bear the extra cost of its expanded corporate responsibility. For example, this is what the village councillors in Upenekang, a village close to Inua Eyet Ikot said in an interview:

> When in 1992 under community pressure, Mobil decided to provide us with electricity just as it has done in Inua Eyet Ikot, government insisted that if Mobil provided electricity for us, then it must also provide for the rest of the core communities. As a result, Mobil withdrew altogether from electricity provision to the village.

This political contestation that often engulfs CC practices at both national and local levels often means communities lose developmental benefits that are neither provided by government nor oil TNCs. This suggests that CC rather than being a domain of shifting responsibility is in fact a site of contestation with negative consequences for community development.

Emerging issues and conclusion

There are two main emerging issues. The first is that this chapter presented concrete empirical evidence in support of the extended view of CC as theorized by Crane et al. (2008), by so doing the chapter attempts to address and begin to resolve some of the core tensions that continue to mar the recent effort to rethink the concept of CC. For example, by explicitly focusing on the notion of community reciprocal responsibility, the findings here directly address Van Osterhout's (2005) concerns with regard to whether state or citizens are willing and able to do what the corporation demand, albeit at the micro-level society. In addition, the way local communities seem to conceptualize their relationship with oil TNCs help to explain the providing, channelling and enabling role that

Crane and Matten (2005) theorize that the corporation can play. This is particularly important given the tendency in mainstream literature to attribute the demand for TNCs to play these roles to prevalence of victim mentality or the failure of government in developing countries. In contrast, findings here suggest that community expectation for TNCs to play these different roles is rooted in their lived experience, and a reflection of their socio-cultural, historical and economic context that are often glossed over in mainstream literature. The implication is that findings here lend credence to Palazzo and Scherer's (2008) argument that any effort geared towards theorizing CC must seek to find a balance between universalized expectations and local reality.

Second, rather than being conceptualized as a domain of shifting responsibility as Crane et al. (2008) might suggest, evidence presented here suggests that CC is more of a domain of stakeholder contestations at the macro and micro levels of society. This is reflected in the acceptance or rejection of reciprocal responsibility by local communities, communities' views of appropriate balance of stakeholder developmental responsibility and the limited coordination between governmental and oil TNCs' developmental efforts in the survey villages. These contestations have material and discursive dimensions to them. Materially, they are manifested in the buck-passing attitude of both government and oil TNCs in an attempt to avoid the cost often associated with community development CC initiatives. Discursively, these contestations can also be seen in either how the Nigerian government or the oil TNCs blame each other for the problems in the Niger Delta while absolving themselves from any wrong doing. Due to these contestations, local communities are often effectively relegated from the status of citizens to that of fragments (see Mir et al., 2008) manifested in the tendency of the Nigerian government and oil TNCs to always prioritize the flow of oil over human security and human rights in the region. The benefit of conceptualizing CC as a space of contestation over shifting responsibilities is that it allows for the explicit consolidation of power (i.e. material and discursive) and its consequence for how corporations not only inform citizenship but also how their own conception of citizenship might shape their behaviour.

Notes

1. The author acknowledges financial support for his research from the Social Sciences and Humanities Research council (SSHRC) of Canada.
2. The corporation can be conceived as a bearer of rights and responsibility akin to the rights and responsibility of a person (see French, 1979) or as a vehicle for co-ordinating different activities for the purpose of achieving specific

goals and therefore not a person (see Ladd, 1970); or the corporation can be conceived as having rights that are derived from, dependent upon and secondary to individual rights. Hence, while not a person, certain respects, concepts and functional normally attributed to persons can be attributed to organizations made up of persons (Goodpaster and Mathews, 1982).

3. See Matten and Crane, 2005; Crane and Matten, 2005; Crane et al., 2008 versus Van Oosterhout, 2005 and Jones and Haigh, 2007; and Néron and Norman, 2008 versus Van Oosterhout, 2008; De George, 2008; Wood and Logsdon, 2008.

4. Indeed, Wood and Logsdon (2008) who are pioneers in CC thinking have argued that organizations should not have equal status with persons, but can be seen as secondary citizens with rights that are subordinate to the rights of humans and with prescribed duties reflecting their special place in society and power asymmetries that typically apply between persons and large, complex, economic organizations.

5. The data reported here are part of a larger study conducted in Akwa Ibom State in the Niger Delta Area of Nigeria (see Figure 6.1) in which 160 households were surveyed and 360 semi-structured interviews were conducted with local communities, government officials, staff of non-governmental organization that are active in the region.

6. See also (Wood and Lodgson, 2000; Néron and Norman, 2008) for similar classification but with different labelling of the categories.

7. This particular conception of CC has received the harshest criticism of the different conceptions of CC put forward by Crane et al. (2008), and therefore it is at the center of the analysis to be undertaken in this chapter (see Van Oosterhout, 2005; Jones and Haigh, 2007).

8. Only two broad criticisms that are directly pertinent to the analysis to be undertaken here are discussed.

9. This position is consistent with the equivalent view of CC as adopted by Carroll (1998) in the pyramid of CC.

References

Akinola, S. R. (2008) 'Coping with Social Deprivation Through Self-Governing Institutions in Oil Communities of Nigeria', *Africa Today*, 55, 1: 89–107.

Amaeshi, K. (2009) 'Corporation as Citizen: Book Review', *Journal of International Management*, 15, 457–477.

Birch, D. (2001) 'Corporate Citizenship: Rethinking Business Beyond Corporate Social Responsibility', in J. Andriof and M. McIntosh (eds) *Perspective on Corporate Citizenship*, London: Greenleaf Publishing, pp. 53–65.

Bowie, N. (1991) 'New Directions in Corporate Social Responsibility', *Business Horizons*, July–August, 34, 4: 56–65.

Burke, M. E. (1999) *Corporate Community Relations: The Principles of the Neighbour of Choice*, London: Quorum Books.

Carroll, A. B. (1998) 'The Four Faces of Corporate Citizenship', *Business and Society Review*, 100/101, 1–7.

Crane, A. and D. Matten (2005) 'Corporate Citizenship: Missing the Point or Missing the Boat? A Reply to van Oosterhout', *Academy of Management Review*, 30, 4: 681–684.

Crane, A., D. Matten and J. Moon (2008) *Corporations and Citizenship*, Cambridge: Cambridge University Press.

De George, R. (2008) 'Reflections on 'Citizenship, Inc.' *Business Ethics Quarterly*, 12, 1: 43–50.

Dobbers, P. and M. Halme (2009) 'Corporate Social Responsibility and Developing Countries', *Corporate Social Responsibility and Environmental Management*, 16, 5: 237–249.

Ferguson, G. (1998) 'Transnational Topographies of Power: Beyond the State and Civil Society in the Study of African Politics', in Manussen, H. S. and Arnfred, S. (eds) *Concept and Metaphors, Ideologies, Narratives and Myths in Development Discourse, International Development Studies*, Roskilde: Roskilde University.

Freeman, R. E. and J. Liedtka (1991) 'Corporate Social Responsibility: A Critical Approach', *Business Horizons*, 34, 4: 92–96.

Freeman, R. E. and S. R. Velamuri (2006) 'A New Approach to CSR in Company Stakeholder Responsibility', in A. Kakabadse and M. Morsing (eds) *CSR – Reconciling Aspiration with Application*, London: Macmillan, Palgrave, pp. 9–23.

French, A. P. (1979) 'The Corporation as a Moral Person', in T. Donaldson and H. P. Werhane (eds) (1993), *Ethical Issues in Business: A Philosophical Approach*, 4th ed., Englewood Cliffs, NJ: Prentice Hall, pp. 120–129.

Frynas, J. G. (2005) 'The False Development Promise of Corporate Social Responsibility: Evidence from Multinational Oil Companies', *International Affairs*, 81, 3: 581–598.

Goodpaster, E. K and B. J Matthews (1982) 'Can a Corporation Have a Conscience?' *Harvard Business Review*, 60, 1: 132–141.

Idemudia, U. (2008) 'Conceptualising the CSR and Development Debate: Bridging Existing Analytical Gaps', *Journal of Corporate Citizenship*, 29: 1–20.

Ite, U. E. (2004) 'Multinationals and Corporate Social Responsibility in Developing Countries: A Case Study of Nigeria', *Corporate Social Responsibility and Environmental Management*, 11, 1–11.

Jones, M. T. and M. Haigh (2007) 'The Transnational Corporation and the New corporate Citizenship Theory: A Critical Analysis', *Journal of Corporate Citizenship*, 27, 51–69.

Ladd, J. (1993) 'Morality and the Ideal of Rationality in Formal Organisations', in T. Donaldson and H. P. Werhane (eds) *Ethical Issues in Business: A Philosophical Approach*, 4th ed., Englewood Cliffs, NJ: Prentice Hall, pp. 130–142.

Logsdon, J. M. and D. J. Wood (2002) 'Business Citizenship: From domestic to Global Level of Analysis', *Business Ethics Quarterly*, 12, 155–188.

Ludescher, C. J., Mc Williams, A. and D. Siegel (2008) 'The Economic View of Corporate Citizenship', in A. G. Scherer, A. G. and G. Palazzo (eds) *Handbook of Research on Global Corporate Citizenship*, Cheltenham: Edward Elgar, pp. 315–342.

Matten, D. and A. Crane (2005) 'Corporate Citizenship: Toward an Extended Theoretical Conceptualisation', *Academy of Management Review*, 30, 1: 166–179.

Matten, D., A. Crane and W. Chapple (2003) 'Behind the Mask: The True Face of Corporate Citizenship', *Journal of Business Ethics*, 45, 109–120.

Mir, R., R. Marens and A. Mir (2008) 'The Corporation and Its Fragments: Corporate Citizenship and the Legacies of Imperialism', in A. G. Scherer and G. Palazzo (eds) *Handbook of Research on Global Corporate Citizenship*, Cheltenham: Edward Elgar, pp. 527–551.

Moon, J., Crane, A. and D. Matten (2005) 'Can Corporations Be Citizens? Corporate Citizenship as a Metaphor for Business Participation in Society', *Business Ethics Quarterly*, 15, 3: 429–453.

Néron, P. and W. Norman (2008) 'Citizenship Inc. Do We Really Want Business to Be Good Corporate Citizens?' *Business Ethics Quarterly*, 18, 1: 1–26.

Palazzo, G. and A. G. Scherer (2008) 'The Future of Global Corporate Citizenship: Toward a New Theory of the Firm as a Political Actor', in A. G. Scherer and G. Palazzo (eds) *Handbook of Research on Global Corporate Citizenship*, Cheltenham: Edward Elgar, pp. 577–590.

Van Oosterhout, J. (2005) 'Corporate Citizenship: An Idea Whose Time Has Not Yet Come', *Academy of Management Review*, 30, 4: 677–684.

Van Oosterhout, J. (2008) 'Transcending the Confines of Economic and Political Organizations? The Misguided Metaphor of Corporate Citizenship', *Business Ethics Quarterly*, 18, 1: 35–42.

Waddell, A. (2000) 'New Institutions for the Practice of Corporate Citizenship: Historical, Intersectoral and Developmental Perspectives', *Business and Society Review*, 105, 1: 107–126.

Ward, H. and T. Fox (2002) *Moving the Corporate Citizenship Agenda to the South*. Retrieved online at www.iied.org/docs/cred/moving_agenda.pdf (accessed 17 July 2004).

Windsor, D. (2001) 'Corporate Citizenship: Evolution and Interpretation', in J. Andriof and M. Mcintosh (eds) *Perspective on Corporate Citizenship*, London: Greenleaf Publishing, pp. 39–52.

Wood, D. J. and J. M. Logsdon (2001) 'Theorizing Business Citizenship', in J. Andriof and M. McIntosh (eds) *Perspective on Corporate Citizenship*, London: Greenleaf Publishing, pp. 83–103.

Wood, D. J. and J. M. Logsdon (2002) 'Business Citizenship: From Individual to Organizations', *Riffin Series in Business Ethics*, 3, 59–94.

Wood, D. J. and J. M. Logsdon (2008) 'Business Citizenship as Metaphor and Reality', *Business Ethics Quarterly*, 18, 1: 51–59.

7
Various Corporate Citizenships in BoP Markets

Céline Cholez and Pascale Trompette[1]

Introduction

'Access to energy is a major preoccupation for the 1.6 billion people who at present live without electricity. [...] By setting out its solutions for access to renewable energies, Schneider Electric is reaffirming its social commitment to contribute to the improvement of the quality of life for populations 'at the bottom of the pyramid' and to facilitate access to care, treatment and education (Press release: 'Electrification of the village of Marovato in Madagascar', June 2009). Providing clean and responsible energy solutions for populations in situations of extreme poverty, such is the radically new challenge, listed as a Corporate Social Responsibility (CSR) initiative, taken up by a team of engineers from Schneider Electric, a global energy company specializing in industrial electrical equipment. Like other multinationals, Schneider Electric has become involved in the design of products affordable to the poorest populations of emerging countries.

Of recent origin, the concept of 'Bottom of the Pyramid markets' (Prahalad, 2010), close to concepts such as 'social innovation', 'inclusive innovation' (Mendoza and Thelen, 2008; Mair and Marti 2009) or 'frugal innovation' (Bhatti and Ventresca, 2012; Sehgal et al., 2010), describes a set of initiatives taken by private investors, and among them by multinational companies, linking the development of innovative products/ services to the fight against poverty (Dalsace and Ménascé, 2010; Mair and Marti, 2009). With regard to the traditional concepts that prevailed up to this point, the driving role of free enterprise, of private investment and more fundamentally of the market, are strongly upheld in this neoliberal model as the potential driving force in the dynamics of development in Southern countries. According to its proponents, the 'BoP' markets vision carries the ambition of promoting a dynamic of market expansion to include the poorest in society (through a logic of economic and financial 'inclusion') (Budinich, Reott and Schmidt, 2007). The companies involved in these experimental projects have been induced to think, to invent, and then to design innovative assemblages in the supply of products/services in connection with the deployment of new value chains 'including' the poorest both as consumers and as producers (Karnani, 2007).

Although they are assimilated to a market strategy that does not require financial aid, most of the firms' BoP projects are developed in the framework of CSR policies. Following the academic instigators of the 'BoP vision' (who mostly come from business schools), the corporate managers present these projects as a new form of CSR which combines both social and economic objectives and deliberately breaks with the 'charity approach'. Each company aims to develop their core competencies by creating a sustainable business model. Assuming that the main problem is one of access to the products (because of the weakness of existing market infrastructures and of the 'consumers' limited capacities for paying), the challenges appear primarily to be technical ones: reducing prices, penetrating the most distant zones and possibly facilitating the act of purchase with leasing or credit systems. However, the ethnographic studies of these projects (Dolan and Johnstone-Louis, 2011; Cholez, Trompette et al., 2010) show that the firms are confronted not only with questions of technical innovation but also of 'market design' and that these questions carry political concerns.

Based on in-depth empirical research in partnership with Schneider Electric, we follow here how actors of a BoP project face various political concerns in the multiple demands for reconciling responsibility and mass consumption, ecological norms and low-cost criteria, sustainable development and poverty. We observe how the different market designs either 'enlist' the support, or on the contrary sideline the multiple actors concerned (governmental institutions, NGOs, intermediaries of local enterprises, BoP consumers, etc.).The company explores two distinct solutions. The first is based on electrification through the setting up of small decentralized electricity power stations in rural villages functioning on the basis of renewable energy. The second follows a parallel but less visible market, involving the provision of individual diesel generators or batteries. Both of these alternative paths involve chains of associations and interdependencies, which combine technical assemblages, public framing (rules, requirements, financing devices), and economic formulas (business plans, tariffs, payment systems, etc.), and partnerships (entrepreneurships, co-operative associations ...). Moreover, as we shall demonstrate, they are also related to different forms of corporate citizenship (Matten and et al., 2003; Matten and Crane, 2005). It is our contention that these forms of corporate citizenship are organized around the alternative between, on the one hand, a rational-legal context of public service where the corporation acts as substitute for the government, and on the other hand, a market circuit around a product sustaining new forms of economic and ecological values. Therefore, these two solutions may diverge in their respective mode of regulation (framing/overflowing) and accountability. In the following, we develop these points according to this plan: we first present the BoP strategy and how it is related to issues of corporate citizenship; second, we outline our theoretical background and our methodology broadly inspired by pragmatic approaches of markets and technologies; then we expose the two solutions explored the firm of our case study; and finally we discuss the different forms of corporate citizenships the different designs markets involve, and the issues of accountability and associated regulation of overflows.

The BoP strategy: a corporate citizenship object

Developed in the early 2000s, the concept of 'Bottom of the Pyramid' markets (Prahalad, 2010), rests on what its proponents see as a win-win gamble that associates the search for profits and the presumed willingness of poor people in developing countries to consume and to develop entrepreneurial skills. The idea – theorized by famous scholars in management strategy, notably C.K. Prahalad and S. Hart (2002) – is that the delivery of 'quality products and services', affordable to the 4 billion potential consumers whose daily incomes do not exceed $5 represents some considerable business opportunities for corporations at the same time as acting as a driving force for sustaining the economies of the developing countries.

Associated to CSR approaches, 'BoP vision' is often presented as a radically new perspective on the way in which corporations can support social issues. Its instigators insist on the necessary break with the common charity approach that would make the poor dependent and even 'child-like' without effectively alleviating poverty over the long term. Each company in its own sector has to identify the societal issues it is best placed to resolve, without requiring financial aid, as a condition of attaining economic sustainability. For international companies, it is not simply about introducing a societal concern into its product or supply strategy, but stretching the market towards a hitherto excluded space: that of poverty. In theoretical terms, this proposition places 'BoP vision' as a direct opposite of the 'social business' model of Muhammad Yunus (Yunus and Weber, 2007): the BoP goal is clearly to make profit while the social business goal is to solve social issues with the market as one of the means of achieving success.

Initially, the 'BoP concept' aroused both enthusiasm and controversy. The main critics came from the academic arena and were about the efficiency of the market as a means of alleviating poverty (Walsh et al., 2005), the over-estimation of the purchasing power of the poor (Crabtree, 2007; Landrum, 2007) and the moral condemnation of the 'value-conscious' consumerism philosophy (Karnani, 2007). The critics of the first experimentations, including those of an American global company that developed a large distribution of some daily sachets of detergent in India, led to a significant change in the BoP approaches (Simanis et al., 2008). The involvement of the local producers, and the wish to contribute to the development of a local value chain as well as the introduction of environmental criteria reinforced the concept but also made its implementation more constraining. At the heart of the questioning in the scientific community as well as among the economic and political actors lies the problem of creating a market and 'making it work' with lots of uncertainties, both because of the 'improbable' consumer market (the weakness of market infrastructures, the limited capacities for paying off the targeted market and the existence of consumer practices remote from western anthropological models) and also because of the attendant high social expectations (the fight against poverty and the need for solutions which are ecologically clean/sound). The result is a complex equation that leads corporations to different design formulas: from entirely integrated markets (Cholez, Trompette, Vinck and Reverdy, 2010), to co-development with NGOs and local users (Burdinich et al., 2005).

Following a neo-liberal conception of the market and its efficiency, the BoP literature pays little attention to local and national political institutions in the developing countries. Public authorities are considered as absent or weak (Seelos and Mair, 2007). The BoP strategy message is often based on mistrust of local institutions, which need to be overcome or 'bypassed' as far as possible. In a sense, the BoP strategy is presented as an authentic 'auto-regulation' of social or societal problems by the company itself, which would be able to deal with or assume the regulatory or financial incentive constraints. The BoP vision promotes the corporation as an agent of regulation, which can compensate for the weakness of local government, a rather simplistic vision which misses out the political issue of reciprocal responsibility between the state, the corporation and local communities, as demonstrated by Idemudia (this volume).

There has been much emphasis in the literature on tackling the link between business and social issues (Valor, 2005). Considering the issues we have described above, we think it relevant to analyse BoP projects in the light of Corporate Citizenship (CC) as Crane and Matten reconceptualized the concept (Matten and Crane 2005; Crane et al., 2008). In fact, unlike the concept of CSR, the citizenship metaphor provides an extended view of the political role of the corporation. Crane and Matten suggests three different ways of playing this role: first, corporations as citizens, which contribute to the democratic debates, for example when corporations offer services and products dedicated to minorities; second, corporations as governments when they substitute themselves for public administration and government; third, corporations as an arena for governance issues including a variety of stakeholders. The development of BoP markets could present lots of implications for understanding corporate citizenship processes and, in the opposite sense, the corporate citizenship perspective allows some interesting political issues concerning BoP strategy to be addressed, specially concerning the management of overflows associated with these markets and the making of accountabilities. As shown by Gerencser (this volume), accountability is central to display the social benefits of the corporation initiative.

Understanding the market as a design process

Within the sociology of markets, the dynamic aspects of market design have been adequately studied through pragmatic approaches (Callon, 1998), with attention paid to the growing role of experiments in the governance of markets (Muniesa and Callon, 2007). In this text, this background will be combined with two complementary theoretical strands, included here because of their potential contribution in dealing with the political dimensions of market design: the 'politics of technology', i.e. assuming that technologies participate in 'the ordering of social collectives' (Berg, 1998); and also 'accountability' as a combination of calculative and narrative accounts as witness to the company's commitment to citizenship requirements.

A pragmatic approach to market design

This analysis of the company's exploratory activities prior to the market design stage is associated with a pragmatic position, in order to trace the emergence of entities and overflowing throughout the building of new assemblages. This position offers an alternative to traditional institution-alist and relational approaches in economic sociology, by emphasizing the process of 'enacting the world through action' (Overdevest, 2011): the 'reality test' is central to the experimentation of 'shifting assem-blages', through which failure or success are experienced. We therefore propose to examine the activity of the company and its commitment in BoP innovations as an 'on-going experiment' (Callon, 2009; Muniesa and Callon, 2007), or more over an 'on-going exploration' in the design of a new market. Even if, in Callon and Muniesa's programme, the experimental setting mainly refers to the expertise of economic science and, beyond, to its performativity on the market governance, in our case, the 'in situ' experiment consists of testing various solutions in order to delineate the sociotechnical network and the value chain.

The company explores, at the same time, the potential offers, afford-able to the poor, the feasible socio-technical 'agencements' and the spe-cifically related BoP market designs (Caliskan and Callon, 2010). As the authors suggest concerning the different types of market experimenta-tion: 'the list of actors actually involved in this kind of experiment (i.e. the identity and power of the different actors that are to be engaged in the experiment with the potential to alter its course) is not defined a priori' (Muniesa and Callon, 2007, p. 178): the exploration of a market around a technical solution, a particular branch of activity or a public programme necessitates taking into account certain actors (govern-ments, local small and medium-sized enterprises, co-operatives, NGOs, the BoP consumer, the micro-entrepreneur) while excluding others. The analysis of this exploration follows a chain of interdependencies which has its own dynamic; it progressively defines a sociotechnical 'agence-ment' that 'combines material, textual and procedural elements' but also seeks to pinpoint possible overflows and the constraints of alignment.

The politics of technology: framing and overflowing

From this pragmatic background, we draw on a set of research on the 'politics of technology' (Berg, 1998; Lavelle, 2009; Winner, 1999). The pragmatic approach of techniques has long shown that artefacts play a role in 'ordering' the world: artefacts incorporate scripts of use, provide 'grasps' (i.e. affordance) (Bessy and Chateauraynaud, 1995), structure interdependencies, configure the user, assemble distributed cognition (notably as calculative agency). In short, they achieve association and alignment. This technical mediation 'folds in' and produces moral and political relations (Latour and Venn, 2002). In Foucault's tradition, the 'political technology' supports the governmentality of society in various ways. Von Schnitzler (2008), for instance, has shown how the development of prepayment technology in South Africa can be interpreted as a central piece in the re-building of a new biopolitic infrastructure connecting the citizens to public services in a context of neoliberal reforms. In a less 'panoptic' perspective, Latour's programme confers moral properties to technologies in the way they 'displace, translate, modify, or inflect' the ends themselves.

This line of investigation meets the pragmatic approach to markets, notably in emphasizing the central role played by 'agencements'. The market design as an 'arrangements' of 'agencements' describes a lengthier chain of actors or agencies, of different or even asymmetrical status (political actors, intermediaries, consumers and also texts, devices, technologies, etc.). Our analysis pays attention to the way political ends are translated into instruments, technologies, and accounts as various forms of 'political agencing'. Indeed, following the corporation in the exploration of rural electrification solutions, we explore the properties of the solutions as two types of 'political agencing': the local station, as a public service infrastructure, which relates to a complex assemblage combining a host of actors (local and national government, local companies, MNC, banks, etc.), procedures (heavy administrative burdens) and techniques; and in the opposite case, a very simple technology (a 'nudge' for Thaler and Sunstein, 2008) performing interactions and behaviours: the product itself incorporates a set of incentives to support ecological and economical practices through its ordinary use by the poor.

Distinct forms of citizenship accounts (or Régimes of Citizenship Accounts)

In the field of organization theory, the concept of 'accountability' relates to a long-standing tradition of research on the accounting practices within the companies and their cultural meanings, focusing either on the financial reporting or on the ordinary management practices. With the rise of democratic and societal requirements addressed to the private sector, the concept is spreading to a certain extent: corporations do not have to account only to their shareholders, but also the civil society, with reports on their social responsibility and ecological impacts. Responsible reporting becomes dominant in regard to the pure accounting activity, even if these two dimensions remain inseparable. Close to this idea, D. Stark (Stark, 2009) proposes the notion of 'account' (of worth) to refer both to 'accounting' and 'narrative' activities within the company.

If the issue of accountability, especially relating to this societal or citizenship definition, is attendant on any BoP project, the question of how the corporation addresses this accountability requirement remains. As mentioned by Crane et al., corporations are not initially set up for political tasks and their accountability procedures remain rather undeveloped. In our innovation story, we investigate the way a new product or service becomes 'accountable' and who are the main stakeholders involved in the accountability process: what are the calculation procedures carried over by each solution? Who is accountable to whom and for what? Which types of citizenship demands are delineated by the different solutions? Again, we suggest two forms of accountability relating to each solution. One refers to bureaucratic accountability procedures: the electrification solution, defined as a local public service infrastructure, is part of the off-grid electrification plan of the government. It is closely framed by procedures for allocating rights and duties, control of equity, business planning, involving numerous institutions. On the other hand, the second solution relates to an accountability attached to the product itself and its use: it depends on the way it generates new forms of consumption and calculation during its use and throughout the market transactions.

Method

As already stated, this chapter is based on collaborative research carried out within Schneider Electric, a global energy company specializing in electrical equipment. This firm entrusted university researchers with carrying out an ethnographic study of one of the test countries and then subsequently associating these researchers in the creative work which formed part of the first phase of the project design stage.[2] The ethnographic information produced both from the work done jointly with the company's engineers and during the field survey on the investigated sites, includes:

internal discussions within the company's staff, observed or recorded during BoP market project meetings;
a set of emails exchanged between the different actors involved in the experiments from the beginning of the project through to delivery of the equipment and a set of documents produced or collected by the engineering team at the beginning of the project;
transcripts of interviews and observations realized during a survey of four rural villages in a developing country (two electrified and two others in the process of being electrified): 52 interviews with local energy

operators, political actors and representatives of public institutions (politicians, religious and traditional leaders and a representative from the local national electrification agency), potential customers from the local business community and local project partners (NGO members, engineers from the local subsidiary responsible for the BoP projects, development personnel from other multinationals involved in the experiment). The survey also includes two filmed studies of local actors' diagnostics of technical and organizational dysfunctioning in the devolved electrification systems.

The material collected has been subjected to analysis at three levels: the network of institutional and political actors attached to the electrification project, the role of energy as a consumer good in the BoP economies, the relationships of interdependence between operators, users, maintenance and other staff introduced and regulated by technical systems.

Innovating for the BoP: between accountability and peripheral markets

The CRS approach began for Schneider Electric in 1998, with the creation of a foundation and then a sustainable development department in 2002. The BoP programme was launched in 2008 with highly ambitious objectives: giving access to electricity for one million BoP households in three years, training 10,000 young BoPs and supporting 500 entrepreneurs in the local development of the energy sector.

Searching for long-lasting innovation for developing countries whose political and economic systems seem totally foreign to such an aspiration, the R&D team launched themselves into the BoP adventure with totally open and enquiring minds (even to the point of considering frugal solutions independent of all forms of generated energy, holes for stocking ice, for example). This exploration initiative was undertaken when the basic properties of the equipment to be used were still undecided on the technical level (solar panels, wind-power, biomass, hybrid solutions, etc.) as also on the economic and social levels (decentralized power stations or individual equipment, private operator or co-operative venture, etc.). For each possible solution, it was a question of identifying and defining the chains of dependencies which the solution entailed without presuming of course to dictate thereby the nature of the links and forms of co-ordination which would be in play (political exchanges, technical chain links, legal forms required, etc.) (Akrich, 1989). It involved calling into question the specific properties of the assemblages and the forms of alignment which ensue. The exploration work was supported by the analysis of some 'reference situations' (for example the study of villages already electrified by other actors working with decentralized network power stations), through experimentation (for example setting up an ad hoc electrification pilot project) and the analysis of existing systems (notably solar home systems or individual equipment).

The decentralized power station: the weight of bureaucratic devices, the discipline of the BoP consumer

The first electrification solution explored by Schneider Electric was based on the concept of a decentralized (off-grid) power station. The assemblage would associate an electricity production power unit from a renewable energy source (photovoltaic, hydraulic or bio-mass) and a mini-transmission network (for a village of less than 100 houses) through aerial wires, controlled from a command post for directing pro-duction and consumption. Two experiments[3] have served as feasibility studies: Antetezambato, a village of a hundred or so houses on the High Plateau of Madagascar where 15 years ago, through an NGO initiative, a localized power station had been installed based on a hydraulic energy source; and Marovato, a village of 20 or so houses on the east coast of the island where Schneider Electric set up in 2008 a localized electricity supply based on photovoltaic energy.[4]

An institutionalized technical solution

The initial idea of developing a decentralized network power station came as an almost 'natural' choice for the Schneider engineers, even if from the beginning its advantages were balanced by more individual-ized solutions (solar home systems) and other hybrid solutions based on extending the station's range over a wider rural zone (through coupling with mobile batteries, for example). The concept of a decentralized power station benefits from a sort of cultural heritage and institutional legitimacy: coupled with technologies based on renewable energy, it figures high, and has done so for several decades, among the develop-ment programmes proposed in the fight against energy scarcity in the countries of the South supported by the main actors in development, including both the big international organizations (the World Bank and NGOs) as well as the governments and local NGOs concerned.

In Madagascar, the decentralized power station is seen as the all-embracing solution to be developed on a national scale and has been promoted for the rural sector by the reform of the electricity sector which was initiated in 1999.[5] Supported by the big financial donors (the

World Bank and the SFI (*Société Financière Internationale*), this reform very much favours the independent private initiatives undertaken apart from the National Electricity Company (Jirama). So exploring the development route based on the concept of the small independent power station is supported by a series of public initiatives, of either a normative or strongly incentive nature. These initiatives are operated by the main government actor, the ADER,[6] an agency in charge of the rural electrification programme, which exists to assist, give advice and expertise, to subsidize and seek financial aid for projects and their subsequent implementation by small and medium-sized enterprises or by the NGOs. With its own specific policy for developing and regulating the electricity sector, the government negotiates its priority investment programmes with the relevant regional and local authorities, and these negotiations can involve complex political manoeuvres. Private operators receive strong incentives to opt for technologies based on renewable energies, through exoneration of custom duties and often with additional financial aid. Legal concessions grant operators a local monopoly as a way of guaranteeing return on investment. If this agency has largely contributed to facilitate the subsidizing of the installations, this institutionalization of decentralized power stations as part of official governmental electrification programmes has also brought with it more rigorous regulatory controls in terms of price-setting and management procedures: the price of the kw/hour is aligned with a national tariff (even though initial production costs are much higher than any return possible on the prescribed tariff), the rules for standing charges for customers must conform to standardized fixed rates or monthly metered charges and these conditions of sale are strictly controlled by the ORE, the National Office for Electricity Regulation.

With its heavy commitment to immovable property investment (the power station and transmission network), its high investment costs in clean energy, together with its public governmental authorization costs, the decentralized power station option is characterized by a panoply of investment formulas, long-term economic planning instruments (business plans), legal frameworks (monopoly, norms) and regulatory arrangements, all of which are essential elements for upholding the stability of business commitments covering the whole chain of actors: the financial investors, the public authorities, the local operator and the links through to the final consumer, a consumer permanently tied to the network through long-term contracts. The network therefore constitutes a first type of assemblage in which solid technical and institutional links provide a powerful framework of interaction between the various market actors.

Developing innovations associated with such a network system means establishing well in advance a market design which is both clearly structured at the same time as being prone to risk because of the combination of the following factors: investment in publicly-controlled procedures which rigorously define the socio-technical system accompanied by *accountability* requirements (Chapman, Cooper and Miller, 2009; Neyland, 2007); the involvement of public actors who can be both advocates of a legal-rational model at the same time as being participants in a politically unstable situation; an economic investment formula based on long-term planning, but for which the profits appear improbable from the outset (on the one hand costly technical choices to be made, on the other price-setting at low levels). Even with the initial grants for installation, the price controls operated by government agencies weigh heavily on its medium-term profitability, a situation made worse by unpaid debts (see below). These constraints limit the capacity of entrepreneurs to get involved, especially in the context of the political instability of a country such as Madagascar which makes long-term economic and financial commitments potentially hazardous.

The local level: 'managing the overflows'

Covering every link in this chain of actors, the field studies carried out in Madagascar have thrown light on the forms of organization and of local life which operate around such a decentralized network. They have also afforded a good insight into the so-called 'BoP' populations, as consumers or future consumers of these installations.

The studies carried out in the electrified villages have revealed in a quite striking way the level of investment agreed to by the local operator – either an entrepreneur or a co-operative venture – in the continuous process of adjusting and inventing official or tacit rules, in the managing of interactions with the consumers or more widely with all the 'groups concerned' with the network. The strong socio-technical interdependence between production and consumption calls for constant regulation in order to tackle problems of reliability and availability or to cope with the need for constant adjustment between the electricity supply and the fluctuating demand.

In the village of Antetezambato, the use of rare natural resources for electrification, in this case the water used for the hydraulic station, has generated periodic shortages for other peripheral economic needs. In a period of drought, the operator finds therefore himself in competition with local agricultural interests for monopoly of use of the water. He then has to suspend operations and deal with tensions with clients over the ensuing constant electricity cuts.

But the opposite can also happen whereby the operator has to face real overflowing of network demand and the consequent difficulty of any rigorous control of production flow. In the case of the electrified villages, there are multiple reasons for overflowing demand, sometimes even drastic overflows, as for example: illegal extensions to the network through unofficial users installing makeshift connections to neighbouring houses which are officially supplied; the re-sale of electricity by regular consumers to households around them; the over-consumption by regular fixed-rate users, using equipment over and above that written into the contract; peaks of consumption in the evening when, over a whole village, all the households are watching television or using the radio or DVD players, and who quickly use up the batteries of solar panels; or times of family gatherings or parties when makeshift extensions are used to link several households together, etc. One can also find examples of almost official 'arrangements' made, by some who are concerned with the political relations with non-electrified neighbouring villages: tensions and jealousies between villagers can be partially resolved by the concession of an indirect access to free services offered by electrified households (such as recharging telephones).

One of the principal activities of the operator is therefore playing the role of arbiter to take into account external factors (such as water), to channel flows and establish the frontiers of the network, controlling uses which very easily go beyond the fixed rules in the contract. These constant adjustments themselves generate an intensification of the regulatory processes and the work of checking up on the user:

Do you tell people you are coming to inspect them or do you make surprise visits?

It tends to be surprise visits. Because when we visit, it's not just a question of inspecting the installations but also checking how much power they are using. For example you find some who are using electric irons whereas that is not in the contract. (Head of the Antetezambato co-operative)

But to the problem of the undisciplined user can generally be added that of the 'irregular payer': a monthly bill for electricity charges imposes a time framework which is far remote from the way the money comes in to the household, which is rather on a one-day basis for work done and in any case is extremely irregular for the local population.

It depends on the circumstances of each consumer and almost all the network heads know the financial situation of each client, and all the clients are aware of this. So the operators can discuss with the client so that they can pay what is owed at the right time, or just a little bit late. The recovery rate of debt is now running at 75% [...] So it [the money] comes in but a little late. They just can't make it.

Do you accept payment in instalments?
Payments spread out over a period of time, yes we do.
And do people sometimes offer you payment in kind, like food crops or something like that, say with their livestock?
With chickens and hens, yes that has happened, but it is the network head who will have to sell them every day. That is arranged between the 'network head' and the clients. But not between the co-operative itself and the clients.

Depending on the neighbourhood and the layout of the houses, the network is managed locally by 'network operators' who have the job of providing access to the network, looking after its basic running and collecting consumer payments. These roles cannot be dissociated from the personal relations cultivated by agents recognized locally for their moral authority, relying on their strong political legitimacy in relation to consumers as much as in relation to the local political authorities (always with the possible threat of embezzlement or other misappropriation). These individuals, as recognized members of the village, combine technical, managerial and social roles: they fulfil a sort of supervisory role concerning the uses made of electricity in favour of local development, advising for example that the electric light should be used for homework and other household work rather than for television, and also for promoting educative projects (such as a computer room for the school) or for promoting craftwork and other educational and professional uses of electricity. The question has to be asked about the long-term future of the enterprise when such reliable and trustworthy staffs are no longer there. The major question therefore remains concerning the long-term (and permanent) future of such an innovatory enterprise.

The network can therefore be seen as a rigid socio-technical 'agencement' largely supported by a series of formal operational systems (rational and legal) – norms, legal status, price-setting, etc. – which incorporates both public requirements (ecology, collective service, uniform tariffs) and at the same time a formula for paying off the initial economic investments (subsidies, monopoly). But it is faced with two major difficulties. The first stems from the relative fragility of long-term agreements and formal arrangements as a part of a much larger political system in countries where its stability is uncertain. The second concerns the fact that this rigid assemblage presupposes a degree of consumer discipline in order to guarantee usage which can meet these requirements and alignments over a long period of time. Faced with consumer volatility (in terms of payments) and the many irregularities at the periphery of the network (fraud, political manoeuvring, etc.), the network can generate institutional re-arrangements of an ad hoc nature as a way of coming to terms with the many necessary adjustments. This can effectively mean a superfluity of control regulations but can also lead to a system of community relations which will constantly provide back-up to this socio-technical system.

Exploring individual forms of electrification: a 'liberal' model to ecologize

Starting with the objective of evaluating the social acceptability of the micro-network small power-station solution, the research team in the field wished to find out more about existing practical uses of electricity. This is how they discovered the important role played by individual installations, and particularly the car battery. A real and thriving market exists around the working of this system. Batteries are in massive use for storing and transporting electricity in rural zones where there is no electricity station. They are also to be found in towns as a way of making up for the deficiencies of the national electric grid. They are in fact alternatives to the generator for less well-off households. Investigating the existing market which operates around this form of energy distribution has led Schneider Electric to consider a new form of assemblage which brings together a socio-technical system which is weak and flexible in terms of interdependencies, a chain of micro-entrepreneurs which is informal but relatively stable and economically long-lasting, with instruments of regulation which are essentially trade-based and founded on confidence and professional reputation, the sort of regulation which has nothing to do with – and is also ignored by – the executives and other political actors and investors engaged in electrification programmes. As in the previous case, we propose to follow the chain of action associated with this system, but this time reversing the process: we shall start with the specific uses and practices 'in the field' and then trace back to the intermediaries of the system and only then consider how such a basic system is treated institutionally by government agencies.

A stable and flourishing second-hand sector

In Madagascar, the battery mainly found in circulation for domestic use is a so-called 'starting' battery, designed to be used in a road vehicle (car or lorry). The socio-technical rationale on which its utilization is based is relatively simple and flexible. Although it is costly and relatively inefficient, it affords certain autonomy to its users, both through the makeshift do-it-yourself way in which it can be used and the relative contractual freedom that it bestows on those involved.

Linked by a rough contraption of wires to a set of socket outlets, the battery can be used to recharge mobile phones, to listen to music or watch a programme broadcast on the national channel or power a DVD reader connected to a television which is generally black-and-white. Batteries are often used in a sub-optimal fashion, for one piece of equipment. The performance of the battery in this case is quite mediocre: a full battery is used up in about three weeks for a radio and lights. On the technical level, batteries present major drawbacks, notably in terms of restrictions in their use linked to breakdowns and maintenance as well as the question of the ready availability of the financial means or the time necessary to go to the nearest town to have a battery re-charged. It was noted moreover that, if a household sometimes had the money to make an initial purchase, it did not necessarily have a budget for its regular use and for repairs. Households rarely save up in order to pay for these things, let alone anticipate them in a regular budget. So recharging the battery and thus having access to electricity appears like a luxury to be indulged in occasionally when the occasion, or the money, presents itself. It is not like school expenses or a mobile phone which have to feature as regular items in the family budget. Compared with the micro-network, we can say that there are no dependent relationships causing problems of consumption: when a person does not have the means of paying to re-charge the battery, nobody covers the transaction; there is no debt or recovery of debt to think about.

This does not mean that the market in 'starting' batteries is unorganized. There exist on the market two types of battery: new batteries that can be bought in hardware or DIY shops and used batteries bought in the market-place or from specialists in re-charging and repairs. These latter can be found for the most part scattered through rural poor neighbourhoods, constituting a stable chain of local micro-entrepreneurs who ensure the circulation, recharging and the maintenance of the products from the time they are imported into Madagascar to their final recycling, when some of the batteries are put to other uses, notably artistic (the battery cases can be repainted and resold as plant tubs). These micro-entrepreneurs generally carry out this business of repairing and recharging batteries together with other second-hand trading such as selling other electrical equipment or tyres. They effectively offer a supply of electricity which is accessible to the poorest both through the multiple forms of recycling practised and through the relative guarantee of competence and professionalism which the personal links which are at the base of these transactions ensure.

Situated upstream from the urban retail market, the supply of second-hand batteries relies on two completely informal but highly organized chains: the illegal trade in second-hand cars imported from neighbouring countries and also the purchase at low prices of old batteries from local drivers and transport companies. These two flows complement each other. 'Working the import trade' depends on being 'in the know' with well identified trading partners so that the traders can have regular access to a good stock of batteries.[7] The drivers and transport companies represent a smaller source of supply, with drivers either taking the old battery directly to the repair workshop or giving it to door-to-door salesmen who work as middlemen. But in all cases, the forms of transaction (where they take place, the exchange rituals, the way of fixing the price and who gets what) are based on stable rules which are known by all the participants in the trade.

In these transactions, it is the expertise of the re-sale agent in evaluating the state of the merchandise, the nature and the cost of the repair operation, its re-sale potential and its wholesale value, which is the essential factor. The best batteries go on sale just as they are to individuals, some of them need small repairs, and yet others, called 'grafts' are entirely rebuilt from parts taken from old batteries beyond repair. The professionalism of the retail micro-entrepreneur is also in evidence in the exchange with the customer at the end of the chain. Reputation plays a big role in building relations of confidence at the re-sale stage, as in the repair and re-charging of the batteries. Rarely technically competent themselves, the end customers can judge the quality of the entrepreneur by comparing the durability of the product after a repair or a battery's life-length after a recharge. It is not only a question of the vendor's reputation; there are other material ways in which the reliability of the purchase can be assessed, giving a relative stability to the market arrangements. In the workshops, the sale prices and recharge prices are clearly displayed. Sales are accompanied by a three to six-month guarantee, and the circulation of the batteries to be recharged is rendered secure by a ticket system stating the date, the power of the battery and the name of the client. The depositing and the recovery of a battery for recharge or for repair are accompanied by systematic controls of the state of the product carried out in the presence of the client.[8] In short, judging the matter as an economic process, the second-hand battery market is a

Posting up the different prices of recharges according to the battery size

The commercial entrance to a workshop: the used batteries serve to advertise the business

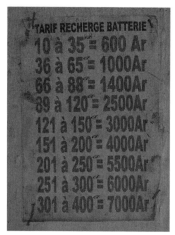

Ticket given to the client when leaving a battery for recharging

Batteries continuously connected for recharging

Figure 7.1   The exchange facilities in the second-hand battery market
Source: Cholez, Trompette.

market which relies on interpersonal arrangements with a minimum of contractualization and a maximum of trust.

Flexible, well organized, and reliable for the customer, the second-hand battery market is a permanent fixture and even a flourishing one.

The micro-entrepreneurs encountered take calculated advantage of their connection to the national electricity network by integrating this cost in their profitability calculations in which the resale of electricity through their battery recharging service finances an electrical consumption reinvested in new battery repair services and the sale of various sorts of electrical equipment. The accumulation of profit on this initial diversification allows some of them to develop new activities (transport, taxi services, etc.). The second-hand battery market appears as an economic activity with few barriers to competition: several battery-charging entrepreneurs of a certain size and portfolio of activities can easily coexist and can be a springboard to constructing real entrepreneurial take-off careers, so sought after in development initiatives. Surely, the specific properties of this second-hand battery market that we have just described should make them immediately eligible for the ambitious promotion of BoP market initiatives?

An invisible market on the periphery of the electricity market

With the use of old batteries being an activity close to the salvage and reclamation sectors, this second-hand market is totally ignored from the point of view of local, national or international authorities. There exist in effect no regulations and political framework around this practice: for one thing, these are not necessary (with limited investment required and no new infrastructure) and for another, it is not subject to control by outside authorities, in particular concerning the kw/per hour price. Moreover, the very sale of these second-hand batteries upstream in the economic chain has a clandestine side to it: the batteries are hidden in second-hand cars and in tyres on the inside of imported containers. Everything happens as if this underground economy is invisible to the public authorities who are concerned only with regulating new batteries used in road vehicles. This is why there are no statistics to evaluate the real dimensions of this market. This field of activity which we have just described is therefore part of the very developed informal economy of the country. For those in the field who are involved in the recharging business, or the battery repair business and all the other intermediaries, it is precisely the fact that they escape economic control and regulations which makes this field of activity an attractive one. Those battery rechargers that we met do not want to make official declarations concerning their activity and accept a legal framework for their practices, arguing that this would have an automatic knock-on effect on prices.

In spite of its technical weakness and the relatively high cost of functioning in terms of supply of electricity, the battery is used on a massive scale and its market is well developed. It reflects a market which is much more directly adjusted to the forms of material life of the BoP populations: on the one hand an economic supply coming from minor local commerce sources (rechargers, repairers) and on the other hand consumers, if not 'the poor' (Cholez et al., 2010), whose income is scarce and irregular and who are only concerned with short-term expenditure. The second-hand car battery recharged in the same sector with only short distances involved would thus seem to be an extreme form of an economically liberal logic of gaining access to electricity. But compared with the localized power-station presented above, the battery is an individual solution of little ecological value: expensive, with a short lifespan, of suboptimal use (poor battery use damages the re-charging potential) and polluting, with dead batteries littering the streets and houses of the villages.

How does Schneider Electric plan to get involved? Interested in the opportunity that such an existing market presents in terms of putting down local roots, the company remains nonetheless circumspect as to the manner in which it can be associated with such BoP innovative projects. There are plenty of 'technical' paths which could be followed up. But on the other hand, in designing a possible assemblage around an innovation plan in this area, the virtual absence of political concern and in particular of macro-actors with institutional back-up would appear as a weakness in such a project. One idea is therefore to join this market by adding a few elements to the existing assemblage (a technical device to the battery) to optimize and ensure a better re-charge and subsequent use. The development of this technical advance would be accompanied by a support for the 'battery sector' through training programmes, an increase in battery rental points, and forming partnerships with local entrepreneurs in a better position to invest in inexpensive solutions. Village micro-entrepreneurs and medium-sized enterprises are the key-players in a project which could be thought of as a form of 'ecologization' of a local market. Its widespread practice is therefore a good indicator of territories which are only weakly institutionalized, spaces on the periphery. But this strength is also its principal limitation: the essential question for Schneider Electric is promoting its visibility.

The conception of a new assemblage based on the battery and its network of local micro-entrepreneurs amounts to a very different market design from what was first envisaged by the company: it places great emphasis on strong autonomy compared with institutionalized macro-actors, but is nonetheless of much more direct interest to the BoP considered both as micro-entrepreneurs as well as consumers. At the same time, it exposes the company to much criticism concerning strong external factors such as pollution and could thus require considerable investment and monitoring (training, close control of recharging operations, etc.) in order to reduce these externalities and satisfy the accountability requirements which would be demanded by the many institutional macro-actors. Ecologized, regulated, controlled, even subsidized, the battery energy system could receive its institutional authorization but its 'civilizing' character is not without question.

Discussion

The BoP vision was built as a business strategy (for corporations and consumers), free from any political concern. Our study shows that, in BoP projects as well as in other business activities, corporations are involved in political issues of citizenship in different ways. First, designing an offer dedicated to the poor, corporations 'take part in the political deliberation' of the countries and of the international institutions: they participate in the classification of populations, the qualification of poverty, the definition of the poor's needs and the best way to address them. Second, corporations are involved in 'governing citizenship' when they position themselves as providing people with their basic needs (food, water, energy, etc.), especially in some contexts where there is a lack of local governance and public infrastructures.

The examination of the political role of corporations in the design of the BoP market extends the reflection about Corporate Citizenship in two respects: (a) the management of the overflow issues associated with the handling of public services; (b) the complex equation to be solved concerning the making of an accountability (depending as it does on the type of public concerned). Accountability and overflows and with them the way of framing, defining and involving the BoP consumer, constitute the critical points around which the essential arbitration between the two separate paths takes place. In the first case, the company substitutes for the government in providing a public service, hence setting out a visible and bureaucratic accountability. But this assumes a high issue of framing the overflows (Callon, 1998), as witness the numerous social arrangements around the power station. Does the corporation have the skills and resources to manage locally the political regulation of a public service? Does it have the legitimacy to assume this role? Such a requirement disappears in the second case. Here the corporation answers to societal expectations with a product 'plugged in' to existing markets and consumer practices. Affordability and frugality are properties which are incorporated in the sociotechnical device itself and in its use. It releases the corporation from the management of overflows. However, this solution opens up questions concerning its more invisible and controversial accountability.

By following innovative process in the development of BoP markets, we observe that the same problematization (in this case energy shortage for rural poor people) can open up to a plurality of market designs, around socio-technical assemblages which are distinct in their basic properties. These market designs relate to very different configurations of actors, and these actors do not carry the same weight in the regulation game, in making themselves heard and asserting their conception of what is at stake for them and/or a matter of political concern.

The first solution, associated with the setting up of local electricity stations, can be qualified as an 'institutionalized technical solution'. As a responsible ecological solution satisfying international norms, both ecological and economic, it is eligible for financial and political support. In their formal dimension, the framing of national governments and international organizations reflects a system of exchange between economic and juridical resources (monopoly, finances) and the satisfaction of ecological and social needs. The market design here operates in a space dominated by a rational-legal legitimacy, which is structured around public involvement, economic planning and a legal framework. The assemblage requires a high institutional investment to justify long-term financial calculations (investment and amortization) and technical choices (renewable energy, capacity restriction). The benefits for the Company (Schneider Electric) are much of a moral order: it can assert itself as a fully-fledged actor in the fight against energy shortages in developing countries and gain in social legitimacy in environments which are more sensitive to demands for responsibility (Fourcade and Kieran, 2007). In a way, institutionalized technical involvement represents a visible and direct accountability (Boström and Garsten, 2008; Neyland, 2007) that could be qualified as 'rational-legal accountability'.

The second path reveals opposite properties: at the margins of the institutional market, it offers a technical arrangement, which is deprived of institutional links (norms, taxes, price-setting, etc.). Its quasi-invisibility attaches itself imperceptibly to existing informal markets. Being part of an informal economy, it is better described as an 'economic circuit', in the sense advanced by V. Zelizer (2004), meaning incorporating unwritten conventions for evaluating goods, regulating transactions based on social networks operating their own circulation of goods and information, etc., without necessarily requiring formal institutional frameworks for regulating exchanges. The limitation of such a solution is that it remains sub-optimal on the ecological level, except in so far as further investment would perceptibly reduce its polluting effects (through enhanced training and product refinement to meet ecological requirements, normalization of the second-hand battery market, etc.). In this case, the multinational company provides incentives and plays a supportive and facilitative role by grafting innovations on this local economic circuit, based on interpersonal arrangements and entrepreneurship. The assemblage conforms to the BoP vision, notably because it supports an existing value chain. But its polluting effects and its informal (even quasi-illegal) circuit hinder the construction of the firm's visibility as a moral actor. To make such a solution accountable in the arena of development programmes requires a host of investments in 'translations', 'interpretations', calculation and the making of equivalence (MacKenzie, 2009).

These two solutions also reveal variations in the corporation managing of overflows. Through the concept of a 'civilizing market', M. Callon suggests that the market capacity to take on political issues (such as sustainable development) requires taking into account externalities and the 'concerned' groups which appear throughout the experimentation. How do these innovation projects taken up by a multinational company and adopted within a BoP market perspective rise to the ambitious challenge of a civilizing market?

The experiment based on the power-station brings up two kinds of overflows issues. On the one hand, as part of a vast political and social system, its stability is far from being assured, either on the institutional level (political instability, with the fragile legitimacy of governments) or on the economic level (its long-term profitability). Local political uncertainties hamper the corporation's involvement despite the significant political gains in terms of social legitimacy. On the other hand, it entails the (re-)invention of numerous supplementary institutional back-up supports to manage the multiple overflows which result from its rigid framing. Notably, it requires a high level of consumer normalization and disciplining in its use (Von Schnitzler, 2008) as in the economic requirements. The corporation has to create morally legitimate uses and economic habits, which can incorporate relatively, restricted definitions of the 'right way of consuming'. That presupposes defining the consumption needs of the poorest people which consuming values appear remote from western consumer models.

Concerning the second market option, the promotion of battery use fits in much more directly with BoP business model strategies: a low-cost product, a scattered entrepreneurial force, informal local markets and local cultural habits. It is free from the constraints that weigh on the world energy market and epitomizes a chain of transactions based on a relative economic and technical flexibility attuned to the material ways of living of the BoP populations. Moreover, it is totally aligned to BoP consumer requirements, including its labile use, the volatile capacity of consumer payment, its adaptability to multi-functions, and especially to collective leisure use (TV, music). The design of this market favours 'plugging in' (literally as well as metaphorically) to this existing economic circuit by enrolling its stakeholders. The whole question remains here nonetheless whether this system has the capacity to incorporate the environmental dimension that is to say whether this volatile and informal but also extremely polluting system can be ecologized.

Conclusion

Working with the theory going by the same name, BoP market design could be directly linked with the enterprise of civilizing markets, a phrase also used for hybrid co-ordinating structures but in this case recognizing other 'piloting' participants, such as the multi-national companies. The challenge of the BoP is that of claiming that the market can constitute a lever for social and economic inclusion, which is more powerful than development programmes. But treating BoP experimentation as a place where alternative market design forms can be explored highlights the tensions which are implicit in these grand globalizing concepts: should we be promoting and supporting a 'rational-legal civilization' based on administered markets which as a consequence incorporate governmental concerns for ecology and equity? Or should we be concentrating our help on existing but informal markets, which are resolutely anchored in local social configurations? We are concerned with what is 'accountable' for the governmental and international political organizations – but does this accountability also apply to the BoP consumer? Should we be civilizing the undisciplined consumers or ecologizing the informal economies where the potential mechanism exists for the economic and social inclusion of the poor populations?

Behind all this lies the question of the very process of civilizing markets, and once it is recognized that we are talking about mass markets targeting several billions of the world's poor, this primordial question now reveals a major tension. Should the 'civilizing virtues' be confined to politics and rational instruments to control and influence economic interaction and the forms of mass consumption, or should we recognize that the democratic taking into account of the multiplicity of the 'voices' involved in the market, and in particular those of the weakest, those at the bottom of the pyramid, can challenge our initial definition of what constitutes the 'common good'? This opens up stimulating exchanges about the multiplicity of the ways in which a corporation can be both citizen and accountable.

Notes

1. PACTE (Political Science and Organization) – CNRS, University of Grenoble. pascale.trompette@iepg.fr and PACTE (Political Science and Organization) Grenoble Institute of Technology, University of Grenoble, celine.cholez@grenoble-inp.fr.
2. The university team reformulated the commission to assess the 'acceptability of solutions' into a study of existing local practices and systems. In this way it can be said that the university team played an integral part in the process of assessing the different assemblages and that this case constitutes a stimulating perspective on the question of how sociological and anthropological knowledge can be integrated into market design (Callon, 2009).
3. A third study was also carried out in a non-electrified village on the east coast where we monitored a Madagascan entrepreneur working in collaboration with the ADER (Agency for the Development of Rural Electrification) on a market study plan prior to requesting authorization for its implementation.
4. The Antetezambato network is supported by a French NGO working in association with big international investment funds. The Marovato network is part of a local development programme sponsored by the World Bank.
5. http://www.riaed.net/spip.php?article35.
6. http://www.ader.mg/index.php?go=news&id=2.
7. About eight times per year for a supply of 10 to 30 batteries per trader.
8. With instruments which are more or less sophisticated depending on the size of the workshop: from a simple electric wire to check the charge level of the battery to measuring tools for acidity and voltage.

References

Akrich, M. (1989) 'De La Position Relative Des Localités. Systèmes électriques et Réseaux Socio-Politiques', *Cahiers du Centre d'Etudes pour l'Emploi*, 32: 117–166.

Berg, M. (1998) 'The Politics of Technology: On Bringing Social Theory into Technological Design', *Science, Technology & Human Values*, 23, 4: 456–490.

Bessy, C. and F. Chateauraynaud (1995) *Experts et faussaires: pour une sociologie de la perception*, Métailié.

Bhatti, Y. A. and M. Ventresca (2012) 'The Emerging Market for Frugal Innovation: Fad, Fashion, or Fit?' *SSRN eLibrary*, January (15).

Boström, M. and C. Garsten (2008) *Organizing Transnational Accountability*, Cheltenham: Edward Elgar.

Burdinich, V., K. Manno-Reott and S. Schmidt (2005a) 'Hybrid Value Chains: Social Innovations and the Development of the Small-Farmer Irrigation Market in Mexico', *Business Solutions for the Global Poor*, San Francisco: Jossey-Bass, pp. 279–288.

Çalışkan, K. and M. Callon (2010) Economization, Part II: A Research Programme for the Study of Markets', *Economy and Society*, 39, 1: 1–32.

Callon, M. (1998) *The Laws of the Markets, Sociological Review Monograph*, Oxford: Blackwell.

Callon, M. (2009) 'Civilizing Markets: Carbon Trading Between In Vitro and In Vivo Experiments', *Accounting, Organizations and Society*, 34, 3/4: 535–548.Chapman, C. S., D. J. Cooper and P. Miller (2009) *Accounting, Organizations, and Institutions: Essays in Honour of Anthony Hopwood*, Oxford: Oxford University Press.

Cholez, C., et al. (2010) 'The BoP Market : The MNF Facing Political Uncertainties'. *1st Interdisciplinary Market Studies*. Stockholm.

Cholez, C., et al. (2010) 'L'exploration des marchés BoP', *Revue française de gestion*, 9: 117–135.

Crabtree, A. (2007) 'Evaluating the "Bottom of the Pyramid" from a Fundamental Capabilities Perspective', *CBDS Working Paper Series*, April.

Crane, A., D. Matten and J. Moon (2008) 'The Emergence of Corporate Citizenship: Historical Development and Alternative Perspectives', in Scherer, A.G. and Palazzo, G. (eds), *Handbook of Research on Global Corporate Citizenship*. Cheltenham, UK, and Northampton, MA: Edward Elgar, pp. 25–49.

Dalsace, F. and D. Ménascé (2010) Structurer le Débat 'Entreprises et Pauvretés'. *Revue Française de Gestion*, 9: 15–44.

Dolan, C. and M. Johnstone-Louis (2011) 'Re-Siting Corporate Responsibility: The Making of South Africa's Avon Entrepreneurs', *Focaal*, 60: 21–33.

Fligstein, N. (2002) *The Architecture of Markets: An Economic Sociology of 21-Century Capitalist Societies*, Princeton, NJ: Princeton University Press.

Fourcade, M. and K. Healy (2007) 'Moral Views of Market Society', *Annual Review of Sociology*, 33: 285–311.

Karnani, A. (2007). 'The Mirage of Marketing to the Bottom of the Pyramid', *California Management Review*, 49, 4: 90–111.

Landrum, N. E. (2007) 'Advancing the "Base of the Pyramid" Debate'. *Strategic Management Review*, 1, 1: 1–12.

Latour, B. and C. Venn (2002) 'Morality and Technology: The End of the Means', *Theory, Culture and Society*, 19, 5/6: 247–260.

Lavelle, S. (2009) 'Politiques des Artefacts', *Cités*, 3: 39–51.

MacKenzie, D. (2009) 'Making Things the Same: Gases, Emission Rights and the Politics of Carbon Markets', *Accounting, Organizations and Society*, 34, 3: 440–455.

Mair, J. and I. Marti (2009) 'Entrepreneurship in and Around Institutional Voids: A Case Study from Bangladesh', *Journal of Business Venturing*, 24, 5: 419–435.

Matten, D. and A. Crane (2005) 'Corporate Citizenship: Toward an Extended Theoretical Conceptualization', *The Academy of Management Review*, 30, 1: 166–179.

Matten, D., A. Crane and W. Chapple (2003) 'Behind the Mask: Revealing the True Face of Corporate Citizenship', *Journal of Business Ethics*, 45, 1: 109–120.

Mendoza, R. U. and N. Thelen (2008) 'Innovations to Make Markets More Inclusive for the Poor', *Development Policy Review*, 26, 4: 427–458.

Muniesa, F. and M. Callon (2007) 'Economic Experiments and the Construction of Markets', in MacKenzie, D., F. Muniesa and L. Siu (eds), *Do Economists Make*

Markets? On the Performativity of Economics, Princeton: Princeton University Press, pp. 163–189.

Muniesa, F., Y. Millo and M. Callon (2007) 'An Introduction to Market Devices', *The Sociological Review*, 55, 1: 1–12.

Neyland, D. (2007) 'Achieving Transparency: The Visible, Invisible and Divisible in Academic Accountability Networks', *Organization*, 14, 4: 499–516.

Overdevest, C. (2011) 'Towards a More Pragmatic Sociology of Markets', *Theory and Society*, 30: 1–20.

Prahalad C. K. and S. Hart (2002) 'The Fortune at the Bottom of the Pyramid', *Strategy+ Business*, 26: 54–67.

Prahalad, C. K. (2010) *The fortune at the bottom of the pyramid: eradicating poverty through profits*, Upper Saddle River, NJ: Wharton School Publishing.

Von Schnitzler, A. (2008) 'Citizenship Prepaid: Water, Calculability, and Techno-Politics in South Africa', *Journal of Southern African Studies*, 34, 4: 899–917.

Sehgal, V., K. Dehoff and G. Panneer (2010) 'The Importance of Frugal Engineering', *Strategy+ Business*, 59: 1–5.

Simanis, E., S. Hart and D. Duke (2008) 'The Base of the Pyramid Protocol: Beyond "Basic Needs" Business Strategies', *Innovations: Technology, Governance, Globalization*, 3, 1: 57–84.

Stark, D. (2009) *The Sense of Dissonance: Accounts of Worth in Economic Life*, Princeton, NJ: Princeton University Press.

Thaler, R. H. and C. R. Sunstein (2008) *Nudge: Improving Decisions about Health, Wealth, and Happiness*, New Haven, CN: Yale University Press.

Valor, C. (2005) 'Corporate Social Responsibility and Corporate Citizenship: Towards Corporate Accountability', *Business and Society Review*, 110, 2: 191–212.

Walsh, J. P., J. C. Kress and K. W. Beyerchen (2005) 'Book Review Essay: Promises and Perils at the Bottom of the Pyramid', *Administrative Science Quarterly*, 50, 3: 473–482.

Winner, L. (1999) 'Do Artifacts Have Politics?' *The Social Shaping of Technology*, 29, 3: 28–40.

Yunus, M. and K. Weber (2007) 'Creating a World without Poverty: Social Business and the Future of Capitalism', *Global Urban Development Magazine*, 4, 2: 16–41.

Zelizer, V. (2004) 'Circuits of Commerce', in Alexander, J. C., G. T. Marx and C. L. Williams (eds), *Self, Social Structure, and Beliefs: Explorations in Sociology*, Berkley and Los Angeles, CA: University of California Press, pp. 122–144.

8
Citizenship, Choice and Social Equality in Welfare Services

Paula Blomqvist

Introduction

The provision of welfare services has been re-organized in many countries in the last two decades. Inspired by ideas best known under the label New Public Management (NPM), policy-makers have introduced organizational features like privatization, contracting and consumer choice into the welfare service sector. Prominent goals behind such reforms were to make the provision of public welfare services more cost-efficient and to raise their quality. Another important goal was to empower users by offering them more choice between different service alternatives. The introduction of NPM into the welfare sector has given rise to new questions regarding the relationship between organizational market dynamics and the preservation of political control over resource distribution in such policy areas. Is it, as suggested by the proponents of NPM, possible to vitalize welfare service provision with the help of organizational features like choice and competition while at the same time preserving the universalistic character of such services? This question has been much discussed by researchers and policy makers alike in the last twenty years (see, for instance, Le Grand and Bartlett, 1993; Le Grand, 2007; Greve, 2009), but few conclusive answers have been given. In relation to this, there have also been questions asked regarding the relationship between the marketization of social service provision and the changing nature of social citizenship. As citizens become re-cast in the role of 'consumers', asked to make choices between different welfare service producers and hence use their consumer power to distribute resources between them, what is added to their citizenship and what, if anything, is lost? Is there a risk, as perceived by some, that the ideals of social equality and social integration are undermined if some groups exercise their right more skilfully than others? Or can 'choice' policies, which imply that services are still *funded* collectively through the state, be crafted in such a way that the freedom of citizens to make choices is enhanced without this negative side effect?

In this chapter I address these questions by reviewing the Swedish experience. The Swedish case can be regarded as particularly interesting in this respect for several reasons. Welfare services like primary education, health and social care in Sweden are financed almost exclusively by the public sector and were, until recently also *provided* foremost by this sector. In order to address criticisms after 1980 that this virtually all-public system provided too little opportunity for service users to choose between different alternatives, Swedish policy makers have gradually expanded opportunities for choice in the welfare sector. With reforms like the school vouchers in 1992 and steady expansion of private providers in health- and care of the elderly services through contracting with private providers after 1991, Sweden became one of the first countries where NPM ideas like choice and privatization of provision were implemented on broad scale in this area. Hence, Sweden constitutes a case where such policies have been pursued for a relatively long period while at the same time the values of social egalitarianism and extensive social citizenship rights have remained strong. Given the (still-) broad political commitment to social equality in Swedish politics, choice reforms have been carefully designed to avoid undermining this value, which can be understood as the right of all citizens to have access to high quality welfare services on the same conditions. In addition, Sweden is one of the countries with the most even distribution of income in the world, which means that user choice is taking place in a context of relative economic and social equality. In this sense, the conditions for informed choice-making on equal terms might be considered better than in countries where social cleavages are wider. For all these reasons, Sweden can be said to constitute a good 'test' case for answering the question whether it is possible to combine choice in welfare services with the ideal of social equality. If there is evidence to suggest that user choice undermines this value in Sweden, chances are that the same logic applies elsewhere.

In order to answer the question about the effects of user choice in a universalistic welfare state, I review the effects of introducing choice and competition between public and private providers in four policy welfare policy sectors in Sweden during the 1990s and 2000s: primary education, child care, health care and elderly care. In particular, I ask what we know about the choice patterns of different groups and whether such patterns can be linked to any known differences in service quality. Given the lack of systematic data on choice patterns and quality differences in most of these sectors, the analysis focuses primarily on so-called *private exit*, that is, if there is any tendency for some social groups, like the better-educated, to leave the public sector in favour of private alternatives and, if so, if this can be said to provide them with higher-quality services than those who remain in the public sector.

The main finding presented in the chapter is that there is evidence of a slight 'middle class-bias' in the utilization of choice in Sweden. Generally speaking, those with higher education are more likely to take advantage of the right to leave the public sector in favour of private service providers than the population in general. In total, however, the group which leaves the public service sector is still relatively small. Moreover, the empirical evidence reviewed in the chapter points to that there are no or very small differences in service quality between public and private service providers. This suggests that even if the better-educated middle class is more likely to make active use of their new right to choose private, rather than public welfare service providers, there is no indication that they thereby receive better services.[1] These findings indicate that, as long as the state manages to regulate and monitor the quality of the services provided in the increasingly 'marketized' Swedish welfare state so that there are no stark quality differences between private and public service providers, the universalistic aspects of the system need not be undermined by the fact that there is a tendency for different social groups to utilize this choice in different ways. Social integration, in the sense of all citizens using the *same* kinds of services, may, however, be jeopardized by this pattern.

The findings in the chapter also reveal, however, that there are developments underway in some welfare sectors that may pose a threat to the egalitarian values of the system in the longer term. One such 'warning sign' is that there are indications that the Swedish school system has become more educationally stratified in recent years and that this is at least in part due to the increasing socio-economic and ethnic segregation within the system. Differences between poorly performing schools – and students – and well-performing ones have grown. Given that Swedish society has undergone other social changes that may affect the performance of schools during this period, such as widening income differences, increased immigration and growing residential segregation, it is hard to know to what extent the introduction of school vouchers has contributed to this development, but most observers seem to agree that it has, even if the effect is marginal. In the health care sector, the possible threat to the social equality of the system is not related to the choice mechanism itself, but rather to the emergence of a market for privately *financed* health care services that has developed as a result of the establishment of commercially oriented health care providers within the system. A similar development appears to be underway in the elderly care sector, where the establishment of for-profit service providers had led to the elderly now having the opportunity to supplement publicly financed services with privately purchased ones. Taken together, these developments indicate that the Swedish system may become somewhat more socially stratified in the future, even if such tendencies are not yet clearly visible.

The chapter is arranged in the following way. In the next section, I give a brief account of the NPM trend and what it implies for the organization of social service provision. I thereafter turn to literature on social citizenship, giving a brief account of this concept and the way its content can be said to have been transformed in recent decades. In the fourth section of the chapter, I discuss more specifically the relationship between NPM and social citizenship, focusing on the question of choice of welfare services. After this, I turn to the Swedish case, reviewing how choice has been introduced in various welfare service areas in Sweden and what we know today about the effects of such policies. The final section summarizes the empirical findings.

NPM and social policy

The recent tendency to market-orient modes of public governance by adopting managerial techniques which draw on the organization of the market is a broad and complex phenomenon with many different policy expressions. This phenomenon is known under different names, the most common of which are managerialism, marketization or New Public Management (NPM).[2] Common elements of this reform trend, which has affected policy-making in most industrialized countries during the 1990s and 2000s (albeit to different degrees) include decentralization, de-regulation, contracting out public tasks to private providers (privatization of provision), full privatization, separation of purchaser and provider functions within the public sector, new forms of performance measurement and consumer choice (Walsh, 1995; Clarke and Newman, 2004). In some countries, including the US, the UK, New Zealand, Australia, Sweden and Denmark, the impact of NPM seems to have been particularly strong (Taylor-Gooby, 2008). Arguably, the worldwide spread and pervasive impact of market-inspired ideas about how to renew the public sector constitutes one of the most remarkable political developments of our time, reflective of the general liberalization of world politics as well as the weakened position of the nation state (Djelic, 2008).

The core ideas underpinning the NPM movement are drawn from neoclassical economics and neo-liberal thought. They build on the notion that markets are inherently more effective in producing goods and services than the state, since these are exposed to competitive forces and price signals (Self, 1993; Savas, 2000). In addition, NPM places great value on the choices of users, or consumers, of public services. 'User choice' is seen as a market mechanism which serves to allocate resources between competing service providers and gives them signals about how users view the quality of their services. In this way the choices of users are seen both as competition-enhancing and as a way to improve service quality: producers have to start taking into account the preferences of the people who use their services in order to attract consumers. In neo-liberal thought, user choice is also seen as an important value *in and of itself*, in that it empowers users in relation to service producers by providing them with purchasing power as well as an exit mechanism if they are dissatisfied with the services they receive (Friedman and Friedman, 1980).

One of the areas in which NPM has been most widely practiced is social services (Gilbert, 2002). 'Social services' typically refer to services like health- and social care and primary education; services which are in most developed countries either provided directly or at least in part financed by the state. This is an area where full privatization is often rejected both by policy makers and the public, as this would imply a very uneven access to services which are seen as essential to a dignified human life. Therefore, most states have chosen to continue to finance such services and retain regulatory control over them (Gilbert, 2002). Given they are costly, and that citizens have a strong interest in their quality, policy makers in many countries have been attracted to the idea of making them more cost-efficient and raise their quality through the introduction of market features such as privatization, competition and choice.

The most common organizational practices used to introduce privatization, competition and choice in the production of social services can be said to be two: contracting and voucher systems. *Contracting* refers to an organizational form where the state enters contractual agreements with private organizations and firms to mandate these to provide social services. Typically, contracting implies a system where there is open competition among private (and frequently also public) service providers for public contracts and where the contracting public agency selects a bidder on basis of price or quality or both. Contracting is thus a form of privatization.[3] *Voucher systems* are characterized by an arrangement where a number of providers (public or private) are authorized by public authorities to provide a certain service in a given geographical area. Citizens are then given real or fictive 'vouchers' for the service in question, which means they can choose freely among the authorized providers at no (or very little) cost to themselves. These will thereafter be reimbursed by the public authorities on basis of how many users they manage to attract (Savas, 2000).

In countries were there has previously been a large private sector in areas likes primary education and health care, NPM reforms have often focused on increasing the competitive element in these areas and widened the scope of choice for users. Examples of this are reforms undertaken in Germany and the Netherlands which introduced wider opportunities for citizens to freely choose health care insurance during the 1990s and 2000s, while the health insurance sector in both countries underwent a development towards increased market competition and commercialization (Brown and Amelung, 1999; Helderman et al., 2005). In countries where social services were previously provided foremost by the public sector, such as in the UK and the Nordic countries, the introduction of NPM led to private service providers being given an opportunity to enter into policy areas which had previously been largely protected from market forces while 'choice' was introduced to citizens as a novel policy feature (Blomqvist, 2004; Pollitt and Bouckaert, 2004). Policies creating free choice of providers for citizens in such systems thus imply at least partial privatization as well as the introduction of competitive mechanisms through some form of choice *system*.

NPM and social citizenship

NPM is a form of governance that introduces market dynamics into the realm of public social services. By emphasizing choice, it creates a new role for the users of social services, turning them into 'choosers' or consumers, rather than just service recipients. In this way the introduction of NPM in welfare services also has implications for how we understand social rights, or citizenship, in contemporary welfare states. 'Citizenship' is a complex and multi-faceted term, but can be said to refer broadly to the rights and obligations of humans formally recognized to be citizens of a nation state.[4] One of the most famous theories of citizenship, which influenced the way many thought of this concept in the postwar era, is that of T. H. Marshall. According to Marshall, there are three main types of citizenship rights: civil (liberties like free speech), political (related to participation in communal decision-making) and social. Social citizenship rights were understood by Marshall as the responsibility of the state to ensure basic levels of economic security to its citizens as well as the ability to 'live the life of a civilized being according to the standards prevailing in the society' for instance by gaining access to primary education and health care in the case of illness (Marshall, 1950). Social citizenship can thus be seen mitigating the social inequalities generated by market capitalism (Turner, 2001:190–91). During the post-war era, Marshall's notions of social citizenship became incorporated in the idea of the modern welfare state. More recent citizenship theories have addressed the struggles of marginalized groups (women, minorities, etc.) to be granted full citizenship rights, or gain recognition of their special needs in order to be able to exercise such rights in full (Young, 1994; Kessler-Harris, 2001). It has also been recognized that the struggle for and exercise of citizenship is not a mere question of political participation or social security but also of identity-formation, and that such processes also frequently involve other actors than the state such as nongovernmental organizations, markets and firms (Heather, 2004; see also Crane, Moon and Matten in this volume). In the Nordic political setting, the understanding of social citizenship has been strongly connected to the specific type of welfare system which was constructed in the region during the 20th century, influenced in large part by strong labour movements. These systems were – and are – characterized by relatively generous systems for social protection and income replacement in case of illness, unemployment and old age, but also, by more uniquely; comprehensive and universalistic systems of public welfare service provision, for instance with regards to health, education and social care. The political rationale behind the extensive systems for social service provision that were developed in the Nordic countries in the post-war period was that the state should provide (directly or through local governments) high-quality services that would meet the needs of all citizens, not just the poor, which, in turn, would ensure their broad public support and financial viability through income taxation (Rothstein, 1998). In this manner the welfare service sector would contribute to the overriding goal of social equality through re-distribution of life opportunities and social integration (Olsson, 1993). This political logic implied that the systems should be *public*, both in their financing and provision; an idea which became challenged on a broad base in the Nordic countries only in the 1980s. The policy conception that welfare services should be universalistic and socially integrating in the sense that they are financed by taxation, publicly provided and accessible to all citizens regardless of ability to pay, is also found in welfare systems outside the Nordic countries, primarily in education but also in health and social care.

When 'choice' policies are implemented in welfare service systems based on universality and direct public provision, they transform the role of the users, e.g. the *citizens*, in several different ways. 'Choice' refers here to policies which provide users with a free choice between public and private service providers while the funding of these providers remains public. Perhaps the most fundamental way in which the practice of citizenship is transformed through choice policies is that it, at least in part, such policies tend to recast citizens in the role of 'consumers'. As *consumers* of welfare services, citizens should, proponents of NPM argue, have the right to freely choose between a range of different types of welfare services, including ones provided by private actors; not, as was often the case in the bureaucratically organized welfare systems found, for instance, in the Nordic countries, directed to a single public service provider. By restoring to the users of social services the right to choose freely among different providers (like consumers in a regular market), they will, Milton Friedman and others argued, regain some of the freedom and consumer power that they were deprived of when these types of welfare systems created virtual public monopolies on social service provision (Friedman and Friedman, 1980; Osborne and Gaebler, 1992). Furthermore, seeing the utilization of social services like health care and primary education foremost as a matter of service *consumption* implies that this citizenship right is something that is granted to and carried out primarily by *individuals*. Thus, it has been argued by some critics of NPM that this ideational movement serves to promote a citizenship ideal based on individual, rather than collective, rights (Clarke et al., 2007; Higgs, 1998). Seeing citizens foremost as consumers of public services also implies that these *have to be active* – by making choices – in order to fully utilize their citizenship rights. This difference is stressed by Hvinden and Johansson, who make the distinction between the 'passive' form of citizenship that was created in the post-war Nordic welfare state and the 'active', choice-based, citizenship which characterizes the relationship between states and citizens in the Nordic welfare states today (Hvinden and Johansson 2007).[5] The development of more active forms of citizenship can also be seen as reflective of broader shifts in society. Sociologists like Anthony Giddens and Zigmont Bauman have argued that after the 1960s, in the period referred to as 'late modernity' (or 'postmodernity'), social and cultural developments are characterized by *individualization*. This implies an increased tendency to focus on the individual as the basic unit of human society and the growing need for individuals themselves to construct their own identity and cultural belonging though a variety of life-style choices. This represents a shift in relation to earlier periods, where collective identities relating to occupation and social class governed much of people's lives, thus creating less need, or desire, to make individual choices regarding life-style and consumption (Giddens, 1994; Bauman, 1998).

A second way in which the introduction of 'choice' in welfare services transforms the role of the citizens who use them is what might be referred to as the *individualization of responsibility* for one's well-being. This implies that not only do citizens have to be more active in order to realize the full potential of their citizenship rights, but they are also more responsible for the *outcomes* of these choices. Choosing a poorly performing health care provider, for instance, may have direct and dramatic consequences for an individual's health status. Likewise, the choice of school on part of the parents will have a substantive impact on a child's educational development. While the freedom of making such choices gives more power to the individual, it also involves the possibility of making bad or 'wrong' choices. As stated by Paul Higgs: 'Instead of the state administering health and seeking out disease these concerns have been privatized' (Higgs, 1998: 180). Giddens discusses the same issue in terms of the uncertainty and risk. He argues that individuals today are to a higher extent responsible for making informed choices regarding their health and social well-being, which implies that they are also exposed to the uncertainty and risks that come with making such choices (Giddens, 1991, 1994). This general condition of higher uncertainty contributes to making the exercise of choice not just a matter of empowerment for the individual, but also a burden, since it is virtually impossible to know which choices are 'right'. In this light, the marketization of the welfare services can be seen as a further extension of the condition of uncertainty in that it extends the obligation of the individual to make lifestyle choices to new domains, such as education and health, where the risks are higher than with most other consumption choices. Other sociologists have argued that the individualization of risk also gives rise to a new form of social inequality as individuals can be seen as having different resources to find and interpret useful information in order to make informed choices (Beck, 1992; Bourdieu, 1997; Bourdieu and Passeron, 1990).

A third implication of choice policies for the exercise of citizenship is the social and cultural fragmentation that may follow from the increased variety of social services offered and the possibility to choose freely between them. In the all-public model of standardized social services-provision (one-size-fits-all), individuals had to be content – in most cases – with the services offered and had little opportunity to express their own lifestyle choices in relation to these. With the creation of voucher systems in primary education and the possibility for different kinds of actors to open schools funded by the state, there is now a growing diversity in the school sector in many countries, both in cultural, pedagogical and linguistic terms. In addition, the growing competition between schools in such programs have led to an increased tendency of the schools themselves, public and well as private, to market themselves through different 'profiles', for instance with regard to curricula and educational orientation. This growing diversity also implies, however, that children will receive different kinds of education depending on their parents' choice. In health and social care, different choice patterns can create more social differentiation if, for instance, certain groups choose private alternative while others 'stay' in the public care sector. The down side of this may be a more culturally fragmented society where there are fewer common public arenas where different groups meet (see, for instance, Clarke and Newman, 2004). In this way, the partly transformed citizenship ideal that choice policies can be said to represent has an opposite logic from what might be called a more traditional (in Marshall's terms) understanding of citizenship, where the utilization of universal social services like a public school or health care system was seen as a way to integrate different groups into a national community. The fragmentation effects of choice policies can also be *institutional* in the sense the systems themselves – for instance educational or health care systems – become more organizationally fragmented with a multitude of different types of actors (public, private, voluntary organizations) and hence more difficult to navigate in for individual users. In this regard too, group variations in resources and skills related to, for instance, social class could become more determining of who gets access to what services. If quality differences between service providers come to vary more, as these become different in orientation and ownership form, this 'class' effect can be even more pronounced.

In sum, it is apparent that at least in theory, the introduction of choice within the welfare sector could transform our understanding of what social citizenship entails. Taken together, the more active and individualized forms of social citizenship that results from these policies points to a shift from a more communitarian citizenship ideals, where the state through its provision of a certain type of social services expresses a preference for what is 'best' for the citizens, to a more libertarian view of citizenship, which leaves to the individual to decide this for themselves (Kymlicka and Norman, 1994). Critics of this development have raised the question what this shift means for the universality of social citizenship, or, in other words, it has the potential to generate increased social equality, which, as noted above, was a central political goal behind the expansion of the welfare state and social citizenship rights during the post-war era in the Nordic countries as well as many others. Can all individuals be counted on making informed choices regarding their health and the education of their children? If not, does this imply that universal social citizenship is undermined by choice policies? This argument draws on the reasoning of those who, like Beck, argue that the capacity to make informed choices is not equally distributed among citizens but follows lines of social privilege like education, income and class (for a different view, see, for instance, Le Grand, 2007). Some, as Ball, go as far as suggesting that the creation of market-like systems and introduction of user choice in the school sector represents a 'class strategy', whereby the middle classes can rid themselves of the poorly performing children of the lower classes and educate their children in their 'own' schools (Ball, 2003).

In the rest of the chapter I examine empirically the proposition that the introduction of choice and voucher systems in the area of welfare services will undermine the universalist character of social citizenship in a social democratic-type welfare state. Reviewing experiences within the Swedish welfare system, I ask how citizens use their right to choose in four welfare areas: primary education, child care, health care and elderly care and whether their choices lead to more pronounced differences in the quality of the services they receive. Given the rather limited information available regarding choice patterns as well as service quality in Sweden at present, I will largely limit myself to discuss differences between public and private service alternatives. When it comes to group differences, the most common distinction between social groups is their educational level, which is strongly related to concepts like class, or socio-economic status. In some cases, information about choice patterns of groups with different ethnic background is provided. Three basic questions will be asked in each area. The first (1) is what choices have been created for users; the second (2) how the right to choose has been utilized by different social groups and the third (3) is whether there are any known quality differences that can be related to differing choice patterns.

User choice in Swedish welfare services: What are the effects for social equality?

Sweden was one of the first countries to introduce NPM policies in its welfare system in the early 1990s. After a non-social democratic coalition government won the national elections in 1991, there was a strong political desire to widen the scope of user choice in this area and to open it to private service providers. In 1992, there was also a change in the so-called Municipal Act (*Kommunallagen*) which made it possible for local governments (municipalities and county councils) responsible for the provision of health and social services like elderly and child care to contract out these to private actors, including for-profit firms. In the same year, a nation-wide school voucher system was introduced that has been described as the most liberal and market-conforming in the world (Chubb, 2007), and which gives all kinds of private actors, including faith-based organizations and for-profit firms, the right to establish schools to compete for public funding on the same terms as state schools. Taken together, these reforms marked a turning point in the development of the Swedish welfare state, where private alternatives to publicly provided services previously had been highly marginalized (representing, on average, about 1–2 per cent of total service provision) and where there had been very few opportunities for choice on part of the service users (Blomqvist, 2004). Over the following two decades, the share of private service providers grew slowly but steadily in all areas, reaching between 10 per cent (in the school sector) and 20 per cent (in elderly care services) of total service provision.

Choice in primary education

The Swedish school system is locally operated by the 290 so-called municipalities. After the introduction of school vouchers in 1992, Swedish parents were offered a free choice of school for their children within their municipality. The voucher system implied that the old principle of allocating children to a municipal school of basis of geographical proximity was abandoned and that private actors could establish schools to compete with the municipal ones (Andersson and Nilsson, 2000). The privately operated schools, known in Sweden as 'free' schools (*friskolor*), have their own admission system but are, in principle, not allowed to select students on any other basis than the municipal schools.[6] In 2009, about 65 per cent of the privately operated schools were operated by for-profit firms. In terms of educational orientation, the overwhelming majority (83 per cent) was 'general' (*allmän*), while about 10 per cent were confessional while the rest (6 per cent) had special educational phi-losophies, like Waldorf or Montessori (The Swedish National Agency for Education, 2010a). The choice of school is constructed so that a form is sent to parents when their children start school at the age of six. Many of the privately operated schools actively market themselves to parents. Basic facts about the characteristics of schools are usually found on the internet, for instance through municipal web sites, but generally there is not much information available about their quality. To make an informed choice, parents have to take the initiative in gathering such information on their own. It may not be surprising, therefore, that the evaluations from the Swedish National Agency of Education (SNAE) show that most parents choose the closest municipal neighbourhood school (Blomqvist and Rothstein, 2000). Data on which parents are most likely to choose another municipal school than the nearest is not available however, why the best indication of active choice is the decision to attend a privately operated school. Vlachos reports that in 2009, pupils with highly edu-cated and high-income parents were clearly overrepresented in the pri-vately operated school sector. This pattern was most pronounced in the non-profit schools. Students with immigrant backgrounds are slightly underrepresented in the private school sector (Vlachos, 2011: 81–84). The effects of school choice have been much discussed in Sweden. Critics have claimed that the system is discriminatory and benefits the better-off at the expense of the less advantaged. This critique has been most pronounced in the bigger cities, where it is claimed that the better-performing students leave the disadvantaged areas, leaving behind more impoverished schools. In some municipalities, the vouchers are weighted on the basis of various residential characteristics in order to compensate for the weaker pupil composition, but according to the Swedish National Agency of Education this does not seem to be enough to off-set the trend towards growing differences in educational attainment between schools in different socio-economic areas (SNAE, 2012). How, then, can we assess the ability of parents to make educational choices? Studies from other countries have shown that those who have been through higher educa-tion are more likely to make 'good' choices of schools for their children in the sense of the schools being better-performing (Reay and Ball, 1998; Reay, 2004; Yoon and Gulson, 2010). There are, however, few systematic studies in Sweden on the motives behind school choice on the part of parents. What is known is that, in 2009, privately operated schools on the whole, did not have better pupil performance (measured as results in national achievement tests) than municipal schools (Vlachos, 2011: 84ff.). This indicates that those who choose a privately operated school do not automatically get a better education than those who stay in the public sector. However, several studies indicate that the privately operated schools tend to give higher grades (relative to performance) than public ones: a characteristic which can be seen as an advantage for those attending such schools (Wikström and Wikström, 2005; Vlachos, 2010).

As for the question of ethnic segregation, there are studies which indicate that there probably are such effects in Sweden, but they are likely to be insignificant. First, residential segregation in larger city suburbs is pronounced, which implies that schools in such areas are strongly segregated 'to start with'. Whether user choice patterns add to this segregation is hard to determine, given that there are also choice patterns which go in the opposite direction, when parents in such areas move their children to less segregated inner city schools (Bunar, 2008). Lindbom draws the conclusion that an ethnically segregating effect of the school voucher system cannot be ruled out, given that he finds some variance in ethnic composition between schools that is not explained by residential segregation (even if this explains most of it), but that if such effects exist, they are most likely to be marginal (Lindbom, 2010). A more negative conclusion is drawn by Andersson et al., who argue that the wider performance differences between schools in areas with large ethnic minorities point to an effect of educational stratification which is enhanced by ethnic segregation: a pattern created by the tendency of ethnic Swedes to avoid schools with high proportions of non-European immigrant children (Andersson et al. 2010).[7] Other studies indicate that there is also an increase in the *social-economic segregation* within the system, as parents with higher income and higher education are more likely to choose schools were such groups are overrepresented (SNAE 2012; Böhlmark and Lindal, 2007; Söderström and Uusitalo, 2005). Taken together, these tendencies indicate that differences between schools with regard to the socio-economic and ethnic composition have increased and that the 1992 choice reform has contributed to this development, even if it is contested how big its effect is in this regard. This development points to the possibility that choice policies might contribute to a less equitable educational system in Sweden, where educational choices on part of the parents become more decisive of the quality of education that their children receive. So far, however, there appears to be no systematic quality differences between the public and private school sectors.

Choice in child care

In international comparison, the Swedish welfare system distinguishes itself in that it provides publicly subsidized, high-quality child care to all children from the age of one. As a result, a very high share of all pre-school children aged 1–5 (85 per cent) in 2012 attend day care facilities. Until the 1990s, child care was an almost exclusively public service in Sweden, provided by the municipalities. Following the legislative change in 1992 which made it possible for municipalities to allow also for-profit private providers to establish themselves, their share has risen gradually and is today about 20 per cent. The child care system in Sweden functions today as a voucher system, where parents enjoy free choice of provider and providers – public as well as private – are reimbursed on basis of enrolment. As of 2006, private providers have the right to free establishment in the municipalities.[8] The privately operated child care centres are mandated by law to accept all children. Like the privately operated schools, they have their own enrolment systems and waiting lists. Recent data from SNAE reveals that there are significant differences in choice patterns between parental groups, at least with respect to the public–private distinction. The higher educated are, it seems, significantly more likely to place their children in a privately operated child care centre. In 2009, the share of children in privately operated schools with parents with two years of post-secondary education was 7 per cent, to be compared with 23 per cent of those whose parents had longer post-secondary education (more than three years of university studies). This implies that the children from the first category (lower educated) were strongly underrepresented, while those of the highly educated were overrepresented (Hanspers and Mörk, 2011: 50).

As for quality differences between public and privately operated child care centres, data from SNAE analysed by Hanspers and Mörk (2011) indicate that such differences are probably small, if they exist at all. The most common quality measures in child care are group size, staff education and staff density. Of these three, only one, staff education, had any marked differences between the sectors: a slightly lower share of teachers in the private sector had pedagogical education, as compared to those in the public sector. In the public sector, 55 per cent had a university degree in child pedagogy (*förskollärarutbildning*), while in the private sector the corresponding number was 37 per cent. Average group size was about the same (albeit somewhat lower in the private sector). Hanspers and Mörk also note that the private sector displays larger variety in this respect: the smallest groups (under 15) were more common, as were the very large ones (over 26) (ibid., p. 58, see also Persson, 2012, for a similar conclusion). Taken together, this evidence cannot be said to support the claim that the better-educated, even though they are more likely to choose private care providers, also choose better services.

Choice in health care

The right of patients to choose freely among health care providers has been gradually strengthened in Sweden over the last two decades. In 2010 the Law on Choice Systems (*Lagen om valfrihetssystem*) was passed. This law makes the right to choose a primary care health centre mandatory. It also gives all providers the right to free establishment within county councils *and* right to reimbursement on the same terms as publicly operated health centres. The choice law, thus, introduced a sort of voucher system in the primary care sector. Choice in the secondary care sector has been gradually strengthened over the years by increased rights for the establishment for private specialists as well as several recommendations to the county councils to allow patients choose, or at least be consulted, when they are referred to specialists. In 2010, only about 10 per cent of all care in Sweden was provided by the private sector. In primary care, the share was substantially higher at 25 per cent (Anell, 2011: 186).

As for the choice patterns of individual users, there is not much systematic knowledge in Sweden yet. A study by Glenngård et al. (2011) pointed to that younger patients were more liable to make an active choice of care provider than older ones. It is known from previous studies that the better-off consume more specialist care than then those with lower incomes, despite the fact that they have higher care needs. This can be seen as an indication that the former are better at voicing their demand for specialist care, also when there is 'gate-keeping' in the form of referrals and waiting lists (Blomqvist and Rothstein, 2000). Given the fact that the early experiences with the primary care choice reform points to it leading to a general increase in the number of care providers – mainly due to new establishment of private, for profit actors – it has been argued that this reform benefits those with lesser incomes as it increases the availability of this more accessible form of care (Anell, 2011). Early evaluations of the reform have also shown that, contrary to what critics expected, establishments of new private health centres have taken place also in less privileged areas (Rhenberg et al., 2009). In specialist and hospital care, there are as of yet no studies conducted in Sweden on how patient choice rights are used (which are weaker in this sector since they are not legally sanctioned) by different groups. Studies from other Nordic countries as well as the UK indicate, however, that the better-educated use this right more actively than those with lower education (Ringard, 2012; Birk et al., 2011; Dixon et al., 2010).

Another question concerns the ability of individuals to make informed choices in health care and what kind of information is available to them. A recent study by Winblad and Anderson showed that most county councils in Sweden do not provide even a minimum level of information to users of primary care services to guide them in their choice of care provider (Winblad and Anderson, 2011). As a result, patients often have to rely on informal information such as rumours and advice from acquaintances to make their choice; a pattern which may lead to an advantage for resource-strong groups with extensive social networks. There are also studies of the effects of choice in Swedish health care indicating that patients who have made an active choice of care provider are more content with the care they receive. Whether this is a result of the care these patients receive being of better quality, or an effect simply of having made an active choice, is not known (Winblad, Isaksson and Bergman, 2012).

As for quality differences between private and public care providers, there is no indication today that any such differences exist in Sweden. Internationally, there is evidence to indicate that for-profit hospitals have poorer results than ones operated by non-profit organizations, but it is questionable if such studies can be generalized to Sweden. There are yet no studies which have tried to measure systematically quality differences between private and public care providers in Sweden. Note can be taken, however, that there is evidence from international studies that the profit motive can lead actors in this area to exchange quality aspects for cost gains, which indicates that even if there might be a tendency for the better-educated in Sweden to use the opportunity to leave the public primary care sector for newly established private care providers, there is little to suggest that they would be raising the quality of the care they receive if they did. A bigger concern for the social equity dimension in this regard might be the growing number of Swedes, albeit still very small in international comparison,[9] who purchase private health insurance and thereby get quicker access to health care than those who stay in the publicly financed system.

Choice in elderly care

Elderly care in the form of residential and home-based services for those in need is a universal right in Sweden and in hence accessible to all, regardless of income. Elderly care has until very recently been one of the areas in Swedish welfare state where the right to choice has been most restricted, despite political calls for user empowerment and choice also in this domain. The gradual privatization of both residential and home-based elderly care that took place after 1992 has primarily taken the form of contracting. After being awarded the contact, the private actor (usually a firm) takes over the operation of these units, including the care of all elderly people who live there. Choices open to the elderly themselves have in practice often been limited. Likewise, when the provision of home-based services in geographical districts have been put out to tender by the municipalities and taken over by private firms, the elderly persons living there have often not had much choice but to accept services from the firm in question.

This situation changed in 2009 following the adoption of the Law of Choice Systems; see above) which states that *if* municipalities want to offer privately provided elderly care (in contrast to the primary care sector, they are not mandated to) they must follow this law, which stipulates that privatization should be carried out through a so-called authorization system, where elderly users should be offered a choice between all authorized providers in the municipality.[10] In 2011, about 50 per cent of all municipalities had introduced or planned to introduce such choice systems.[11] With the new law, thus, it seems that choice opportunities in this area will increase. It is also likely that this law will further stimulate the establishment of private providers. In 2010, about 20 per cent of all elder care, as measured as the share of elderly treated by private providers, was carried out by private actors (Szebehely, 2011).[12]

So far, there has been little systematic evaluation in Sweden of how the elderly utilize their right to choose a care provider. A study by Edebalk and Svensson in 2005 carried out in municipalities which were forerunners in creating choice rights for the elderly pointed to the fact that many have difficulty choosing without help and that it is hard for this user group to make informed choices. The study also showed that the most common reason for choosing a care provider was geographic proximity and recommendations from friends and family. Another observation was that the longer the opportunity for choice had been available, the higher the likelihood that the elderly would choose a private care provider. No data on differences in choice patterns based on socio-economic characteristics seem to be available in the elderly care sector in Sweden at this point. As noted by Szebehely, there might, however, be other ways in which distributional patterns in this area are affected by the tendency towards choice and an increased share of private providers. The most important might be that the elderly who are financially better-off are shown to be more to be more likely to supplement publicly financed help with the private purchase of services like cleaning by using the right to tax deduction for such services. Given that the choice law gives private care providers the right to sell such services 'on the side' to their users, it is likely that this pattern will be reinforced when choice systems become more common (Szebehely, 2011). Szebehely also reports that working-class elderly were found to be more likely to rely on relatives for help, while those with middle-class backgrounds were more likely to turn to the welfare system to articulate their needs (ibid.). If such differences in the ability to take advantage of the system are complemented with an emerging *private* market for care services in close proximity to the public system, the result might be that the more advantaged will also get better access to care services. So far, however, the market for privately financed care services is very limited in Sweden.

A final question is whether there is any documented variation in care quality between public and private elderly care providers. As of yet, there are few studies in Sweden which have systematically investigated this. One exception is a study by Stolt, Blomqvist and Winblad (2011) which is based on quality indicators for publicly and privately operated residential homes for the elderly. This study demonstrated that there are in fact such differences, foremost in that certain types of quality criteria, such as staff density and the share of part-time employees, which wer found to be higher in the public sector, where other, more service-oriented qualities such as user involvement in care planning and options to choose between meal alternatives, were higher in privately operated homes. The results of Stolt, Blomqvist and Winblad were confirmed by the report of the Swedish National Board for Health and Welfare Services (*Socialstyrelsen*) in 2012 which also found staffing levels to be lower in the private sector. This finding is supported by several international studies, particularly in relation to for-profit care providers, which have often been found to have lower quality in terms of key quality criteria like staffing levels than non-profit and public actors (Commondore, 2009; Hillmer et al., 2005). However, since there has yet been little opportunity for the elderly to choose a residential home in Sweden, there is no indication that such quality differences are related in any systematic way to differences in the social composition of user groups.

Conclusions

The review in this chapter of the experiences so far with choice reforms in the Swedish welfare system gives a mixed and somewhat inconclusive picture with regard to their effects on the social equality of the system. First, it can be noted that there is a marked tendency in most areas – more clearly documented in primary education and child care – for the higher-educated to use the right to choose. This has led to the fact that there is a higher share of these citizens who have left the public sector and chosen alternatives in the emerging private sector. Second, even if the better-off are more inclined to choose private alternatives (in some areas, at least) there is no systematic evidence of this leading to them receiving services of higher quality. In no sector reviewed here is there any clear indication that private services are of higher quality (generally speaking) than public ones; if anything the pattern seems to be the contrary. Hence, at least if we limit the analysis to the effects of private exit, or the tendency of some citizens to leave the public sector when the opportunity is given through choice reforms, there appears to be no cause for alarm: even if the better-educated turn to private service providers to a slightly higher extent, this does not translate into higher inequality with regard to service quality. Thus, as long as there are no substantive quality differences between the two sectors, the universal character of social citizenship in Sweden cannot be said to be undermined by the fact that some groups are more likely to prefer private providers.[13]

On the other hand, there are also warning signs that there are developments underway that pose a threat to the egalitarian nature of the system in the longer run if they are not moderated. One such sign is the indication the Swedish school system has become more educationally stratified in the last twenty years and the differences in performance between schools have increased. In this case, it does seem that choice reforms have led to an undermining of the universal character of social citizenship rights in Sweden in the sense that the educational background and ethnic origin of the parents seem to play a larger role then before in determining the quality of education received by their children. Another problematic tendency can be witnessed in the health and elderly care sectors, where the establishment of market actors, including both health insurance companies and commercially oriented care providers, has led to the emergence of markets for privately *financed* care services alongside the public system. If this development, which is still very marginal, continues, income, rather than medical need, will play a bigger role in determining access to health and social care services in Sweden in the future. It should be noted, however, that both these threats to the egalitarian ideals of the Swedish welfare system – the tendency of middle-class parents to make more active educational choices for their children and the development of a complementary private health care market alongside the publicly financed system – are common occurrences in most other welfare systems. In this sense, the introduction of choice and privatization in the Swedish welfare state during the 1990s and 2000s may not undermine the system, or threaten its value foundation of universal social citizenship rights as much as orient slightly in the direction of other European welfare systems, where welfare service users have long had the right to choose more freely between different service providers.

Notes

1. Some caution is called for here, however, as there is still relatively limited availability of quality data which distinguishes between public and private providers in the welfare area.
2. In this chapter I will use these concepts interchangeably.
3. Privatization in this sector is usually partial in the sense that it is the provision of services, not their funding, which is being privatized. This implies that private actors such as firms and non-profit organizations are given the task of providing certain services to the citizens in exchange for public reimbursement while the users pay no higher fees than they would in the public sector. Some countries allow only non-profit actors to carry out such tasks on the state's behalf; others have encouraged commercial markets to develop.
4. Sometimes it is also given the meaning of actively engaging oneself in the communal life within that state, for instance in the form of civic activities like community work or voting.
5. The concept 'active citizenship' has also been used, particularly in the UK, to refer to citizenship ideals stressing more active participation in the community, as well as the obligation of citizens to engage in paid labour.
6. There might be exceptions to this, for instance when schools have a certain educational profile, or are oriented towards certain skills, such as music or sports. All schools, public and private, also give preferential treatment to children whose siblings already attend the school.
7. A de facto ethnic segregation can also be said to result from the free schools which have a for instance a Muslim/Arab profile, even if these are few in number.
8. The local variation with respect to the share of private providers is significant however; in 2009 there were municipalities were virtually all children attended private care facilities while 50 municipalities had no private providers at all.
9. About 400,000 Swedes had a private health insurance in 2011.
10. This implies, in effect, a shift from contracting to a voucher-type system.
11. The government has also stated that, if all municipalities have not introduced choice systems according LOV on 'voluntary' basis by 2014, they will make it mandatory to do so.
12. Like in the other service areas there is large local variation: the larger cities generally have a much higher share of private actors.
13. Social integration, in the sense of all citizens using the *same* kinds of services, may, however, be jeopardized this development.

References

Andersson, E., J. Öst and B. Malmberg (2010) 'Ethnic segregation and performance inequality in the Swedish school system: A regional perspective', *Environment and Planning*, 42, 11: 2674–2686.

Andersson, I. and I. Nilsson (2000) 'New political directions for the Swedish school', *Educational Review*, 52, 2: 155–162.

Anell, A. (2011) 'Hälso- och sjukvårdstjänster i privat regi', in Hartmann, L. (ed.), *Konkurrensens konsekvenser*, Stockholm: SNS.

Ball, S. (2003) *Class strategies and the education market: The middle classes and social advantage*, London: Routledge.

Bauman, Z. (1998) *Theory, culture and society*, London: Sage.

Beck, U. (1992) *Risk society*, London: Sage.

Birk, H.O., R. Gut and L.O. Henrikssen (2011) 'Patients' experience of choosing an outpatient clinic in one county in Denmark: Results of a patient survey', BMC Health Services Research, 11: 262.

Blomqvist, P. (2004) 'The choice revolution: Privatization of Swedish Welfare Services in the 1990s', *Social Policy & Administration*, 38: 139–155.

Blomqvist, P. and B. Rothstein (2000) *Välfärdsstatens nya ansikte*, Stockholm: Agora.

Böhlmark, A. and M. Lindahl (2007), 'The impact of pupil achievement, segregation and costs', Discussion paper no 2786, IZA, Bonn, Germany.

Bourdieu, P. (1977) *Reproduction in education, society, culture*, London: Sage.

Bourdieu, P. and J.C. Passeron (1990) *Reproduction in education, society and culture*, London: Sage.

Brown, L.D. and V.E. Amelung (1999) 'Manacled competition: Marker reforms in German healthcare', *Health Affairs*, 18, 3: 76–91.

Bunar, N. (2008) 'The Free Schools "Riddle": Between traditional social democratic, neo-liberal and multicultural tenets', *Scandinavian Journal of Educational Research*, 52, 4: 423–438.

Chubb, J.E. (2007) 'Att få ut det mesta möjliga av marknaden: lärdommar av fritt skolval I USA', in Lindbom, A. (ed.), *Friskolorna och framtiden: segregation, kostnader och effektivitet*, Report, Swedish Institute for Future Studies, Stockholm.

Clarke, J. and J. Newman (2004) *The managerial state*, London: Sage.

Clarke, J., J. Newman, N. Smith, E. Vidler, and L. Westmarland (2007) *Creating citizen-consumers*, London: Sage.

Commodore, V. R. (2009) 'Quality of care in for-profit and not-for-profit nursing homes: Systematic review and meta-analysis', *British Medical Journal*, 339: 2732.

Dixon, A., R. Robertson, J. Appelby, P. Burge, and N. Devlin (2010) *Patient choice – How do patients choose and how do providers respond?* Report, The King's Fund, London, UK.

Djelic, M.-L. (2006), 'Marketization: From intellectual agenda to global policy-making', in Djelic, M.-L. and K. Sahlin-Andersson (eds), *Transnational governance*, Cambridge: Cambridge University Press.

Edebalk, P. G. and M. Svensson (2005) *Kundval för äldre- och funktionshindrade i Norden*, Tema Nord, Rapport 2005: 507.

Friedman, M. and R. Friedman (1980) *Free to choose*, New York: Harcourt Brace Jovanovich.

Giddens, A. (1991) *Modernity and self-identity: Self and society in the late modern age*, Cambridge: Polity Press.

Giddens, A. (1994) *Beyond left and right*, Oxford: Polity Press.

Gilbert, N. (2002). *The transformation of the welfare state: The silent surrender of public responsibility*, Oxford: Oxford University Press.

Glenngård, A, A. Anell and A. Beckman (2011) 'Choice of primary care provider: Results from a population survey in three Swedish counties', *Health Policy*, 103, 1: 31–37.

Greve, B. (2009) 'Can choice in welfare states be equitable?', *Social Policy and Administration*, 43, 6: 543–556.

Hanspers, K. and E. Mörk (2011) 'Förskola', in Hartmann, L. (ed.), *Konkurrensens konsekvenser*, Stockholm: SNS.

Heather, D. (2004) *Citizenship. The civic ideal in world history, politics and education*, Manchester: Manchester University Press.

Helderman, J.-K., F.T. Stout, T.E.D. van der Grinten and Wynand P.M.M. van de Ven (2005) 'Market-oriented health care reforms and policy learning in the Netherlands' , *Journal of Health Politics, Policy and Law*, 30, 1–2: 189–210.

Higgs, P. (1998) 'Risk, governmentality and the reconceptualization of citizenship', in Scambler, G. and Higgs, P. (eds), *Modernity, Medicine and Health*, London: Routledge.

Hillmer et al. (2005) 'Nursing home profit status and quality of care: Is there any evidence of an association?', *Medical Care Research Review*, 62: 139–166.

Hvinden, B. and H. Johansson (2007) *Citizenship on the Nordic welfare state*, London: Routledge.

Kessler-Harris, A. (2001) *In pursuit of equity: Women, men, and the quest for economic citizenship in 20th-century America*, Oxford: Oxford University Press.

Kymlicka, W. and W. Norman (1994) 'Return of the citizen: A survey of recent work on citizenship theory', *Ethics*, 104, 2: 352–381.

Le Grand, J. (2007) 'Choice and competition in publicly funded health care', Health Economics, Policy and Law, 4, 4: 479–488.

Le Grand, J. and W. Bartlett (1993) *Quasi-markets and social policy*, Basingstoke: Macmillan Press.

Lindbom, A. (2010) 'School choice in Sweden: Effects on student performance, school costs and segregation', *Scandinavian Journal of Educational Research*, 54, 6: 615–630.

Marshall, T.H. (1950) *Citizenship and social class*, Cambridge: Cambridge University Press.

Olsson, S.E. (1993) *Social policy and welfare state in Sweden*, Lund: Arkiv.

Osborne, D. and T. Gaebler (1992) *Reinventing government*, Reading, MA: Addison-Wesley.

Persson, S. (2012) *Förskolans betydelse för barns utveckling*, Reportto the Commission for a Socially Sustainable Malmö (Kommissionen för ett socialt hållbart Malmö), Malmö.

Pollitt, C. and G. Bouckaert (2004) *Public management reform: A comparative analysis*, Oxford: Oxford University Press.

Reay, D. (2004) 'Exclusivity, exclusion and social class in urban education markets in the United Kingdom', *Urban Education*, 39, 5: 537–560.

Reay, D. and S. Ball (1998) 'Making their minds up: Family dynamics and school choice', *British Education Research Journal*, 24, 4: 431–447.

Rhenberg, C., N. Janlöv, and J. Khan (2009) *Uppföljning av vårdval Stockholm år 2008*, Report no 2009: 6, Stockholm: Karolinska Institutet.

Ringard, Å. (2012) 'Equitable access to elective hospital services: The introduction of patient choice in a decentralized health care system', *Scandinavian Journal of Public Health*, 10, 1: 10–17.

Rothstein, B. (1998) *Just institutions matter*, Cambridge, MA: Cambridge University Press.

Savas, E.S. (2000) *Privatization and public–private partnerships*, New York: Seven Bridges Press.

Self, P. (1993) *Government by the market?*, London: Macmillan.

Söderström, M. and R. Uusitalo (2005) 'School choice and segregation: Evidence from an admission selection reform', IFAU Working Paper no. 2005: 7.

Stolt, R., P. Blomqvist and U. Winblad (2011) 'Privatization of social services: Quality differences in Swedish elderly care', *Social Science & Medicine*, 72, 4: 560–567.

The Swedish National Agency for Education (Skolverket) (2010a) Skolverkets lägesbedömning 2010, Report 2010: 349. Del 1- beskrivande data.

The Swedish National Agency for Education (Skolverket) (2010b) Rustad att möta framtiden? PISA 2009 om 15-åringars läsförståelse och kunskaper i matematik och naturvetenskap, Report 2010: 1196 (based on the OECD report *PISA results 2009*).

The Swedish National Agency for Education (Skolverket) (2012) Likvärdig utbildning i svensk grundskola, Report 2012: 374.

Szebehely, M. (2011) 'I privat regi', in Hartmann, L. (ed.), *Konkurrensens konsekvenser*, Stockholm: SNS.

Taylor-Gooby, P. (2008) *Reframing social citizenship*, Oxford: Oxford University Press.

Turner, B. (2001) 'The erosion of citizenship', *British Journal of Sociology*, 52, 2: 189–209.

Vlachos, J. (2010) http://people.su.se/~jvlac/pop_pub/Betygens-varde-2010-6.pdf, Konkurrensverket rapport 2010: 6.

Vlachos, J. (2011) 'Friskolor i förändring', in Hartmann, L. (ed.), *Konkurrensensko nsekvenser*, Stockholm: SNS.

Walsh, K. (1995) *Public services and market mechanisms: Competition, contracting and the new public management*, London: Macmillan.

Wikström, C. and M. Wikström (2005) 'Grade inflation and school competition: An empirical analysis based on the Swedish upper secondary schools', *Economics of Education Review*, 24: 309–322.

Winblad, U. and C. Andersson (2011) *Vilken information behöver patienter och medborgare för att välja vårdgivare och behandling?: Patienters och medborgares behov av kvalitetssäkrad och lättillgänglig information*, Research report. Department of Public Health and Caring Sciences, Uppsala University.

Winblad, U., D. Isaksson and P. Bergman (2012) *Effekter av valfrihet inom hälso- och sjukvård – en kartläggning av kunskapsläget*, Report 2012: 2. Myndigheten för vårdanalys.

Yoon, E.-S. and K. Gulson (2010) 'School choice in the stratilingual city of Vancouver British Columbia', *Journal of the Sociology of Education*, 32, 6: 703–718.

Young, I.M. (1994) 'Polity and group difference' in Turner', B. and Hamilton, P. (eds), *Citizenship: Critical concepts*, London: Routledge.

9
Corporate Citizens and 'The War on Terror'

Karin Svedberg Helgesson and Ulrika Mörth

Introduction

In 2005 the EU adopted a directive that stipulated that a range of industries within the EU were obliged to prevent money laundering and terrorism financing (Directive 2005/60/EC). The private actors were expected to take on a new role – as agents of the state – in preventing terrorist attacks. In this chapter we analyse the devolution of authority to corporate actors in the public security domain, and present some implications of this new authority for the responsibility and democratic accountability for designated corporate citizens.

A basic definition of the crime of money laundering is that it is the process through which the illegal source and unlawful application of illicit gains is concealed or disguised to the make the gains appear legitimate (Braithwaite and Drahos, 2000). The fight against this crime – anti-money laundering (AML) – has undergone two waves of transformations during the last twenty years. The first transformation took place in the late 1980s and early 1990s. AML was until then politically perceived as a financial crime to be managed at the national level. Since the inception of the global organization the Financial Action Taskforce (FATF) in 1989, AML has been viewed as a global problem, especially in connection to drug trafficking.

A second wave of transformation in the field is occurring in the aftermath of 9/11, this time associated with 'the war on terror' (Mitsilegas, 2003; Amoore and de Goede, 2008; Helgesson and Mörth, 2012). The war on terror narrative (Hodges, 2011) was evoked by President George W. Bush in his speech to a Joint Session of Congress, on 20 September: 'Americans are asking: How will we fight and win this war? We will direct every resource at our command ... every financial influence ... to the disruption and to the defeat of the global terror network'. With this speech, President Bush aimed to securitize the financial sector by publicly stating, to overwhelming Congressional and public appeal, that finance was as an explicit means to be used in the fighting against terrorism. The banking sector, and later on accountants and lawyers (Seyad, 2012), was from now on now expected to incorporate anti-money laundering as a security issue into its organization and its day-to-day activities. It is this second, and still ongoing, wave of transformation of AML that this chapter analyses.

We start out by delineating an analytical approach to ideas of the responsibility and democratic accountability of corporations in the emerging new public security domain that transgresses the traditional public-private divide. We then place the discussion of whether and how corporate actors can be responsible and democratically in the specific context of the increased transnational regulation urging the banking sector, and other private actors, to engage as partners in 'the war on terror'. We argue that the responsibilities for the surveillance of illicit financial flows have gradually been shifted to private actors, placing these actors in a rather delicate position. Notably, the designated corporate citizens need to strike a balance between complying with the directive on the one hand, and continuing to manage their clients with discretion and confidentiality, on the other. In the third section, we discuss how this balancing act may play out in practice by using illustrations from an on-going study. We show how two Swedish industry associations, in banking and law respectively, have quite different takes on their new position in the public security domain. In the concluding section we summarize our main points and provide ideas for future research. One conclusion is that the corporate actors may well have been made responsible, but it is questionable whether they are, or can be, democratically accountable.

Analytical framework

Security is an important public good. Security can mean many things – from traditional military and state-centred threats, on the one hand, to societal and transnational problems, on the other (Buzan and Hansen, 2009). However, security is always about constituting something that needs to be secured, whether it is the planet or the state. The bulk of the literature on how for-profit actors are participating more in the 'production' of security policy-making, war and imposed war situations is very much based upon public security concepts and theories (Bailes and Frommelt, 2004; Singer, 2003; Avant, 2005). A central tenet of this literature is that the state is challenged by the private actors, and that the very monopoly of legitimate violence is no longer in the hands of the state. There is also an increasing academic interest in new ways of conceptualizing the security concept – from a state centred approach to a more comprehensive understanding of what and which actors are objects for security (Buzan and Hansen, 2009). Moreover, the sociological approach on securitization as a practice (Balzacq, 2011) can be linked to the emerging focus on the interrelationship between the (public) management of security and that of (corporate) risk management (Power, 2012a; Helgesson, 2012), and wider issues of fraud risk (Power, 2012b).

From the perspective of the current volume, these developments in the security field, and analyses thereof, can be considered part of the on-going renegotiation of the relationship between the state and the business sector, a renegotiation that not only questions the role of the state but places new demands on the corporate actors to perform citizenship duties, including political ones. To be sure, there is a definite link between attempts to promote public security and overarching questions on power and governmentality in society (Miller, 1991; Larner and Walters, 2006; Lipschutz, 2005). This link is particularly salient when private actors are enrolled as agents for the promotion of public security (see Amoore and de Goede, 2008). A growing role for corporate actors as citizens, or indeed 'governments' (Moon et al., 2005), calls traditional boundaries and established relationships into question. But can these designated corporate citizens really be held to account for democratic values when enacting that authority?

We define accountability as the technologies, in broad terms, through which an agent is 'held to answer for performance that involves some delegation of authority to act' (Romzek and Dubnik, 1998). A common accountability model across disciplines is the one where agents are accountable to principals (e.g. Woodward, Edwards and Birkin, 2001). With a view to democratic accountability, the focal relationship is that between the electorate, as principals, and the elected politicians, as agents (Bovens, 2006; Strom, Wuller and Bergman, 2003). Alternatively, the parliaments or governments can be considered the de facto principals, with the bureaucracy or administration taking on the role as agent. Be that as it may, in both models, authority, defined as legitimate power, is delegated from principal to agent.

In order to enable agents to behave in accordance with the goals and aims of principals, principals need to keep agents informed about their aims and goals. Yet, what the preferred ends are is not always that clear, and in practice agents may know more about the issues at hand than their principals (Baier, March and Saetren, 1986). When power is delegated between public actors – between the governments and the bureaucracy – problems of accountability (and implementation) may thus arise concerning how principals are to know that agents behave properly. In order to secure that agents do not perform activities that are outside the aims of the principals, principals therefore tend to put a variety of mechanisms in place to monitor and control the behaviour of agents. When power is delegated from public principals to corporate actors, the problem of accountability is even more challenging.

Corporate actors and the public accountability dilemma

Contemporary governance rests upon multiple authorities, including non-profit and for-profit actors (Hall and Biersteker, 2002; Mörth, 2004). The turn to market mechanisms in the public sector, and the use of public-private partnerships and the like, have effects on the construction of accountability in the policy-making process (Dingwerth, 2007; Mörth, 2008). The traditional liberal understanding of democratic accountability is challenged when e.g. close collaborative ventures between the public sector and corporate actors are enacted. It becomes difficult to assess what, specifically, accountable behaviour is. What is more, the virtue of democratic accountability turns into a problem when the authority of public and private agents is intertwined (Behn, 2001).

In the context of public-private interaction in the public domain, there thus exists a public accountability dilemma when private actors are to take on new tasks and obligations involving claims for democratic accountability. The dilemma of democratic accountability is exacerbated by the fact that corporate actors tend to be agents to another set of principals that do not by tradition place democratic accountability at the top of their list of priorities. In fact, corporate systems of accountability are still centred round the promotion and protection of economic interest (Shearer, 2002), a condition that goes contrary to establishing the primacy of democratic accountability. Thus, the tenets of agency theory constitute a yardstick for the development of management and control systems to be used internationally irrespective of local conditions (Lubatkin et al., 2005) or extant renegotiations of roles. Placing private actors in the position of agents with the task of promoting public interests is therefore likely to produce problems and friction.

Interestingly, even in seemingly boundary blurring arrangements that appear to transgress the myth of the public-private divide, corporate actors are still often presumed to follow what Gaddis (1964: 123) described as a 'nineteenth century form of corporate accountability' that is focused on economic value. Corporations tend to be associated with bringing traits like efficiency and innovativeness, and funding, into the collaboration with the public sector (Broadbent and Laughlin, 2003; Peters and Pierre, 2010). It is due to the fact that private actors are considered different, and adding to the democratic accountability dilemma, that they are deemed attractive as partners. The primacy of profit interest in systems of corporate governance further reminds us that the myth of the public-private divide keeps reasserting itself.

In summary, the fact that authority is being delegated to the corporate actors does not automatically translate into these actors turning into more democratically accountable corporate citizens. There are counter pressures from established systems and mechanisms of economic accountability, and it is not always clear how the private actors are to go about behaving democratically accountably – and in relation to what goals.

The developments in the field of security are illustrative of the on-going renegotiation of the relationship between the public and the private sectors. Drawing on the ideas of the new public domain, we use the concept of a public security domain to denote a domain where rules, actors, norms and values from both of these sectors are present and where new, trans-boundary, ones are being developed. The idea of a public domain has primarily been discussed in the field of global politics. Ruggie (2004) draws on the classic international relations theme on the importance of transnational actors and transnational relations when describing a fundamental reconstitution of the global public domain (Ruggie, 2004; Dryzek, 2000). This transformation is a function of the fact that states are becoming embedded in a broader institutionalized arena concerned with the production of global public goods. In this context, the public is not to be interpreted as equivalent to the state. Rather, what the emerging public domain reflects is what is going on in practice (e.g. Ruggie, 2004; Dryzek 1996, 2000, 2010).

We argue that that the public security domain is an emerging area of social life with its own rules, norms and organizations that cut across the public-private divide (see Marquand, 1997). In the public security domain, corporate actors are sometimes explicitly linked to the very object of security being designated as agents, sometimes they count as part of the 'empowered elite' that is engaged in setting the rules and standards. As the domain is emerging, and thus in a process of institutionalization (e.g. Bourdieu, 1996), there is as yet no established agreement on the rules of the game, the main actors, nor on what norms are to govern their relations and so on. In the following, we will use the issue of money laundering to illustrate how the problems of responsibility and democratic accountability of the corporate citizens may play out in the public security domain.

Corporate efforts and public aims in AML/CTF

In essence, money laundering concerns two aims on behalf of criminals: 'preventing "dirty money" from serving the crimes that generated it, and ensuring that the money can be used without any danger of confiscation' (Stessens, 2000: 5). More recently, as we have discussed, this crime has come to be associated with 'the war on terror', and terrorism financing. During the past decades, the regulatory activity concerned with surveilling transnational financial flows deemed potentially suspect in relation to money laundering has intensified, globally as well as on the European and national levels (Amicelle, 2012). As a part of this transformation corporate actors are increasingly enrolled in the fight against these crimes, in efforts of anti-money laundering (AML), and counter terrorism financing (CTF). The merging of AML and CTF has made the discretionary power of law enforcement significantly larger, a change that raised concerns from a legal perspective (McCulloch and Pickering, 2005). Another concern has been that the uniting of AML and CTF regulation, and efforts, create new problems, without effectively contributing to preventing crime due to inherent differences between money laundering, and the financing of terrorism (Roberge, 2007).

The regulation within the field of AML involves multiple types of organizations and authorities. The OECD Financial Action Task Force (FATF) is a major regulator that promulgates best practice (Gardner, 2007; Jakobi, 2010). Recommendations of the FATF are mirrored in EU directives (Directive 2005/60/EC) as well as in national legislation among union members (Bergström, et al., 2011). The banking sector is represented by entities like the Basel Committee on Banking Supervision (BCSB) and the International Organization of Securities Commissions (IOSCO) (see Winer 2003), and the Wolfsberg Group (Pieth, 2002). Another characteristic of the field of AML is that the 'repressive approach' of criminal law is interspersed with the 'preventative approach' of banking law (Stessens, 2000), contributing to the overall complexity of governance.

In addition, there has been a shift in the use of technologies utilized by regulators and other actors in order to counteract money laundering. A so-called 'risk-based approach' (RBA) to anti-money laundering has become dominant (e.g. Directive 2005/60/EC). Transnational AML-regulation thus follows the more general preference for risk-based regulation across various fields of society (Hood, Rothstein and Baldwin, 2001; Power, 2004). As regards the role of corporate actors within AML, this approach presupposes a more pro-active stance, as compared to a 'rule-based approach' where what is legitimate behaviour is laid out in more detail (Unger and van Waarden, 2009). The corporate actors are expected to join forces with the agencies of law enforcement against crime and terrorism.

What then, is it that the corporate citizens are to do? What are the responsibilities they take on, and to what extent are they democratically accountable? A main reason for delegating power according to liberal democratic theory is that the agents have 'that time the principal lacks' (Strom, 2000: 266) and/or certain types of skills or information not available to the principal. In the case of AML, one of the main arguments in favour of involving the corporate actors is that they have access to privileged knowledge. It is they who know their customers, it is presumed. To apply appropriate customer due-diligence, or 'Know the Customer', measures, constitutes an important part of the contemporary AML regime. The risk assessment and risk management of the client relationship is to be a continuous process (Directive 2005/60/EC). In practice, however, the corporate actors do not have all the knowledge needed to perform their citizenship duties. They may therefore have to start additional investigations to put an appropriate knowledge base together themselves, or collect information through recourse to outsourcing where specialized sub-suppliers/sub-agents are being utilized (Favarel-Garrigues, Godefroy and Lascoumes, 2008). Technological developments engender new forms of white-collar crime, and new means to launder money (cf. Mitchell et al., 1998), but such developments are also intrinsic to AML-measures. The corporate actors make use of technological devices (Demetis, 2010) so that new forms of 'dataveillance' (Clarke, 1988) can be performed on behalf of the regulators. However, it is unclear to what extent these measures are effective.

Canhoto and Backhouse (2007) argue that deniability and not efforts at crime prevention drives the level of investment in AML technology by corporate actors. In accordance with their view, Favarel-Garrigues, Godefroy and Lascoumes (2009) report that such technological devices are utilized as tools of 'defendable compliance' (Ericson, 2006; cf. Power, 1999), rather than attempts at pro-active prevention of serious crimes.

Corporate actors are further faced with the task of persuading clients that theirs is a relationship that surpasses the usual business-client one, and goes into the realm of public security. Corporate actors have to invest in technology, new personnel, education and so on. For clients, 'surveillance becomes the cost' (Haggerty and Ericson, 2006: 12) to be paid to safeguard security. One can add that for actors to engage in controversial tasks of surveillance on behalf of others is associated with high reputational risks (Martin et al., 2009). Thus, good citizenship in relation to AML is not without such risks for the corporate actors. As indicated by the findings of Favarel-Garrigues et al. (2009), the risk of sanctions from the regulator is one such risk. Another type of reputational risk is to do with customer relationships. Good client relations constitute a core aspect of many businesses, and is thus very much in the interest of private principals.

In addition, the public aims set for the corporate citizens are not that clear cut. Unger and van Waarden (2009) underline how responsibility for doing the right things in the right way is shifted over to the corporate actors, as regulation gets more imprecise (Unger and van Waarden, 2009). There is thus a transfer of responsibility for ML from public agencies to private agents (Ross and Hannan, 2007). When it comes to customer relationships, this transfer of responsibility may be further reinforced by the monitoring agencies. For the corporate actors, this also means that it is largely up to them to mediate between the demands for public security, and those of profit-interest.

In summary, the corporate actors have taken on additional responsibilities to do with the public good of security (as have their clients). The question remains, though, whether this also includes more democratic accountability on behalf of the corporate citizens. In the next section, we turn to the industry association view.

Corporate citizenship in AML/CTF: The industry association view

This section draws on an on-going cross-industry study[1] of the role of private actors as agents of the state in AML/CTF. In the following, we will focus on how the demands for more proactive citizenship in AML/CTF were encountered by the Swedish Bankers' Association, and by the Swedish Bar Association. We further reflect on some of the differences between their approaches.

The bankers' association

The Swedish Bankers' Association represents banks and financial institutions established in Sweden. The association has twenty eight member companies – financial institutions, mortgage institutions and branches of foreign banks in Sweden. Surveillance of customers for business purposes is an established part of banking, and a means in the management of customer relationships. Yet, in the case of AML, the demand placed on corporate citizens is to extend surveillance of clients in the public interest of securitization, a demand that may clash with good customer relationships. How does the association deal with this and related issues?

First, the Bankers' Association (BA) states that it 'welcomes' the Swedish government's implementation of the third EU directive on money laundering (BA, 2008-12-10: 1). The bankers' association emphasizes the importance of efficient measures against money laundering and the issues have received a lot of attention in designated internal work groups and among major members in the industry. Moreover, the General Counsel at the Swedish Bankers' Association emphasized that 'banks do want to be "good citizens" here and follow the regulation and be part of crime prevention' (Interview).

Yet, citizenship was to be kept within reasonable bounds. The association has published very few position papers on the third directive. In these, the organization aims to establish clear boundaries of responsibilities between the banking industry and public authorities. Banking is about 'doing business', not about 'being an authority' as the General Counsel at the Swedish Bankers' Association puts it (Interview). The banks do what they are asked to do, but it is important for clients to get the message that it is not the banks that have decided on the new rules. In accordance, the Bankers' Association has put a lot of effort into framing the third EU directive as a bank-client relationship issue and in explaining why the 'bank must ask questions':

> In short, the new anti-money laundering act entails that the bank must make an assessment of the risk of exploitation for money laundering. The law places high demands on the bank to have good knowledge of its customers and their bank affairs. The bank must understand the purpose of the business relationship and the customer's various transactions. (BA homepage)

By supplying information on the how and why of money laundering regulation through a specialized homepage, and by providing leaflets that can be handed out to customers, etc., the association has aimed to explain to clients what the role of the banks is, and what it is not. In this aim, the Bankers' Association would have liked more communicative efforts from the public bodies that could have emphasized and explained the division of roles to the general public (B1).

The supervisory authority, the Swedish Financial Supervisory Authority (SFSA) has not been silent, though. It issues its own recommendations and provides advice on how to follow the rules, including education. Following the general template of the risk-based approach, the banks are expected to rely on their own knowledge and judgement when assessing the appropriateness of their own measures and the possible negative impact on clients, and to take the blame if they do not manage to do so. This is also the message from the supervisory authority to the customers of banks:

> Consumers get in touch with us and describe situations that feel insulting to them or where they are questioning the practices of the bank. Considering what we hear it could be that the banks are too rigid. Certainly, it is up to the banks to decide how to implement the regulation in practice based on the risk of money laundering, but their measures must be proportionate to the risk the banks have identified. (Unit Manager at the SFSA quoted in the journal *Privata Affärer*, 2009)

It can be further noted that the bankers' association follows the general European and international trend in the banking sector on how to handle the new requirements, that is, to set up new routines in order to prevent money laundering. In a joint initiative in 2005 by the BCBS (Basel Committee on Banking Supervision), IAIS (International Association of Insurance Supervisors) and IOSCO (International Organization of Securities Commissions it is stated that banks must 'develop policies and procedures in key areas such as customer acceptance, customer identification, on-going monitoring of high-risk accounts and risk management' (The Joint Forum, 2005: 1). The very risk of being investigated is detrimental for the business and constitutes an important incentive for taking on the more challenging demands proposed (B1).

The bar association

The Swedish Bar Association is an association under private law. It performs some public administrative functions such as the requirements for Bar membership and disciplinary measures for the profession. In non-banking professionalized industries, the question of what it means to be a good corporate citizen is likely to be even more complex due to strict notions of client confidentiality. One may ask how law firms can handle the tension between being a good corporate citizen and helping their clients. Or can the fact that one is being loyal to clients be considered a way of being a good corporate citizen?

The importance of independence and client confidentiality constitutes the very core of the professional code according to the Bar Association (Code of professional Conduct, the Bar Association Homepage). Furthermore, the bar association emphasizes its important role in a democratic society:

> An emancipated and independent legal bar acting in line with an ethical framework outlined by an independent bar association constitutes an important part of a democratic society governed by law and is a prerequisite for the affirmation of individual constitutional rights. (Code of Professional Conduct, p. 5)

The representative of the Bar Association emphasized that role of lawyers is unique in a democratic society (L1). The basic position of the Swedish Bar Associations and the European Bar association, CCBE (Conseil des Barreaux de l'Union Europeenne/The Council of Bars and Law Societies of Europe), is that the EU directives on AML ought not to apply to lawyers due their duties to clients:

> A lawyer must serve the interests of justice as well as those whose rights and liberties he or she is trusted to assert and defend and it is the lawyer's duty not only to plead the client's cause but to be the client's adviser. Respect for the lawyers' professional function is an essential condition for the rule of law and democracy in society. (Code of Conduct for European Lawyers, p. 5)

The Swedish Bar Association monitors that members follow the professional code and can in cases of non-compliance issue sanctions. Interestingly, the SBA has increased its supervisory role because of the third Directive (L1). The bar association issued a binding recommendation concerning AML/CTF to its associates before this was done by the Swedish Financial Supervisory Authority (ibid.). The bar has further been very active in following up how the thirty-five of the largest law firms in Sweden follow the legislation (ibid.). It is also part of a national body consisting of various state agencies that evaluates the implementation of the Swedish law (ibid.).

From the perspective of the Swedish Bar Association, the main criticism of FATF's recommendations concern how, and to what extent, the lawyer should make a risk-assessment of the client, for instance, the obligation to identify the client in a risk-based manner. CCBE argues that the regulations could jeopardize the confidential lawyer-client relationship.

'Providing authorities with the competence to access information on an identity from, amongst others, lawyers would clearly interfere with its principle of legal professional privilege and professional secrecy and should therefore be firmly rejected' (CCBE, June 2011, Para. 7). CCBE argues that the importance of a confidential relationship between a lawyer and his client is supported by The European Court of Human Rights and the Luxembourg Court of Justice:

> Therefore, lawyers should at any rate be fully exempt from any obligation to provide information to competent authorities. General principles of the right of access to law, access to justice and human right of privacy would otherwise unjustifiably be infringed. (CCBE, June 2011, Para. 7)

The Swedish Bar Association has been very active towards the Swedish government and parliament in order to influence the Swedish implementation of the EU Directive. The lobbying seems to be rather successful in contrast to the implementation of the Directive in the UK, France and Benelux countries (L1). The Swedish government has been more respectful towards the core values of the lawyers than in other European countries (L1). Still, the Swedish Bar Association argues that the Directive and the national legislation are not compatible with the practice of lawyers. The Directive has a focus on money transactions, rather than on durable client relations in a democratic society. One case in point is how the efficiency of the Directive is measured by the number of reports on suspicious money laundering to the police. Lawyers do not have casual encounters with client as banks and foreign exchange offices do (L1).

Pragmatic citizenship or a quest to uphold the public-private divide

In relation to the new demands for extended responsibility and proactivity in relation to crime and terrorism prevention, as expressed in recent regulation on AML/CTF, the position of the Swedish Bankers' Association could be labelled pragmatic, if not pro-active. The Bankers' Association deemed it possible for banks to be good citizens by complying with AML legislation. Indeed, the representative of the Bankers' Association conceptualized the issue as a question of citizenship. Taking on extended responsibility in the public domain is costly, and could cause irritation in relation to customers, but it is a duty. There is also a business side to the equation. For the banks, AML regulation is considered an additional means to manage reputational risk. Thus, in addition to the increased reputational risks associated with devolved authority (Martin et al., 2009), there exists a possibility of decreasing reputational risk through new devices for client control.

The lawyers have a very different take on the citizenship demands placed on them. The Swedish Bar Association, and its European counterpart, does not want to be good citizens in the sense that they should take on a public role and co-operate with the law enforcement agencies. Instead, it is strongly argued that lawyers should be loyal to their clients and that client confidentiality is the cornerstone in upholding the rule of law in democratic societies. By defending the public and private divide the lawyers could be regarded as good corporate citizens. To quote Logsdon and Wood:

> Yes, a company can be viewed as a corporate citizen, an entity distinguishable from the humans who own and work in it, with rights and duties necessary to maintain its role in preserving community identity and boundaries. (Logsdon and Wood, 2008: 161)

The lawyers defend their rights and duties as lawyers, an important professional identity in every democratic society, by preserving the boundaries between the public and private.

Conclusions and concluding remarks

Notions of corporate citizenship challenge the traditional boundary between public and private. In this chapter, we have discussed how the requirement to engage in the quest against money laundering and terrorism financing imposes a proposed extension of accountability of corporate actors by adding another 'to whom', and the object of public security. The private actors across industries are increasingly pressured to co-operate with the law enforcement agencies. In doing this, they have to set up new routines and procedures in order to trace any illicit financial transaction. They are expected to make decisions that could have major implications for individuals and their rights in democratic societies. We argue, however, that it is difficult to make the corporate actors democratically accountable for the decisions they make.

We argue that the notion of extended corporate responsibility is easier to identify than that of corporate (democratic) accountability. Responsibility is widened to include issues of public security, but in the everyday corporate actors remain economically accountable to their private principals. The practices of the public security domain are not reflected in how we organize democracy and democratic accountability. Democratic accountability is based on the premise of hierarchy, or what liberal democratic theorists call the chain of command and control. In AML, it is up to law enforcement agencies and other public actors to monitor and follow up whether the corporate citizens are fulfilling their duties or not. Still, there are no direct democratic implications of cases of non-compliance. The private sector is not part of the liberal understanding of this chain of command and control. The principal–agent relationship is between the constituency and the elected politicians. Corporate actors are not elected by the people and have no seat in the legislative bodies (though large firms may have significant parts of the public as shareholders). By contrast, in relation to clients, and other business associates, non-compliance likely results in bad-will, as it is negative for the reputations of banks and law firms to be named and shamed by the regulator. Similarly, for shareholders or other incarnations of the private principals, in cases of non-compliance there may be economic repercussions.

Finally, we have shown that when corporate actors, like banks, are taken on to safeguard the common good of public security, their clients are simultaneously expected to accept additional levels of control and information provision in their dealings with these actors. In short, when demands for corporate citizenship are raised and corporations aim to comply, this affects the citizenship of individuals as well in that their duties may be extended. When corporations turn into citizens, so may their clients. We would therefore like to like conclude with a call for further analyses of the co-construction of corporate – and individual citizens.

Notes

1. We wish to thank the Ragnar Söderberg Foundation (Grant E8/10) for the funding of this research project.

References

Amicelle, A. 2012. 'Trace my money if you can: European security management of financial flows' in: K. Svedberg Helgesson and U. Mörth (Eds), *Securitization, accountability and risk management. Transforming the public security domain*, pp. 110–131, London: Routledge.

Amoore, L. and de Goede, M. (Eds) 2008. *Risk and the war on terror*, London: Routledge.

Avant, D. 2005. *The market for force*, Cambridge: Cambridge University Press.

BA 2008-12-10. *Framställning. Genomförande av tredje penningtvättsdirektivet* (prop 2008/09:70), Stockholm: Svenska bankföreningen.

Baier, V.E., March, J.G. and Saetren, H. 1986. 'Implementation and ambiguity', *Scandinavian Journal of Management Studies*, 2: 150–164.

Bailes, A. and Frommelt, I. (Eds) 2004. *Business and security. Sector relationships in a new security environment*, Oxford: SIPRI/Oxford University Press.

Balzacq, T. (Ed.) 2011. *Securitization theory. How security problems emerge and dissolve*, London: Routledge.

Behn, R. 2001. *Rethinking democratic accountability*, Washington, DC: The Brookings Institution.

Bergström, M., Helgesson, K. Svedberg and Mörth, U. 2011. 'A new role for-profit actors? The case of anti-money laundering and risk management', *Journal of Common Market Studies*, 49: 1043–1064.

Bourdieu, P. 1996. *The rules of art. Genesis of structure of the literature field*, Cambridge: Cambridge University Press.

Bovens, M. 2006. *Analysing and assessing public accountability: A conceptual framework*, European Governance Papers. 2006; EUROGOV, ISSN 1813-6826 (http://www.connex-network.org/eurogov) (accessed September 1, 2011).

Braithwaite, J. and Drahos, P. 2000. *Global business regulation*, Cambridge: Cambridge University Press.

Broadbent, J. and Laughlin, R. 2003. 'Public private partnerships: An introduction', *Accounting, Auditing and Accountability Journal*, 16: 332–341.

Buzan, B. and Hansen, L. (2009). *The evolution of international security studies*, Cambridge: Cambridge University Press.

Canhoto, A.I. and Backhouse, J. 2007. 'Profiling under conditions of ambiguity: An application in the financial services industry', *Journal of Retailing and Consumer Services*, 14: 408–419.

Clarke, R. 1988. 'Information technology and dataveillance', *Communications of the ACM*, 31: 498–512.

Demetis, D.S. 2010. *Technology and anti-money laundering. A systems theory and risk-based approach*, Cheltenham: Edward Elgar.

Dingwerth, K. 2007. *The new transnationalism. Transnational governance and democratic legitimacy*, Basingstoke: Palgrave Macmillan.

Directive 2005/60/EC of the European Parliament and of the Council of 26 October 2005 on the prevention of the use of the financial system for the purpose of money laundering and terrorism financing, http://eur-lex.europa.eu/LexUriServ/LexUriServ.do?uri=CELEX:32005L0060:EN:NOT.

Dryzek, J.S. 1996. *Democracy in capitalist times. Ideals, limits and struggles*, New York: Oxford University Press.

Dryzek, J.S. 2000. *Deliberative democracy and beyond. Liberals, critics, contestations*, Oxford: Oxford University Press.

Dryzek, J.S. 2010. *Foundations and frontiers of deliberative governance*, Oxford: Oxford University Press.

Ericson, R.V. 2006. 'Ten uncertainties of risk-management approaches to security', *Revue canadienne de criminologie et de justice pénale*, 48: 345–359.

Favarel-Garrigues G., Godefroy, T. and Lascoumes, P. 2008. 'Sentinels in the banking industry: Private actors and the fight against money laundering in France', *British Journal of Criminology*, 48: 1–19.

Favarel-Garrigues G., Godefroy, T. and Lascoumes, P. 2009. *Les sentinelles de l'argent sale au quotidien. Les Banques aux prises avec l'antiblanchiment*, Paris: La Découverte.

Gaddis, P.O. 1964. *Corporate accountability: For what and to whom must the manager answer?* New York: Harper & Row.

Gardner, K.L. 2007. 'Fighting terrorism the FATF way', *Global Governance*, 13: 325–345.

Haggerty, K.D. and Ericson, R.V. 2006. 'The new politics of surveillance and visibility,' in: K.D. Haggerty and R.V. Ericson (Eds), *The new politics of surveillance and visibility*, pp. 3–25. Toronto: University of Toronto Press.

Hall, R.B. and Biersteker, T.J. (Eds) 2002. *The emergence of private authority in global governance*, Cambridge: Cambridge University Press.

Helgesson, K. S. 2012. 'The multiple positions of private actors in securitization', in: K. Svedberg Helgesson and U. Mörth (Eds), *Securitization, accountability and risk management. Transforming the public security domain*, pp. 132–145. London: Routledge.

Helgesson, K. S. and U. Mörth (Eds) 2012. *Securitization, Accountability and Risk Management. Transforming the public security domain*, London: Routledge.

Hodges, G. (2011). *The 'War on Terror' Narrative. Discourse and Intertextuality in the Construction and Contestation of Sociopolitical Reality*, Oxford: Oxford University Press.

Hood, C., Rothstein, H. and Baldwin, R. 2001. *The government of risk. Understanding risk regulation regimes*, Oxford: Oxford University Press.

Jakobi, A.P. 2010. 'OECD Activities against money laundering and corruption', in: K. Martens and A.P. Jakobi (Eds), *Mechanisms of OECD governance. International incentives for national policy-making?* Oxford: Oxford University Press.

Larner, W. and Walters, W. 2006. *Global governmentality. Governing international spaces*, London/New York: Routledge.

Lipschutz, R.D. 2005. *Globalization, governmentality and global politics. Regulation for the rest of us?* London/New York: Routledge.

Logsdon, J.M. and Wood, D.J. 2008. 'Business citizenship: From domestic to global levels of analysis', *Business Ethics Quarterly*, 12, 2: 155–187.

Lubatkin, M.H., Lane, P.J., Collin, S.O. and Very, P. 2005. 'Origins of corporate governance in the USA, Sweden and France', *Organization Studies*, 26: 867–888.

Marquand, D. 1997. *The new reckoning? Capitalism, citizens and states*, London: Polity Press.

Martin A.L., van Brakel, R. and Bernhard, D.J. 2009. 'Understanding resistance to digital surveillance: Towards a multi-disciplinary, multi-actor framework', *Surveillance and Society*, 2009: 213–232.

McCulloch, J. and Pickering, S. 2005. 'Suppressing the financing of terrorism: Proliferating state crime, eroding censure and extending neo-colonialism', *British Journal of Criminology*, 45: 470–486.

Miller, P. (Ed.) 1991. *The Foucault effect. Studies in governmentality*, Chicago, IL: University of Chicago Press.

Mitchell, A., Sikka, P. and Willmott, H. 1998. 'Sweeping it under the carpet: The role of accountancy firms in money-laundering', *Accounting, Organizations and Society*, 23: 589–607.

Mitsilegas, V. 2003. *Money laundering counter-measures in the European Union. A new paradigm of security governance versus fundamental legal principles*, The Hague, London, New York: Kluwer Law International.

Moon, J., Crane, A. and Matten, D. 2005. 'Can corporations be citizens? Corporate citizenship as a metaphor for business participation in society', *Business Ethics Quarterly*, 15, 3: 429–453.

Mörth, U. (Ed.). 2004. *Soft law in governance and regulation. An interdisciplinary analysis*, Cheltenham: Edward Elgar.

Mörth, U. 2008. *European public-private collaboration. A choice between efficiency and democratic accountability?* Cheltenham: Edward Elgar.

Peters, J.G., and Pierre, J. 2010. 'Public-private partnerships and the democratic deficit. Is performance based legitimacy the answer?' in: M. Bexell and U. Mörth (Eds), *Democracy and public-private partnerships in global governance*, pp. 41–54. London: Palgrave.

Pieth, M. (Ed.) 2002. *Financing terrorism*, Dordrecht: Kluwer Academic Publishers.

Privata Affärer (2009). 'Klaga på övernitiska banker' ('Complain at over zealous banks'), 2009-08-26.

Power, M. 1999. *The audit society. Rituals of verification*, Oxford: Oxford University Press.

Power, M. 2004. *The risk management of everything*, London: Demos.

Power, M. 2012a. 'The managerialization of security', in: K. Svedberg Helgesson and U. Mörth (Eds), *Securitization, accountability and risk management. Transforming the public security domain*, pp. 70–87. London: Routledge.

Power, M. 2012b. 'The apparatus of fraud risk', *Accounting, organizations and society*, http://dx.doi.org/10.1016/j.aos.2012.07.004.

Roberge, I. 2007. 'Misguided policies in the war on terror? The case for disentangling terrorist financing from money laundering', *Politics*, 27: 196–203.

Romzek, B.S. and Dubnick, M.J. 1998. 'Accountability', in Jay Shafritz (Ed.), *International encyclopedia of public policy and administration*, Boulder, CA: Westview Press.

Ross, S. and Hanna, M. 2007. 'Money laundering and risk-based decision-making', *Journal of Money Laundering Control*, 10: 106–115.

Ruggie, J.G. 2004. 'Reconstituting the global public domain: Issues, actors and practices', *European Journal of International Relations*, 10: 499–531.

Seyad, S.M. 2012. 'The EU anti-money laundering legal regime', in: Helgesson Svedberg, K and Ulrika Mörth (Eds), *Securitization, accountability and risk Management. Transforming the public security domain*, pp. 34–55, London: Routledge.

Shearer, T. 2002. 'Ethics and accountability: From the for-itself to the for-the-other', *Accounting, Organizations and Society*, 27: 541–573.

Singer, P. 2003. *Corporate warriors*, Ithaca, New York: Cornell University Press.

Stessens, G. 2000. *Money laundering. A new international enforcement model*, Cambridge: Cambridge University Press.

Strom, K. 2000. 'Delegation and accountability in parliamentary democracies', *European Journal of Political Research*, 37: 261–289.

Strom, K., Muller, W.C. and Bergman, T. (Eds) 2003. *Delegation and accountability in parliamentary democracies*, Oxford: Oxford University Press.

The Joint Forum, 2005. www.bis.ag/bcbs/jointforum.htm (accessed November 2012).

Unger, B. and van Waarden, F. 2009. 'How to dodge drowning in data: Rule- and risk-based anti money laundering policies compared', *Review of Law and Economics*, 5: 953–985.

Winer, J. 2003. 'Globalization, terrorist finance, and global conflict. Time for a white list?' in: Pieth, M. (Ed.), *Financing terrorism*, New York: Kluwer Academic Publishers.

Woodward, D., Edwards, P. and Birkin, F. 2001. 'Some evidence on executives' views of corporate social responsibility', *British Accounting Review*, 33: 357–397.

10
Conclusions: The Political Role of Corporations

Karin Svedberg Helgesson and Ulrika Mörth

Introduction

This volume has addressed the complex and classic questions on the roles of states and markets by analysing how this long-standing debate is manifested in corporate citizenship. Drawing on a range of disciplines, including political science, organization and management, sociology, and accounting, the authors in this volume make use of the notion of corporate citizenship as a device for delineating and analysing the political role of the corporation in the public domain.

In Chapter 1, we delineated the concept of citizenship in terms of duties and rights, identity and participation. One starting point for our analysis was that these conceptions could serve as a point of reference when placing corporations in the position of citizens. These traits and associated values are mirrored in the individual chapters, but our co-authors also raise new questions. Another starting point for our discussion was that the friction and resistance the concept of corporate citizenship may encounter is particularly useful if one wants to understand the political role of corporations. This friction and resistance has come to the fore in several of the preceding chapters, providing a richer, but also ambiguous, view of what corporate citizenship is, and in turn, of what constitutes the political role of corporations.

In this concluding chapter we first provide a summary of the conclusions from our co-authors on what corporate citizenship is about; what metaphors, concepts and values have been brought to the fore in the volume. We offer examples of how these depictions of corporate citizenship are manifested in social practice. We then turn to question on the role of the corporations in the public domain and discuss a set of implications for the political role of the corporation based on our analyses of corporate citizenship. This leads us to ponder whether a political theory on corporations is the solution – or whether the quest for such a theory is in fact an impasse.

The language of corporate citizenship

The most salient connotations of corporate citizenship in our chapters are issues of power, legitimacy, private government, accountability, moral actorhood, identity, duties, responsibility, participation, and social equality. At the same time, the concept of corporate citizenship remains somewhat elusive. In this regard, corporate citizenship is a metaphor in search of a language (Panozzo, this volume). Our chapters also show that corporate citizenship is linked to a more traditional language of business, such as market design, user choice, contracting, and private exit. Moreover, some authors are critical of extending the concept of citizenship to corporations.

The projections on various values on corporations are evident in several of the chapters. They are explicitly linked to a whole range of political, democratic and social values and norms. Like other citizens, corporations are portrayed as political and social agents and thus cannot be reduced to being pure economic entities. On the contrary, they are described as entities that act across the border of the public-private divide. First, the 'citoyen' plays a social role in the public sphere (Holzer, this volume). The expectations on corporations depend on what aspects of the company's publicness are highlighted (Holzer, this volume). As the public sphere in which the corporation is present widens, the corporation may be regarded as a public institution similar to governments. Corporations are driven into moral actorhood by societal expectations and activism, but this citizenship is not necessarily an expression of business ethics. Rather, corporations may be turned into citizens 'inadvertently' through others defining them as citizens (Holzer, this volume). This view of the transformation of the identity of the corporation is thus quite in line with the argument that citizens 'should seek to apply to it [the corporation] modes of accountability and responsibility similar to those they apply to the public government' (Vogel, 1975: 17).

For what are corporations to be accountable, and do they always know to whom they ought to be accountable, and what community to prioritize? These issues are raised in Cholez and Trompette's (this volume) analysis of how Bottom of the Pyramid (BoP) markets emerge in developing countries. The two cases from Madagascar illustrate how private investment, by multinational companies, is confronted with the task to design markets that can accelerate poverty reduction. At first, the very concept of BoP markets was only conceived as a business strategy without any political concerns. Gradually, however, the two projects became more political and transformed into corporate citizenship objects (Cholez and Trompette, this volume). In the presence of no or weak public authorities the social and democratic accountability mechanisms were projected on the corporation. The citizenship projects had to develop accountability mechanisms to live up to these expectations that were not fulfilled by the public actors. Thus, the language of corporate citizenship gets really interesting when the corporation is expected to step in as a private government.

Still, the very idea of associating citizenship with corporations, not least in terms of private government, can be considered quite problematic (Gerencser, this volume). Gerencser argues that corporations fit easily into 'neither the position of the protected citizen, nor themselves being humans with fundamental dignity to be respected, nor the role of rights' securer and enforcer, lacking the traditional foundations of authority and legitimacy that sovereign governments can claim' (Gerencser, this volume). Indeed, corporations are not part of the Universal Declaration of Human Rights (UDHR) established in 1948. They are not bearers of rights. Corporations are instead powerful agents and should therefore take responsibility to act in certain ways towards citizens and governments (Gerencser, this volume). The Global Compact initiative established that corporations were committed to aligning their operations and strategies with universally accepted principles, but these principles did not equate corporations with citizens or governments (Gerencser, this volume). Instead, Gerencser argues that the adoption of a language of citizenship could empower corporations against individuals and even against states because the corporations lack the legitimacy of being either governments or individual citizens. He suggests that a more relevant conceptual framework to analyse corporations in societies that focuses on the power asymmetry between the corporation and its stakeholders is therefore to conceptualize the corporation as the patron with the various clients.

However, this conceptualization could also be (mis)used by the corporations to shift development responsibility to the government and local authorities.

To be sure, as discussed above, the concept and metaphor of corporate citizenship activates questions on to whom and for what corporations are accountable in relation to relevant communities. The recent wave of making corporations more relevant to politics seems to have begun already with the introduction of the concept of stakeholder (Panozzo, this volume). 'The invention of the stakeholder responds to the fundamental discursive precondition of having somebody with whom to exchange narratives and, ultimately, accountabilities' (Panozzo, this volume). With the introduction of corporate social responsibility (CSR), social audit and other social accountability mechanisms, the language of business is redefined. Accountability is not only about being accountable to shareholders but to a larger and amorphous 'public'. Indeed, the concept of accountability as part of the language of corporate citizenship is affected by the practices that are imported from other domains of management and financial accounting (Panozzo, this volume). It is further affected by the intermingling of practices and technologies of risk management, from the business sphere, and with practices and technologies of securitization and crime prevention, from the public sphere (Helgesson and Mörth, this volume). One may further ask, as Helgesson and Mörth (this volume) do, whether being turned into a more responsible corporate citizen really equals being accountable as well.

Another set of issues is to do with how corporations serve as devices and arenas in processes of identity construction. Helgesson and Mörth (this volume) touch upon this issue in their discussion of how clients of banks and law firms are being made to accept the citizenship duty of being scrutinized by the banks and law firms in order to safeguard the common good of public security. This illustrates that not only may the 'persona' of corporate citizen be acquired as a new identity for corporations, as discussed by Burchell and Cook (2006), but corporations are also affecting the identities of individual citizens. When corporations take on more responsibilities for 'the other', this extension of responsibility may spill over to individual citizens.

It follows that when the identity of the corporation changes, the citizen identity of its consumers may change as well. On this note, Crane et al. argue that 'the significance of economics for identity politics is that it challenges the assumption that political struggle can be understood mainly in terms of solidarity and public interests since private interests and commercialisms are inherent to market interactions' (Crane et al., this volume). Corporations have multiple identities themselves and can therefore reflect 'a range of alternative, sub-national, or minority identities based on race, religion, gender, sexual orientation, or other forms of social identity' (Crane et al., this volume). In this way, they may contribute to the forming of new citizenship identities (and inhibit others). In summary, the language of corporate citizenship underscores how corporations are not self-contained economic actors but that they are political in the sense that they take an active part in minority-rights politics and other political issues. The corporation is a political agent rather than an agent of politics.

Relating to this topic, Idemudia (this volume) further shows that the political role of corporations as agents of minority rights may be a required one by communities in developing countries. The transnational oil company in Idemudia's study (this volume) was expected to take on social and political issues, especially when local authorities were weak, that is to help with 'problem solving' in society (cf. Bexell and Mörth, 2010). The villages that were geographically close to the oil corporation's activity, and that had a long relationship with the company, saw oil TNCs as part of the host community. The secretary of the Inua Eyet Ikot village council even argued that 'Oil TNCs operate, and their staff live, in our communities. As part of our communities, we are not supposed to tell them what to do. Our problems should automatically be a priority for them' (Idemudia, this volume). Being present in the community, the oil company was thus considered to have duties towards that community, and was expected to participate in various development projects. The communities in the Niger Delta further argued that the corporation ought to be a good neighbour. As Idemudia shows, the corporate citizenship initiatives were are seen as the result of responses to, legitimate, community pressures, by the communities.

This further meant that the oil companies could not play the 'CC card', in the way that they might be expected to when they tackle social and infrastructural problems. The case of the Niger Delta shows that the language of CC is, not surprisingly of course, about power, but not necessarily about the relationship between the stereotype – the powerless poor community and the mighty oil company. Instead, Idemudia describes how the power asymmetry between the corporation and the communities seems to have generated a community strategy to become less powerless. The community members used different concepts to illustrate the duties and expectations of companies to participate and take responsibility for the communities. The relationship was described as that between the landlord (the community) and the oil TNCs as their squatters (Idemudia, this volume). 'They see crude oil being prospected by oil TNCs, and the land upon which oil TNCs' infrastructures are located as their property. Hence, the oil TNCs are their squatters and like all other squatters, oil TNCs would eventually leave if they no longer derived utility from the leased property' (Idemudia, this volume). The categorization of landlord and squatter is interesting because it does not give the corporation full citizenship in terms of rights and identity. Instead, it is the duties and societal participation that are emphasized.

In concluding this section on the language of corporate citizenship, one may further add that ideas on corporate citizenship cannot be understood unless we understand the changes of the metaphors and concepts in the traditional political sphere. This volume focuses on the language and social practices of businesses but that is of course only half of the story if we want to get a more comprehensive explanation and understanding of why corporations are expected to and need to take on societal responsibilities. The transformation of the state has created concepts as user choice, contracting and private exits. They are all part of the New Public Management trend that was introduced in Sweden and in many other welfare states during the 1990s. Just as publicization of the corporation has created political, democratic and social metaphors and concepts; the marketization of the public has resulted in a market-oriented language of the welfare sector. Blomqvist (this volume) shows how citizens are turned into consumers and users of various public services. The concept of social citizenship, which has been important in the Nordic political setting, is partly replaced by a more libertarian view of citizenship. It is against the major political, economic and social changes of the transformed state, the increasing globalized economy, and the emerging of a global civil society, that the very metaphor and concept of corporate citizenship emerges and becomes part of how we talk about the political role of corporations. This is not a new issue but its 'stickiness' is certainly due to these radical changes during the last twenty years.

The business of citizenship

In the following section, we will turn to the manifestations of corporate citizenship in social practice. Panozzo (this volume) explores the interconnection between how corporate citizenship is defined, operationalized and practised. In so doing, he emphasizes the importance of 'the calculative infrastructure' for the articulation of corporate citizenship. Three tools that are part of such an infrastructure serve to emphasize this point: the triple bottom line, the balanced scorecards, and standards for social and environmental accountability. Panozzo (this volume) discusses how the tools of the triple bottom line and the balanced score card 'create a symbolic and operational connection with both long established and more innovative tools of accounting' while the standards aiming to cover social and environmental issues 'evoke the possibility of conducting audits similar to those performed on financial statements'. The result is something of an illusion of a proper accountable corporate citizen, an entity where different and even conflicting qualities and practices are made commensurable through the common metric(s) supplied by the tools. This, in turn, indicates that the quest for corporate citizenship feeds the expansion of the 'audit society' (Power, 1994, 1999).

Adding further complexity to the highly technical accountability mechanisms Panozzo (this volume) analyses, several other chapters show that many demands that corporations face are quite difficult to cut into clear measurements. Here, commensuration is not achieved. It is not even clear to whom the corporation should be accountable. The demands may come from the local communities, governments or from NGOs in global society. One example of conflicting demands comes to the fore in Holzer's analysis (this volume). He recounts how Phil Watts of Shell observed that 'All multinational companies operate in front of a hugely diverse worldwide audience' (Holzer, this volume). It is often the case that the ethical, social and economic priorities are in conflict, and may be irreconcilable (Holzer, this volume). Another point is the case of AML/CTF, where demands for crime and terrorism prevention are to be balanced with the demands of business, and the integrity of clients (Helgesson and Mörth, this volume).

The complex relationship and interaction between corporate citizens and other actors in the public domain is perhaps best illustrated by the case of BoP markets in Madagascar (Cholez and Trompette, this volume). Schneider Electric faced various political concerns that were expressed in the multiple demands for reconciling different and opposing values. These included safeguarding responsibility whilst enabling mass consumption, being in line with ecological norms whilst promoting low-cost criteria, and working towards sustainable development whilst aiming to reduce poverty (Cholez and Trompette, this volume). The company explored two strategies – 'the first based on electrification through the setting up of small decentralized electricity power stations in rural villages functioning on the basis of renewable energy. The second follows a parallel but less visible market, involving the provision of diesel generator of batteries' (page 2). These strategies were related to different forms of corporate citizenship. They also tell of the interrelationship of corporate citizenship and individual citizenship. The example of the second-hand car battery market as a source of electricity was reliable for the customer, because it escaped public control and attempts to engineer the use of electricity for activities like studying rather than watching TV, which were intrinsic to the power station alternative. What strategy the company chose thus affected the possibilities, and restrictions, of electricity consumption. In fact, one might say that in relation to the car-battery alternative, electrification attempts could be seen as part of attempts to 'faire laissez-faire' (Cochoy, 2007), of creating a free choice market second-hand car battery for the consumer. Here, practices of corporate citizenship enacted the villagers as customers. In the case of the electricity power stations, villagers were to be consumers of electricity, but they were also to be good citizens who used electricity responsibly and agreed to submit to a larger degree of control.

Idemudia (this volume) shows how the extent to which corporations take on citizenship duties, such as solving certain problems in the community, may affect the willingness of the government in a developing country to withdraw from its responsibility. He also discusses how there could be a complimentary relationship between corporations, as governments, and local authorities (Idemudia, this volume). What is salient in his empirical study is how the community members, including ordinary people and senior local officials, argue that there is a need for both local authorities/governments and companies to tackle socio-economic and infrastructural problems. Furthermore, a majority of the respondents in the study claim that the oil companies have more responsibility for community development than the government in cases of weak or failed governmental efforts (Idemudia, this volume). The corporation, on the other hand, contests that responsibility. Indeed, corporate citizenship is a 'domain of political contestation, manifested in the buck-passing policies pursued by government and oil TNCs', Idemudia concludes (this volume).

Idemudia's (this volume) study further shows that most respondents in the four survey villages shared the expectation that the corporation should be active in human development, defined in terms of capacity building and poverty reduction. The corporation was also expected to meet regularly with the communities. There was an implicit psychological contract between the communities and the corporation, rather than an explicit social contract. The expectation and pressure on the corporations from the community members were not always successful. It even sometimes could result in no help from both the company and the government (Idemudia, this volume). One case in point is how the Nigerian government insisted that Exxon Mobil should provide electricity not only in one village but also in another which resulted in the company withdrawing provision of electricity altogether.

In addition, corporate citizens may be likened to governments in that they may be a positive force in alleviating social inequality. Crane, Matten and Moon (this volume) discuss how corporations could play an enhancing role for alleviating social inequality. The authors discuss how corporations can enable marginalized social identities to acquire or develop their citizenship. One way of doing this is to offer jobs to non-citizen immigrant or migrant workers and thus provide them with a status that could give them entitlements of citizenship (Crane et al., this volume). However, they go on to show that there is a darker side to the involvement of corporations in citizenship matters in that corporations may restrain or inhibit citizen identity. There are several ways for corporations to do this such as refusing to employ homosexuals or people with strong religious beliefs; failing to represent the company with groups from the society at large, or supplying products and services to repressive regimes that suppress particular citizenship identities (Crane et al., this volume).

Moreover, corporations may reflect citizen identity by branding or targeting specific market segments. The emergence of 'the pink economy' is an illustration of how corporations may reflect the gay market. The vodka brand Absolut has, for instance, experienced remarkable loyalty from the gay community in the United States 'because of their persistent willingness to advertise in gay media and appeal to gay consumers' (Crane et al., this volume). Furthermore, corporations can employ people that come from a certain group in society, and that have a minority citizenship identity. The corporations can also reflect identities through associations with a founder or owner. One case in point is how IKEA actively promotes itself as a Swedish company (Crane et al., this volume). However, many companies have increasingly severed their connection with a national identity in order to be able to reflect multiple identities. Furthermore, corporate reflections of citizenship identities are not stable. They may change rather quickly due to corporate acquisitions and other changes of market segments.

The complexity of the publicization of corporations and what this might entail for societies in the Global North is illustrated by Blomqvist and her chapter on the privatization of various parts of the Swedish welfare system. She argues that there are developments underway that could pose a threat to the social equality. The Swedish school system has become more stratified in the last twenty years and the differences in performance between schools have increased. The choice reform 'has led to an undermining of the universal character of social citizenship rights in Sweden in the sense that the educational background and ethnic origin of the parents seem to play a larger role the before in determining the quality of education received by their child' (Blomqvist, this volume).

The political role of corporate citizens

As others have observed before us, corporate citizenship is used by students of business firms as a way of understanding their good or bad deeds (Andriof and Waddock, 2002), as well as by corporations as a way of describing good deeds on their web sites and in their annual reports (Néron and Norman, 2008). Throughout this volume, we have discussed how corporate citizenship is used by communities and citizens affected by actors taking on the role of corporate citizens as we have discussed in the previous chapters and sections. A general observation from the chapters in this volume is that corporate citizenship is a theoretical concept, as well as a language or metaphor that is used to depict and construct empirical phenomena. There is a performative side to corporate citizenship that goes beyond the 'as if' of Moon et al. (2005), but also a feedback loop from practice to theory. In this sense, the concept of corporate citizenship is similar to many other concepts in its ability to evolve and travel between practice and theory (Giddens, 1990).

Returning to our basic conceptualization of corporate citizenship as having to do with rights, duties, identity and participation the following summary conclusions can be drawn. First that the notion of corporate citizenship, as a language, and as it is practised, not surprisingly, has little to do with rights. What is emphasized are rather the responsibilities of the corporate citizens. They have duties and they are expected to participate in the community. But what community, and what duties is a debatable question. For one, our chapters show that the 'proper' community is not easily identified. Is it to be the local community where the company is active, the national, and/or the transnational – and who is to determine which community is the appropriate one? Furthermore, our chapters show that even when one does know which community/-ies to take into consideration, it is not easy to know for what and to whom the corporation is accountable. The analysis of Cholez and Trompette (this volume) further illustrates that the 'moral free space' (Donaldson and Dunfee, 1999) where one can make decisions in between local norms and hyper norms is likely to be rather restricted.

Another factor is that that the corporations are selective in what social and economic projects they engage in. Their duties are subject to change. Thus, the private government of the corporation is selective in what social and economic projects it engages in and the companies are often not very stable or reliant community participants. However, in contrast to the cases of Nigeria and Madagascar, most welfare states have chosen to continue to finance the welfare services and retain regulatory control over them. The corporations are unreliable community authorities and the fall-back position in cases of market failure is the state, even though the state is weak and has weak democratic legitimacy. However, the fact remains that corporations may leave communities, but states cannot. Dahl's argument that the corporation should be regarded as a political system (Introduction, this volume) is therefore somewhat misleading. Corporations are complex organizations and they have the power to change people's lives, but they do not have the democratic authority to act as states do.

Another interpretation of when corporations choose to leave a community is that they do that in their role as 'as if' individual citizens who participate in the community. The normative implications of this type of exit are less dramatic than if they leave as governments. Individual citizens may move and reside in another country. This right cannot be denied to corporations. The corporations may take an active part in the development of the community but they may also leave as other citizens do.

In relation to duties, Gerencser further formulates a crucial question and dilemma on how an extended role of corporations as governors can be legitimate. 'On what basis do corporations claim legitimacy for acting with governing authority'? (Gerencser, this volume).

The legitimacy of private governors

In this volume, two sources of legitimacy for corporations to take on the role of private government come to the fore. The first one is the fact that corporations may step in when states are weak or absent. The corporations may then fill the void by providing the community with goods and services. Another source of legitimacy that has also to do with output is efficiency, the idea that the market is a better provider of public goods and services.

The case of the Niger Delta and the oil company and the case of the Bops in Madagascar illustrates the first source of legitimacy (Idemudia, this volume; Cholez and Trompette, this volume). The local authorities in these cases are weak or absent, and the corporation steps in as a participant in the communities. The presence of corporations may entail an increasing number of public and private infrastructure projects, but it may also result in passive public authorities when corporations are located in the community.

The case of the New Public Management reform and the case of identity politics (Blomqvist, this volume; Crane et al., this volume) illustrate the other source of legitimacy. The privatization of parts of the welfare sector in Sweden has turned citizens into consumers who can choose private providers of schools or elderly care. Crane, Matten and Moon have a similar reasoning. When the government's provision of social rights is being increasingly marketized, the corporations take a more active part in different societal and political sectors. Corporations are self-interested actors but they are 'not simply a passive object within the domain of citizenship, but act to shape and construct relations of citizenship' (Crane et al., this volume).

Identity and the co-construction of citizenship

Turning now to the issue of identity, we started out discussing how corporations could acquire the identity of corporate citizen, either through their own acts in the public domain, or via the activities of other citizens treating the corporation like a citizen. Hence, rather than having a traditional identity grounded in the business sphere, the corporate identity would be formulated across the public-private divide. This would further imply that this divide would be questioned in its role as a boundary. With a view to the identity of corporations, it is evident from our chapters that the corporate citizen is indeed identified as an actor that transcends the public-private divide, and one that is indeed active in the public domain. As we have discussed above, this raises questions on the legitimacy of this type of actorhood in the public domain. What is more, our chapters highlight the interrelatedness of corporate citizenship and individual citizenship. Specifically, our findings point towards the co-construction of these forms of citizenship, and towards the co-construction of the roles of the individual and the corporation in the new public domain.

A starting point for the analysis was that ideas on individual citizenship could be used to analyse the citizenship of corporations. In Chapter 1 (this volume) we further discussed how citizens treating corporations like public institutions (e.g. Vogel, 1975), could render these corporations more 'public'. Individual citizens were thus instrumental in shaping corporate citizens through for example processes of 'political consumerism' (Micheletti, 2003). Yet, this is only one of several possible outcomes of the interaction across corporation, consumer, corporate citizen, and/or citizen and we will discuss a wider set in the following section.

Corporate citizens evoking individual citizenship

Notably, we have outlined what could be deemed a reverse form of the process Micheletti (2003) describes. That is, in addition to discussing how citizens may evoke corporate citizenship (cf. Holzer, this volume), we have shown how corporations may evoke the identity of citizen among individuals; through treating clients like citizens rather than (mere) consumers, clients can be induced to accept citizenship duties. The AML/CTF case illustrates this point (Helgesson and Mörth, this volume). Bank clients may prefer to be consumers only, but the more proactive role expected of the banks in the 'war on terror' involves making the clients appreciate the importance of doing their duty as citizens.

Corporations evoking individual citizenship

Another conclusion is that corporate citizenship is not a precondition for corporations to induce clients to take on the role of citizens. Corporations may affect, or even construct, citizenship identities among their clients whilst essentially minding their own business. In fact, standard marketing practices, like selling products to new segments, may have the effect of evoking and supporting (but also inhibiting) new citizenship identities, as in the case of 'pink money' (Crane et al., this volume). In this case, the ordinary corporation is thus implicated in acts of boundary transgression.

Corporate citizens evoking consumer identity

Finally, we would like to emphasize that corporations engaging in forms of corporate citizenship may foster a shift towards the identity of consumer, rather than to that of citizen among their clients. This can be the case when corporations take on the role as government. An illustrative example is the role of corporations as providers of services in the wake of NPM-reforms. Using corporations to solve the public problem of services provision tends to put individuals in the positions of consumers where they previously have been primarily citizens with for example right to care (see Blomquist, this volume).

Concluding remarks: A political theory of the corporation?

The processes of privatization of the public sector and the publicization of the private sector create a new public domain. However, it is very hard to make any generalizations on how these processes could generate a political theory on the political role of corporations (Scherer and Palazzo, 2011). Corporations are political actors and this volume on corporate citizenship has showed that their political actorhood is manifested in multiple ways. Corporations are active in different types of states and political settings. Their decisions and actions affect people, government and local communities and raise fundamental questions on various political values. Thus, what we need to elaborate more is how we can develop different theories and perspectives on how corporations are political actors and the normative implications of being political. There is no size that fits all. In addition, the democratic implications of the social practice of corporations as political actors should be the object for further research.

States and businesses are becoming more embedded in a broader institutionalized arena concerned with the production of public goods and services. The public is no longer equivalent with the state. Business firms engage in the provision of public health, education, security, etc., and are active in a range of other public policy areas. A new type of local and global domain emerges, cutting across the traditional public and private divide.

The liberal understanding of democracy is challenged by an increasingly political role of the firm. The most important test is how the political role of the business firm calls the liberal understanding of democratic accountability into question. The virtue of democratic accountability, which is built on the premise of delegated authority, turns into something of a vice when the authority of public and private actors is intertwined. Indeed, a public accountability dilemma occurs when private actors are expected to take on new tasks and obligations evoking claims for democratic accountability.

Future research should address this dilemma between the democratic ideals in liberal theory and the practice of an increasingly political role of the firm. How can this dilemma be handled according to various democratic theories? Or do democratic theories seldom engage in questions on the political role of firms? In what ways can deliberative democratic theory legitimate the political role of the firm, or does it raise new dilemmas when the public sphere becomes indeterminable? How can firms be part of public reason if political equality is an important condition for a legitimate democratic deliberation?

References

Andriof, J. and S. Waddock (2002) 'Unfolding Stakeholder Engagement', in J. Andriof, S. Waddock, B. Husted and S. Sutherland Rahman (eds) *Unfolding Stakeholder Thinking: Theory, Responsibility and Engagement*, Sheffield: Greenleaf Publishing, pp. 19–42.

Bexell, M. and U. Mörth (eds) (2010) *Democracy and Public–Private Partnerships in Global Governance*, London: Palgrave Macmillan.

Burchell, J. and J. Cook (2006) 'Confronting the "Corporate Citizen". Shaping the Discourse of Corporate Social Responsibility', *International Journal of Sociology and Social Policy*, 26, 3/4: 121–137.

Cochoy, F. (2007) 'A Brief Theory of the "Captation" of Publics: Understanding the Market with Little Red Ridinghood', *Theory, Culture & Society*, 24: 203–223.

Donaldson, T. and T. W. Dunfee (1999) *Ties that Bind. A Social Contracts Approach to Business Ethics*, Boston, MA: Harvard Business School Press.

Giddens, A. (1990) *The Consequences of Modernity*, Stanford, CA: Stanford University Press.

Micheletti, M. (2003) *Political Virtue and Shopping: Individuals, Consumerism, and Collective Action*, New York: Palgrave.

Moon, J., A. Crane and D. Matten (2005) 'Can Corporations Be Citizens? Corporate Citizenship as a Metaphor for Business Participation in Society', *Business Ethics Quarterly*, 15, 3: 429–453.

Néron, P.-Y. and W. Norman (2008) 'Citizenship, Inc. Do We Really Want Businesses to Be Good Corporate Citizens?' *Business Ethics Quarterly*, 18, 1: 1–26.

Power, M. (1994) 'The Audit Society', in A. G. Hopwood and P. Miller (eds), *Accounting as a Social and Institutional Practice*, Cambridge: Cambridge University Press, pp. 299–316.

Power, M. (1999) *The Audit Society: Rituals of Verification*, Oxford: Oxford University Press.

Scherer, A. G. and G. Palazzo (2011) 'The New Political Role of Business in a Globalized World: A Review of New Perspectives on CSR and Its Implications for the Firm, Governance, and Democracy', *Journal of Management Studies*, 48, 4: 899–931.

Vogel, D. (1975) 'The Corporation as Government: Challenges & Dilemmas', *Polity*, 8, 1: 5–37.

Index

Printed and bound in the United States of America